Golf in the Ozarks

I0792632

On the front cover: Payne Stewart celebrating after his 1999 U.S. Open victory. (Courtesy of Winston Luzier); Horton Smith with Sam Reynolds and others outside Hickory Hills Country Club. (Courtesy of Hickory Hills Country Club.)

On the back cover: Horton Smith is pictured here with golf great Bobby Jones. (Courtesy of Photos From the Fairway.)

GOLF IN THE OZARKS

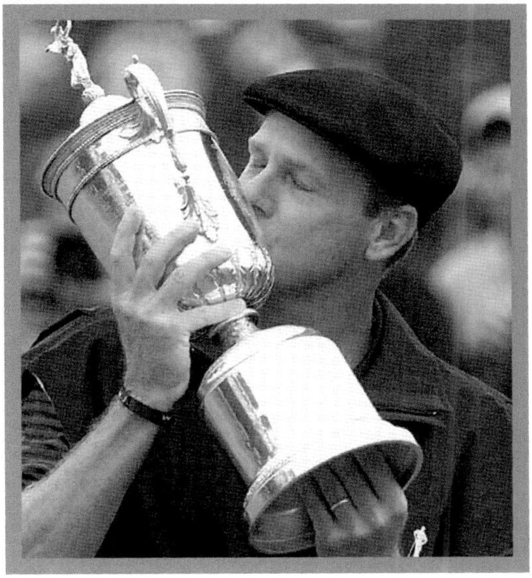

Monte McNew

ARCADIA
PUBLISHING

ISBN 978-0-7385-4033-7

Published by Arcadia Publishing
Charleston, South Carolina

Printed in the United States of America

Library of Congress Catalog Card Number: 2006921001

For all general information contact Arcadia Publishing at:
Telephone 843-853-2070
Fax 843-853-0044
E-mail sales@arcadiapublishing.com
For customer service and orders:
Toll-Free 1-888-313-2665

Visit us on the Internet at www.arcadiapublishing.com

This book is dedicated to my father, whom I loved to talk with about sports, and to my sons, Christopher and Colin, whom I hope to share that same passion with.

CONTENTS

ACKNOWLEDGMENTS

Countless people have helped me amass all of the information found in this book. Personal interviews with local golf historians, including Dr. John Ferguson, Jim Ferguson, Bee Payne Stewart, Perry Leslie, Sam Reynolds, and many more, helped with the flavor of how golf developed in the Ozarks through the years. Accumulating the best photographs for this book was only made possible due to help from Dustin Raymond, Steve Kemp, Bob Zajak, Shirley Burke, Rick Neal, Andrew Smith, Wayne Fredrick, Eugene Robinett, Doug Adams, Rick Grayson, Tom Mast, and Rita Moore. Others who helped me gain the endless amounts of information for this book include Rand Jerris and Patty Moran of the United States Golf Association, Dina Taylor from Joplin Museum, Jean-Paul Herbert, Jim Fryar, Clair Goodwin, and Dr. Paul Gill. While I truly enjoyed the research portion of the book, I needed a lot of help with the writing and designing of the book. Endless thanks go out to Jeff Ruetsche, John Young, Stephanie McNew, Aaron McNew, Shelia Youngblood, Katie Starrett, and my wife, Sarah McNew. Thanks to the guys that make golf fun, including David, Justin, Nick, Joe, Ashley, Steve, and Jason.

I would also like to thank my family and friends for not only allowing me the time to put this book together but also for putting up with me talking about golf for hours on end.

INTRODUCTION

Golf in the Ozarks began in the early 1900s, with Dr. Tom Talbot as one of the golfing pioneers in the region. During the peak of his golfing career, Talbot was listed as one of the top ten amateur golfers in the United States. The first golf courses in southwest Missouri were located in Springfield, with the most notable being the Springfield Country Club and the Glenstone golf course. In 1907, the Springfield District Golf Association, led by Talbot as president, developed the first local tournament, the Springfield City Amateur. The inaugural tournament was held at the Springfield Country Club and was won by Felix Blackwell.

In 1911, golf in the Ozarks spread to nearby Joplin with the development of the first local course, Oak Hill Country Club. The course had legendary head professionals including two-time Masters winner Horton Smith and Ed Dudley, who later became the head professional at Augusta National Golf Club. In 1920, Joplin developed the region's next golf course, named Schifferdecker Golf Course. This soon became the location of one of the oldest tournaments in the region, the Tri-State Amateur, later known as the Ozark Amateur. The inaugural Tri-State Amateur tournament was won by Charles Martin. Other winners of this prestigious tournament include Masters winner Herman Keiser and senior tour professional Jim Hatfield. The expansion of golf courses continued in Springfield with the addition of Hickory Hills Country Club in 1926.

The Ozarks quickly produced golfers that would be known at the game's highest level. Among early professionals were Horton Smith, Ky Laffoon, Leonard Dodson, and Herman Keiser. From the 1920s to 1940s, it was common for professional golfers to tour the country and play in exhibition matches. Southwest Missouri developed a reputation throughout the golfing community as one of the premier areas for golfers to find competition, including "big money games" geared to gamblers.

Many accomplished golfers, such as Walter Hagen, Harry Cooper, Lawson Little, and Joe Kirkwood, would make stops in Joplin and Springfield for exhibition matches, while legendary gambler Titanic Thompson often toured the area to play, commonly leaving with less than he came with. As the popularity of golf grew in the Ozarks, so did the number of courses. By the mid 1970s, the number of area courses grew to over 25, including Honey Creek Golf Course in Aurora, Carthage Municipal Golf Course, and Grandview Golf Course. In the 1970s, golfers including Payne Stewart and Cathy Reynolds began a second generation of elite golfers from the Ozarks.

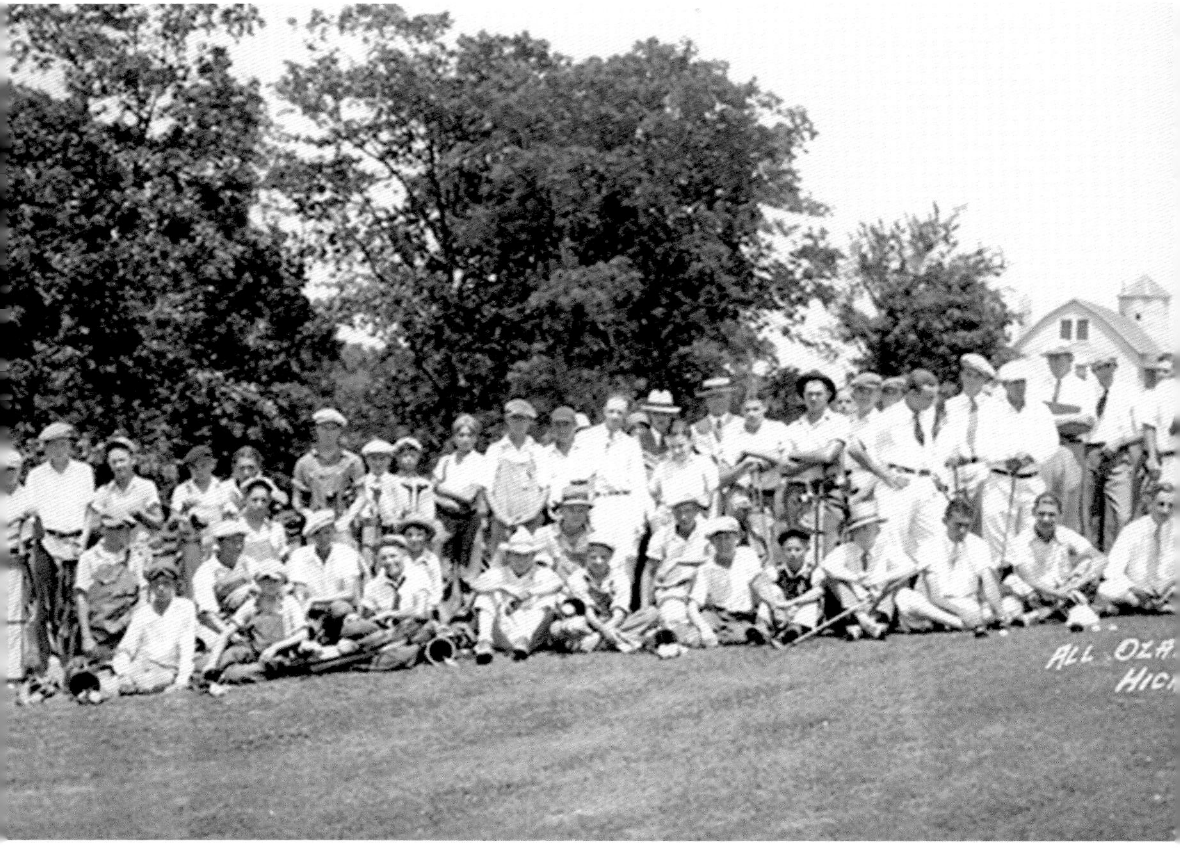

This panoramic photograph was taken at the 1929 All Ozarks Amateur Golf Tournament held at Hickory Hills Country Club in Springfield, Missouri. The photograph depicts many of the founders of golf in the Ozark region. Among those photographed are

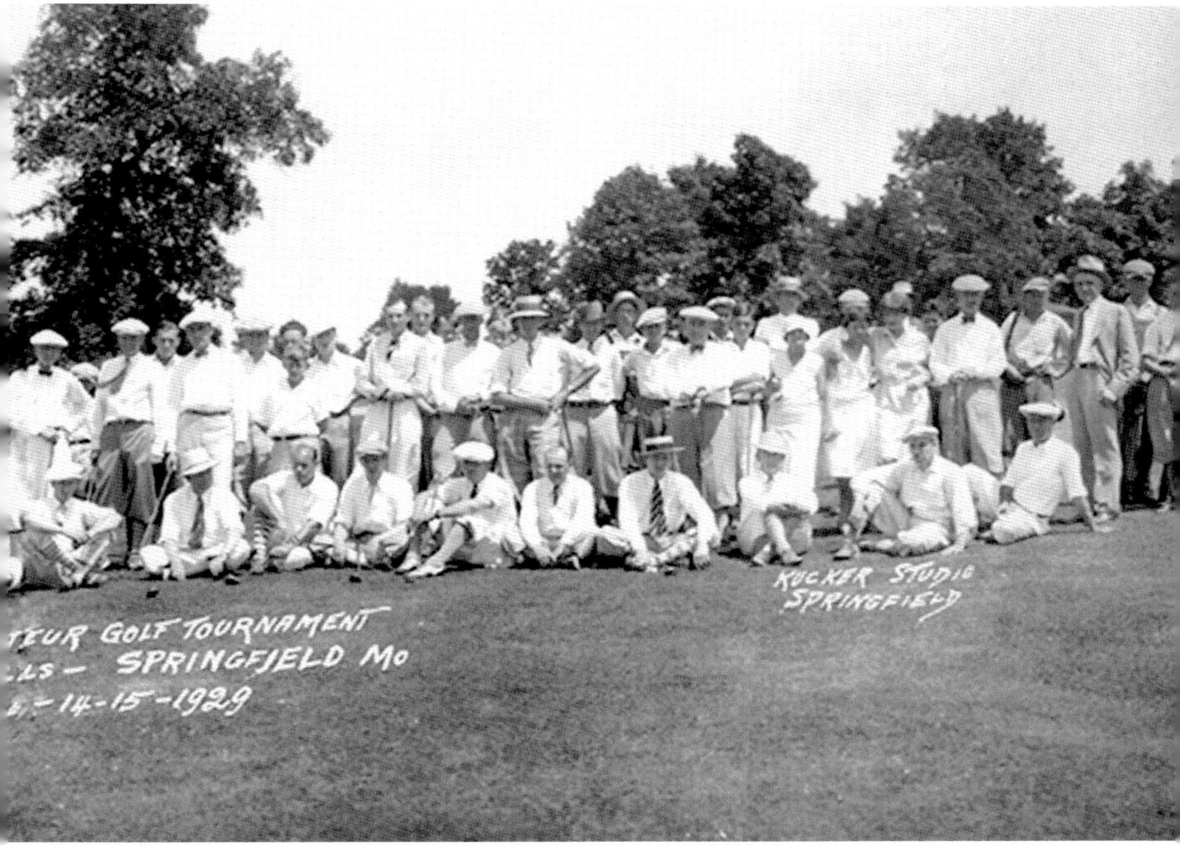

Tom Talbot, Norman Hinds, Tom Woodruff, John Ferguson, and Dick Farrington. The first clubhouse at Hickory Hills can be seen in the background. The club opened in 1926 on the east side of Springfield.

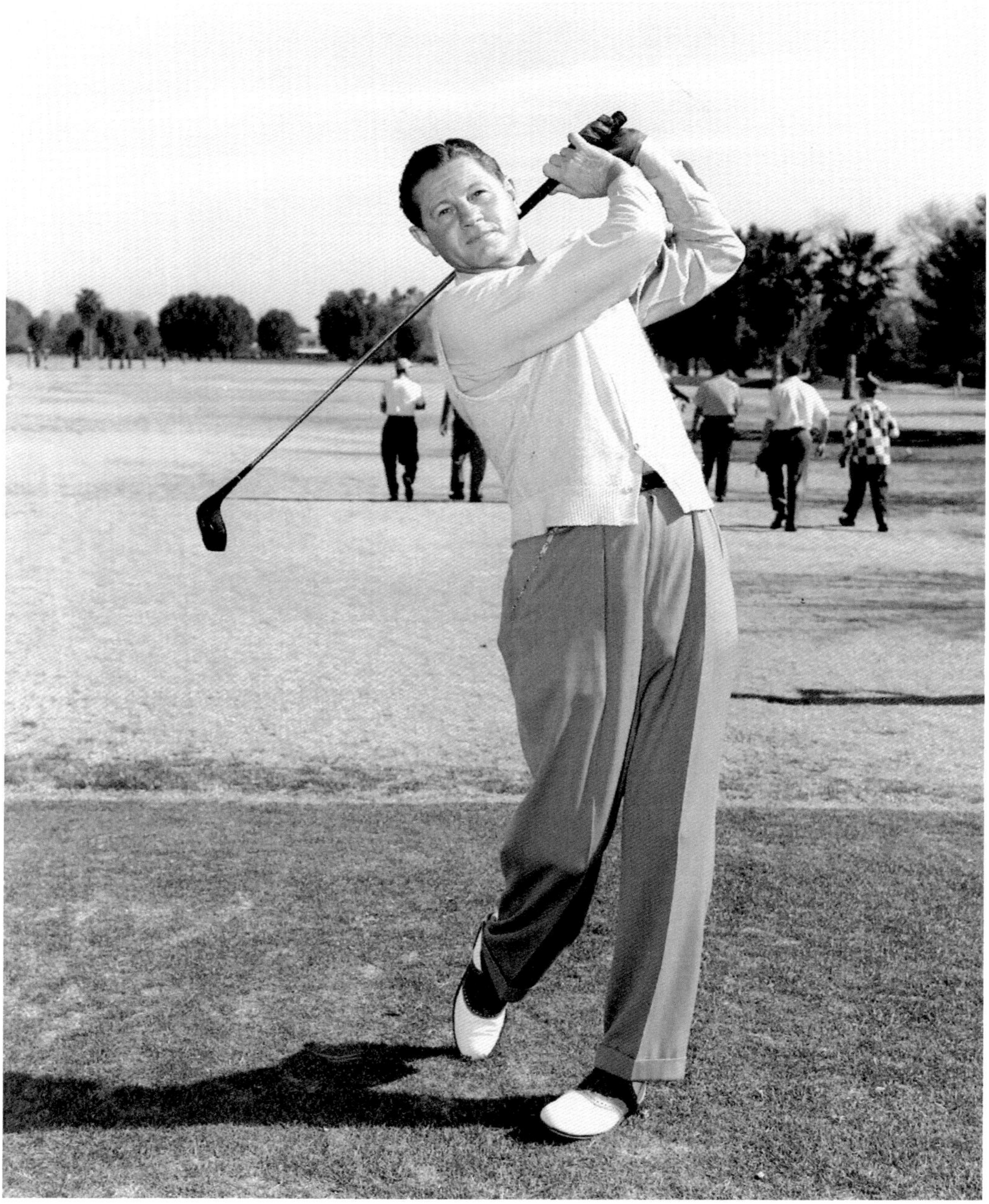

Horton Smith was the first golfer from the Ozarks to succeed on a national level. By winning the inaugural Masters tournament in 1934 at the Augusta National Golf Club in Augusta, Georgia, Horton Smith will forever have a place in golf history. This picture, by legendary golf coach Alex Morrison, shows Horton in his recognizable finish position. (Courtesy of Photos From the Fairway.)

1

THE JOPLIN GHOST

Horton Smith was born on May 22, 1908, in Springfield, Missouri. Horton's parents, Perry and Ann, had a farm seven miles from town. Horton was the second of two boys. While Horton and his older brother, Renshaw "Ren" Smith, were growing up, they helped on the family farm. The Smiths' would eventually move to a farm closer to Springfield, giving Horton the opportunity to be introduced to the game of golf, with Springfield Country Club only a half-mile from the family farm. To make extra money, Horton, beginning at the age of 11, would caddie for the members of Springfield Country Club. Horton would be paid 25¢ for carrying a member's bag for nine holes. After a year of caddying part-time, Horton began to caddie regularly and played as often as possible. Every day after school, Horton would throw his clubs on his bike and head to the course.

The Smith family would eventually join the Springfield Country Club, which gave Horton the ability to play every morning before school and caddie in the afternoon. Recognizing Horton's skill and potential, head pro Neil Crose put Horton under his wing. When Horton was 13 years old, he finished second to older brother Ren in the Junior Club Championship. The following year, at the age of 14, Horton would finally win the Junior Championship at the club.

In 1923, Horton would get the opportunity of a lifetime for a young golfer. At the age of 15, Horton and his brother, Ren, caddied for Walter Hagen and Joe Kirkwood in an exhibition match in Joplin. At the end of the match, Hagen gave Smith some balls and "ready tees." This was the first time Horton had seen wooden tees, as players at the time would typically use wet sand to tee up their ball. Horton would maintain a relationship with Walter for many years. The same year, Horton won both the Springfield Country Club and Springfield City Championship at the young age of 15. Also in 1923, Horton set the Club's course record at 58, by shooting a 26 on the front nine holes that carried a par of 31 and shooting a 32 on the back nine with a par of 35. After high school, Horton spent some time in college at the State Teachers' College in Springfield. While in college, Horton could not deny his dream of becoming a golf professional, and, against his father's wishes, Horton dropped out of college and began working as an assistant professional at Springfield County Club, where he would quickly work to become the caddie master and assistant to Neil Crose.

In 1927, Horton was offered and accepted the position of club pro in Sedalia, Missouri. In the same year, he was invited to also become the head pro at both the golf course in California, Missouri, and the Jefferson City Country Club in Jefferson City, Missouri. Each week, Horton would spend a few days at each course. On Sunday, Monday, and Tuesday, he worked in Sedalia. On Wednesday, he would be in California, and Thursday, Friday, and Saturday, Horton would be at the Jefferson City Country Club. During this time in golf history, it was common to be the head professional at more than one club. Also that year, Horton qualified for the U.S. Open at

Oakmont, in Pittsburgh, and finished in 44th place. During the winter of 1927, Horton competed in golf tournaments across the country, learning about the professional tour.

In 1928, at the age of 20, Horton moved to Joplin, Missouri, to be the head professional at Oak Hill Country Club, which is now known as Twin Hills Country Club. During the same year, Horton would break out for his first professional win at the Oklahoma City Open, where he took home $1,000 for first place. One month later, Horton struck again at the Catalina Open. Horton was in the clubhouse with a three-stoke lead over Walter Hagen, who had three holes left to play. When Horton went back out on the course to watch Walter come in, Walter asked Horton what he had shot. When told, Walter replied with "well I guess I need to shoot a three, a two, and a one to beat you," as the final three holes were a par four, a par three, and a par three. Walter birdied the first two holes. On the final hole, Hagen sent his caddie down to tend the flag. The shot was on line but flew over the flag. Horton would beat the great Walter Hagen by one stroke at the Catalina Open, bagging $2,500.

With earnings of $15,000, Horton's biggest year would be 1929. With thanks to his almost supernatural putting ability, Horton was number one on the money list. Horton was voted onto the Ryder Cup team that year and to date is the youngest player ever to be a member of the team. The U.S. Ryder Cup team would lose that year, as Horton and Leo Diegel were the only Americans to win their singles matches. It would later be Horton's idea to use the point structure that is used today during Ryder Cup play. Later the same year, Horton won the French Open on his 21st birthday. After the round, Walter Hagen presented Horton with a birthday cake on the 18th hole and a party that night at the Ritz. Throughout the year, Horton played nearly 100 exhibition matches with his friend Walter Hagen. The following year, Horton toured Mexico with Ed Dudley for the Mexican Golf Association. Horton also won the 1930 Savannah Open, which was the last time a player would defeat Bobby Jones in formal competition. In 1931, "the Joplin Ghost" won the St. Paul Open and became the head pro at Oak Park Country Club in Oak Park, Illinois. Even after his tremendous successes in golf at such a young age, 1934 was the year Horton would leave his mark on golf history.

In 1934, the great Bobby Jones organized a tournament to be held at his club in Augusta, Georgia. Bobby invited only the finest golfers in the world, including Gene Sarazen, Harry Cooper, and Walter Hagen. Against the finest, Horton posted a four round total of 284 to win the inaugural Augusta National Invitational, later to be renamed the Masters. Horton made a three-foot putt on the final hole to beat Craig Wood by one stroke. He took home $1,500 for the win. Horton would win this tournament again in 1936 to be the first two-time champion. The tournament was hampered by bad weather, forcing the final 36 holes to be played on Monday. Thanks to a 45-foot chip in on the 68th hole, an eight-foot putt on the 69th, and a 16-foot putt on the 71st, Horton was able to pull off the victory by one stroke over Harry Cooper.

During the Masters tournament in 1936, Horton would meet Barbara Bourne, heiress to the Singer Sewing Machine estate. They would marry just two years later in 1938. During the beginning of the marriage, Horton was called to serve in the war. In the fall of 1942, he went to the Army Air Corps. On June 30, 1943, in Baltimore, Barbara gave birth to a son, Alfred Bourne. Horton missed the birth of his son and did not meet him until one week later, upon Horton's return from the war. In 1945, Barbara sought a divorce in Reno, Nevada, based on grounds of mental cruelty. Horton would never remarry.

In 1946, Horton took the head pro position at the Detroit Golf Club, where he had played in the Ryder Cup in 1941. The famous Alex Ross had announced his retirement and asked Horton to take his place. In 1952, Horton sought a larger role with the Professional Golfers' Association

(PGA) by becoming president of the association, where he served for three terms, the most allowed by the PGA. While acting president, Horton made many improvements for the young tour. The most noted change occurred by addressing the issue of African Americans on tour, as African Americans were barred from PGA-sponsored tournaments. In 1952, Joe Louis, former heavyweight boxing champion and avid golfer, was banned from the San Diego Open after promoters had invited him to play. Horton told the committee to incorporate an "approved entry clause," which would allow the independent tournaments to invite whomever they chose to play in their tournaments; Louis was allowed to play.

After the Masters in 1957, Horton developed a persistent cough, which later was diagnosed as Hodgkin's disease. On September 21, 1957, a successful operation removed a growth in his right lung. Horton had enough energy to play in the Masters again in 1958, to become the only golfer to participate in all 22 Masters tournaments.

In 1958, Horton was only the 20th player inducted into the PGA Hall of Fame. In 1959, the PGA of Great Britain made Horton an honorary life member of its organization; at the time, he was the only U.S. golfer to receive that recognition. In 1960, Horton won the Ben Hogan award, which is given annually to the golfer who has overcome illness or injury and continued to play the game.

In 1962, he took a trip to Springfield for the opening of the golf course named in his honor. During the inaugural round at Horton Smith golf course, Horton shot a 36 on the nine-hole, par 34 course. Playing partners Sam Reynolds, Tom Talbot, and Gene Sallee shot 38, 38, and 36 respectfully. Weeks later, Horton played his 26th Masters. In November, he went home to Springfield with his brother, Ren, where after a week at home he entered St. John's hospital. Again, Horton mustered up the strength to play in the Masters in 1963. Just a few months later on Tuesday, October 15, 1963, at the age of 55, Horton Smith died. Smith was inducted into the Missouri Sports Hall of Fame in 1964 and the World Golf Hall of Fame in 1990.

Career Victories

1928 Oklahoma City Open
1929 Catalina Open
1929 Fort Myers Open
1929 French Open
1929 Jacksonville Open
1929 La Gorge Open
1929 North and South Open
1929 Oregon Open
1929 Pasadena Open
1929 Pensacola Open
1930 Berkeley Open
1930 Oregon Open
1930 Orlando Open
1930 Savannah Open
1931 St. Paul Open
1932 Capital City Open
1932 Michigan City Open
1932 Tri State Open
1933 California Open
1933 International Four Ball
1933 Louisville Open
1934 The Masters
1935 Miami Biltmore Open
1935 Oklahoma City Four Ball
1935 Palm Springs Open
1935 Pasadena Open
1935 Toledo Inverness
1936 The Masters
1936 Victoria B.C. Open
1937 Inverness Invitational with Cooper
1937 Oklahoma City Invitational
1937 North and South Open
1940 St. Augustine Pro-Am
1941 Belleair Open
1941 Florida West Coast Pen
1941 Mid South Open
1941 St. Paul Open
1948 Michigan PGA

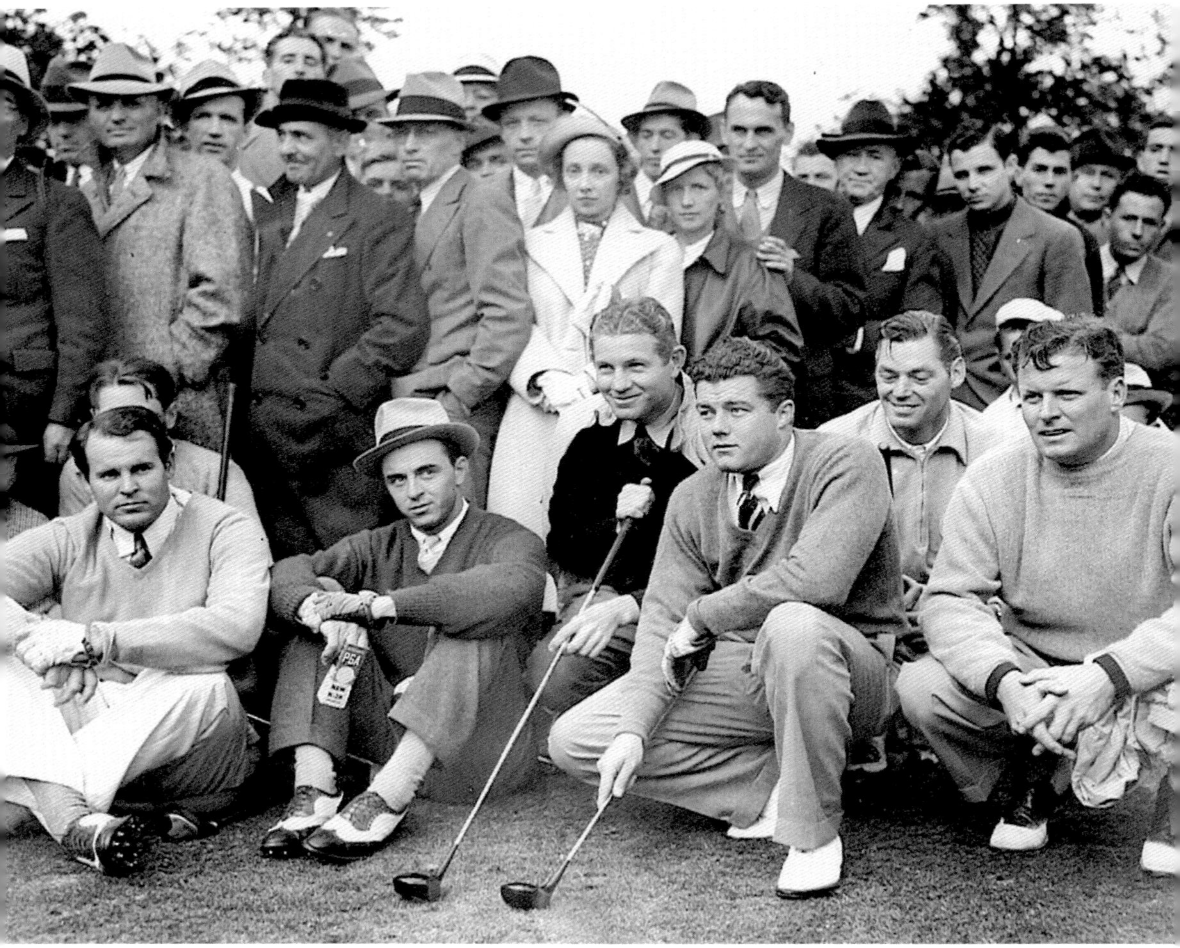

The 1937 Western Open was won by Ralph Guldahl in a playoff over Horton Smith. The players in this photograph, taken at the Western Open held at the Canterbury Golf Club in Ohio, include (from left to right) Ralph Guldahl, Sam Snead, Horton Smith, Lawson Little, gold medal swimmer Johnny Weismuller, and Jimmy Thompson.

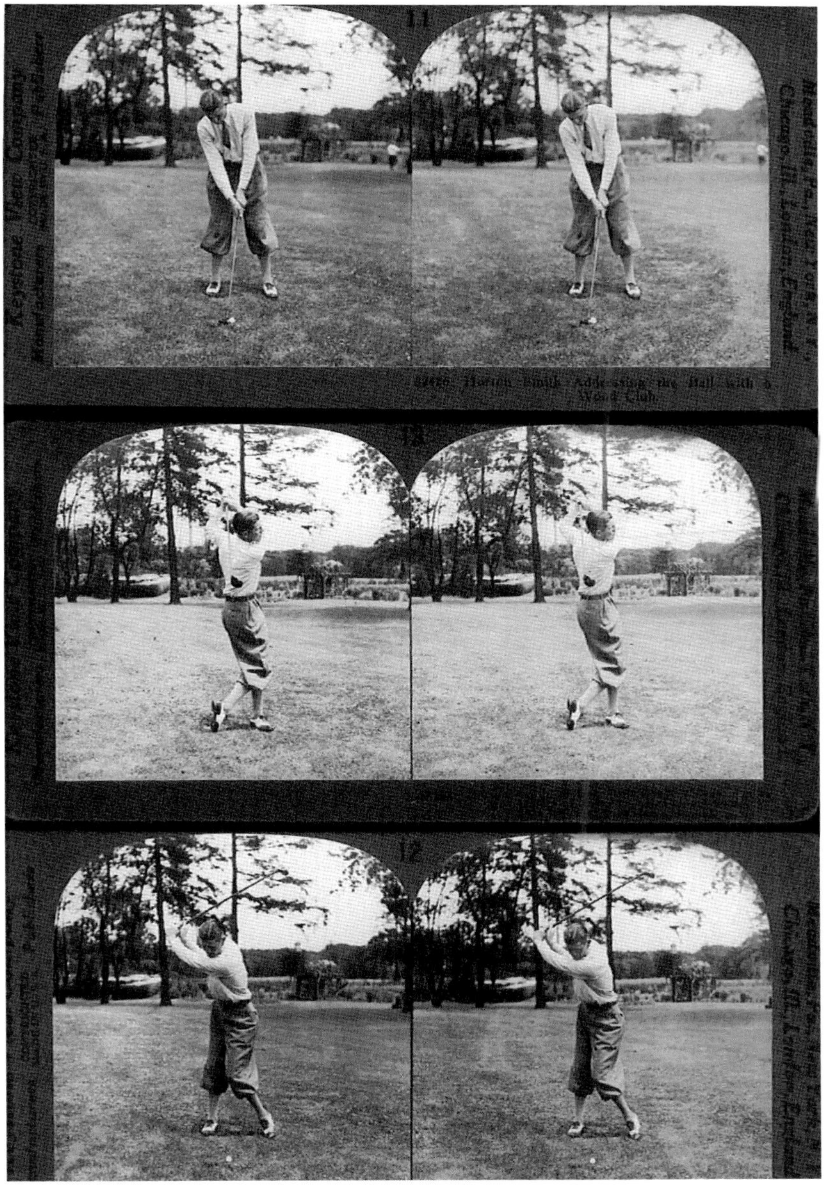

These vintage stereoscope cards, produced by Keystone View Company, could be used to see three-dimensional images of Horton Smith. On the back of each card, the famed golf writer Grantland Rice described in detail Smith's classic swing.

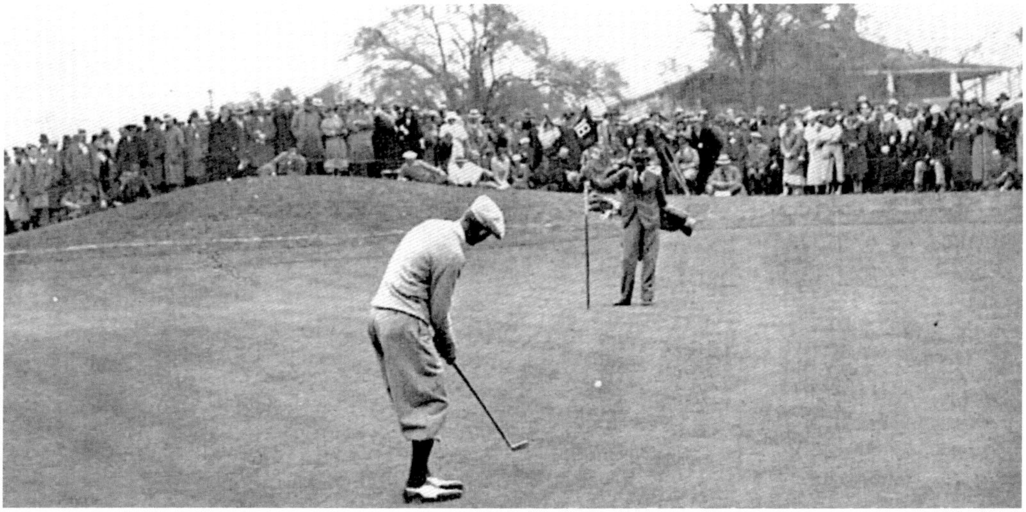

Pictured is Horton Smith's final hole at Augusta National to win the first Masters in 1934. Teeing off on the final hole, Smith knew he needed a par to win. After a long drive and a nice approach shot, his ball finished 20 feet to the right of the hole. The putt pictured rolled past the hole four feet to give him a challenging putt that he would make for the victory.

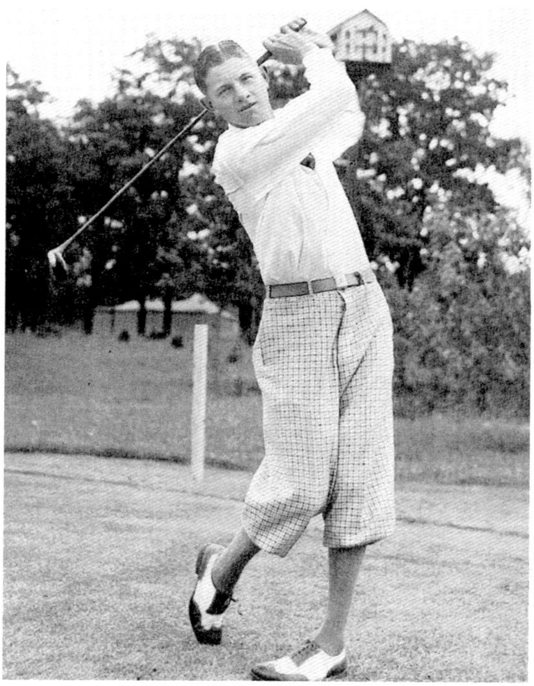

Horton Smith is pictured here at Oak Hill Country Club in Joplin, Missouri, in early 1928. Smith was yet to win a professional tournament but had great showings including the 1927 Oklahoma Open where he finished third, the San Diego Open where he finished second, and the Long Beach Open where he finished fifth.

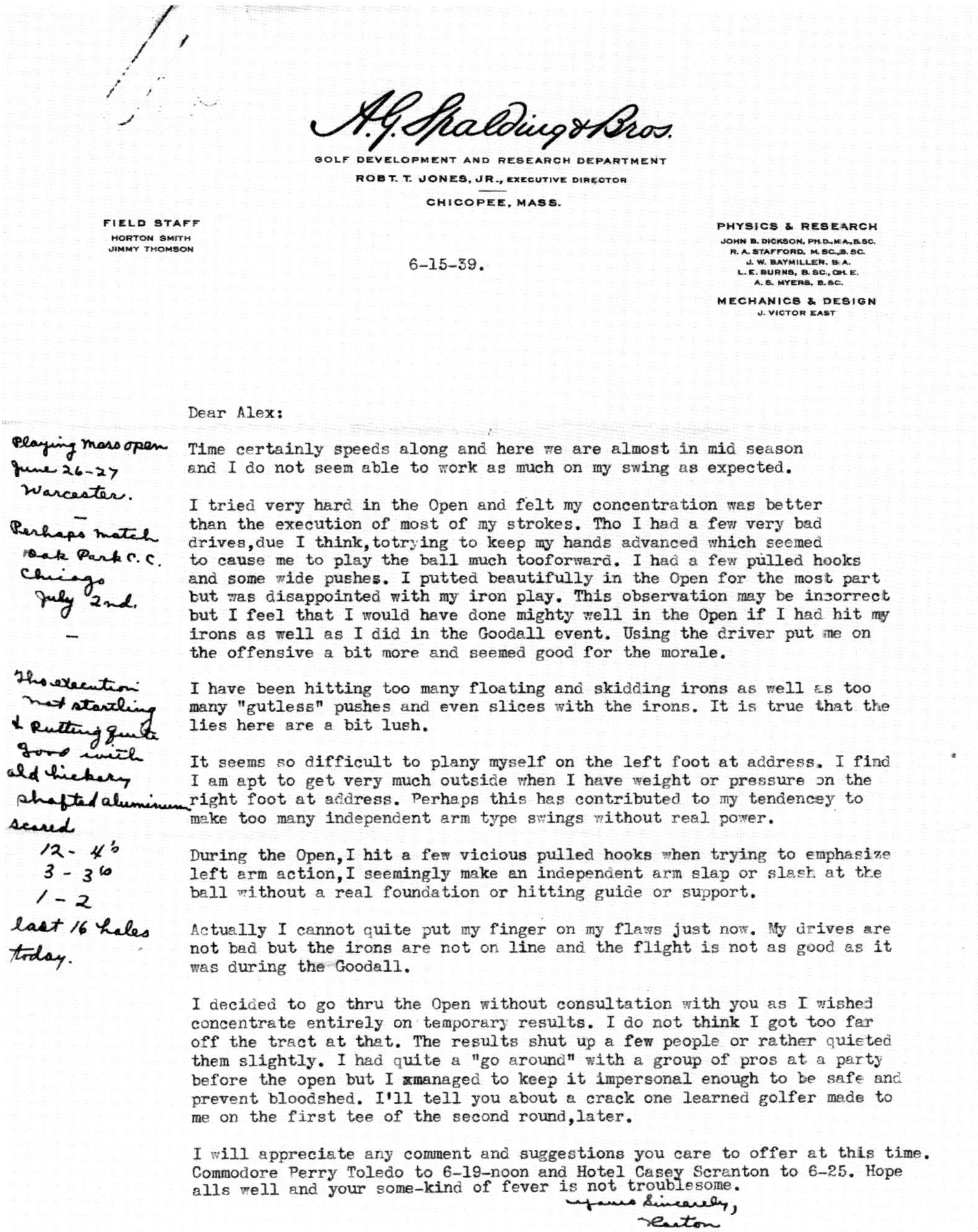

A.G. Spalding & Bros.

GOLF DEVELOPMENT AND RESEARCH DEPARTMENT

ROBT. T. JONES, JR., EXECUTIVE DIRECTOR

CHICOPEE, MASS.

FIELD STAFF
HORTON SMITH
JIMMY THOMSON

PHYSICS & RESEARCH
JOHN B. DICKSON, PH.D., M.A., B.SC.
R. A. STAFFORD, M.SC., B.SC.
J. W. BAYMILLER, B.A.
L. E. BURNS, B.SC., CH.E.
A. S. MYERS, B.SC.

MECHANICS & DESIGN
J. VICTOR EAST

6-15-39.

Dear Alex:

Time certainly speeds along and here we are almost in mid season and I do not seem able to work as much on my swing as expected.

I tried very hard in the Open and felt my concentration was better than the execution of most of my strokes. Tho I had a few very bad drives,due I think,totrying to keep my hands advanced which seemed to cause me to play the ball much tooforward. I had a few pulled hooks and some wide pushes. I putted beautifully in the Open for the most part but was disappointed with my iron play. This observation may be incorrect but I feel that I would have done mighty well in the Open if I had hit my irons as well as I did in the Goodall event. Using the driver put me on the offensive a bit more and seemed good for the morale.

I have been hitting too many floating and skidding irons as well as too many "gutless" pushes and even slices with the irons. It is true that the lies here are a bit lush.

It seems so difficult to plany myself on the left foot at address. I find I am apt to get very much outside when I have weight or pressure on the right foot at address. Perhaps this has contributed to my tendencey to make too many independent arm type swings without real power.

During the Open,I hit a few vicious pulled hooks when trying to emphasize left arm action,I seemingly make an independent arm slap or slash at the ball without a real foundation or hitting guide or support.

Actually I cannot quite put my finger on my flaws just now. My drives are not bad but the irons are not on line and the flight is not as good as it was during the Goodall.

I decided to go thru the Open without consultation with you as I wished concentrate entirely on temporary results. I do not think I got too far off the tract at that. The results shut up a few people or rather quieted them slightly. I had quite a "go around" with a group of pros at a party before the open but I xmanaged to keep it impersonal enough to be safe and prevent bloodshed. I'll tell you about a crack one learned golfer made to me on the first tee of the second round,later.

I will appreciate any comment and suggestions you care to offer at this time. Commodore Perry Toledo to 6-19-noon and Hotel Casey Scranton to 6-25. Hope alls well and your some-kind of fever is not troublesome.

Yours Sincerely,
Horton

Playing mass open June 26-27 Worcester.
Perhaps match Oak Park C.C. Chicago July 2nd.
The execution not startling & putting quite good with old hickory shafted aluminum scored 12-4's 3-3's 1-2 last 16 holes today.

This letter from Horton Smith to his golf instructor Alex Morrison was written on June 15, 1939. Smith had the ability to describe in detail the issues with his swing. He describes the smallest nuances, including getting outside of the proper weight on his back swing, to too much arm action. At this time, Horton was a member of the field staff for Spalding sporting goods. (Courtesy of Photos From the Fairway.)

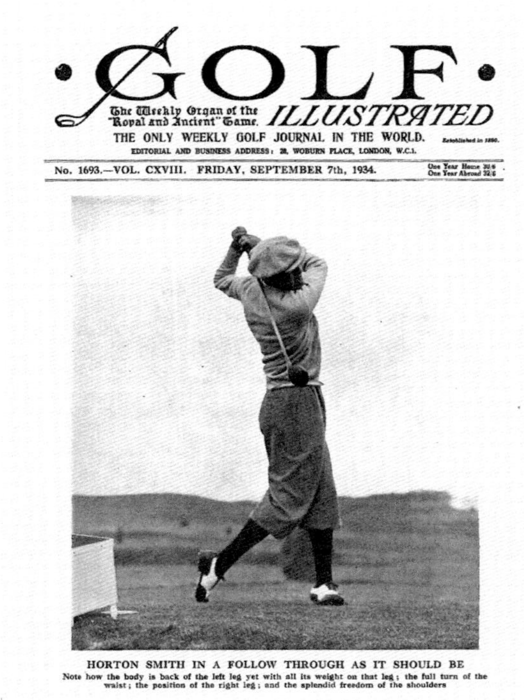

GOLF ILLUSTRATED

The Weekly Organ of the "Royal and Ancient" Game.

THE ONLY WEEKLY GOLF JOURNAL IN THE WORLD. Established in 1890.

EDITORIAL AND BUSINESS ADDRESS: 28, WOBURN PLACE, LONDON, W.C.1.

No. 1693.—VOL. CXVIII. FRIDAY, SEPTEMBER 7th, 1934. One Year Home 30/6 One Year Abroad 32/6

HORTON SMITH IN A FOLLOW THROUGH AS IT SHOULD BE

Note how the body is back of the left leg yet with all its weight on that leg; the full turn of the waist; the position of the right leg; and the splendid freedom of the shoulders

Horton Smith made the cover of the September 7, 1934, *Golf Illustrated,* along with many other covers, after his victory at the inaugural Masters Tournament at Augusta National Golf Club in 1934.

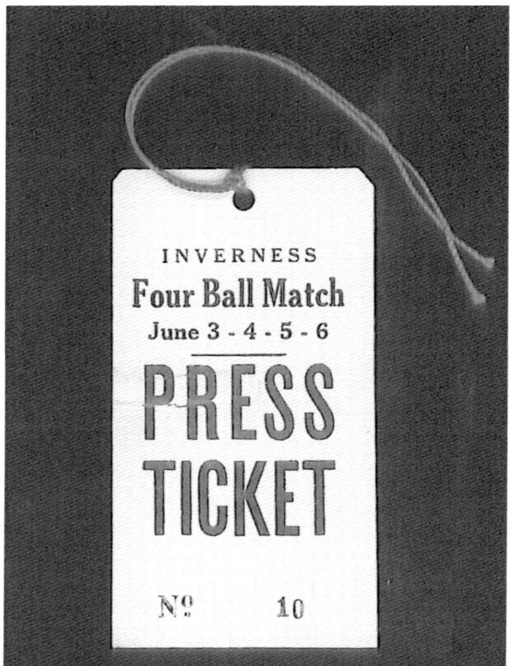

Pictured here is an actual tournament pass from Smith's victory at the 1937 Inverness Invitational in Toledo, Ohio. Smith teamed up with Harry Cooper to win the four-ball tournament over teams such as Paul Runyan and Ky Laffoon, Ralph Guldahl and Sam Snead, and Gene Sarazen and Olin Dutra.

Horton Smith became the first two-time winner of the Masters. In 1936, he topped Harry Cooper for the victory with a score of 285. Weather caused a 36-hole finish on Monday. His final two rounds were 68 and 72, while Cooper shot 71 and 76. Ed Dudley and Ky Laffoon both finished eight strokes back.

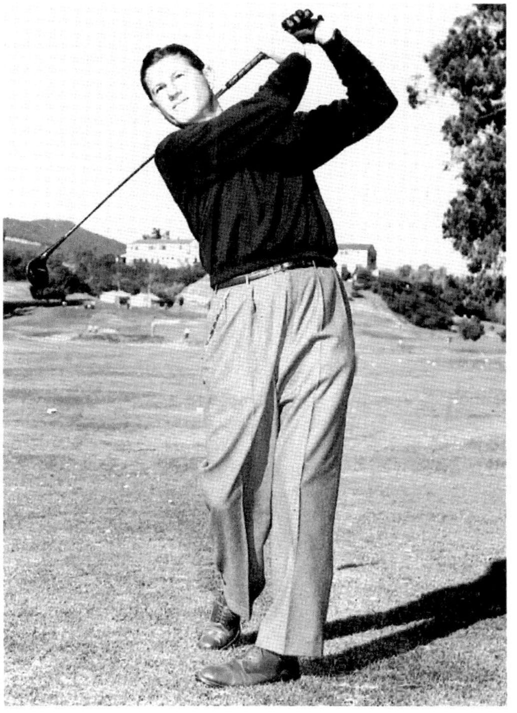

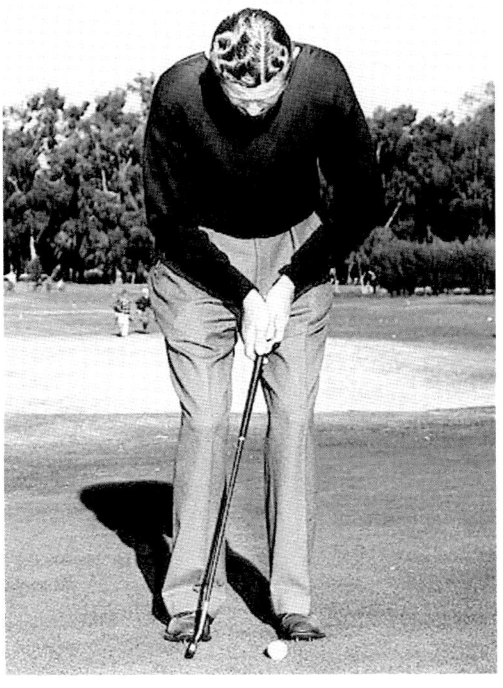

Pictured here is Horton Smith in his recognizable putting stance. Smith authored two books, *The Velvet Touch* and *The Secret of Holing Putts*, and countless articles on the art of putting. According to Bobby Jones, Horton was "one of the finest putters of all time."

CONSULTANT
A. G. SPALDING & BROS.

GOLF

PROFESSIONAL
DETROIT GOLF CLUB
DETROIT 3, MICHIGAN
PHONE UNIVERSITY 16120

1346 E. Grand St
Springfield 4 Missouri.

Jan 19-48.

Dear Alex:

Quite a bit of water has run over the dam since you were in Detroit. We had quite a storm at DGC - it was stated that fiiriction existed between Bush and myself - the friction as I saw it was that Eddie wanted more of my profits or my job if he thought he could get it. Outgoing DGC Pres,on Oct 1, told annual membership meeting that if Bush-Smith combine was not retained that neither would be retained.

We had a "compromise meeting" with Cmtee and Bush agreed to my terms - all was rosy -bugles blew-mouths wagged-printing presses rolled etc. Then when Sam quit Plum Hollow,while I was away at Pinehurst,because of their refusal to pay his requested increase - Bush resigns and applies for P H.

Well Bush is at Brandywine CC Wilmington Dl and I have signed Eddie Kirk to replace him. Two officials,after Bushx quit, sold Bd of Dir on reducing my clubcleaning chgs etc so I guess I have finally found the bottom.

I had the knee operated on by Dr Secord,whom you met, on Dec 18th and the progress seems a bit slow. Had to make a couple of "cuts" - perhaps he was only getting even with me.

I exposed myself to something in PGA but fely I should NOT let my friends down and therefore offered myself as the opposition canditate. I could have gotten votes but election was imposs-ible so no fight was made at election. Some expressed sorrow when convention concluded.

My winter plans are pretty well restricted by this knee tho I hope to make Augusta or some other tourneys before returning to DGC.

I hope you have found a suitable place to live and that you are keeping yourself busy. What have you done withh your Morrison shoe idea or patent ? I thought it was a good idea and helpful to the player. What are your plans for the next few months ?

I just thought I would bring you up-to date on the gossip and thank you for your constructive letter. I had a nice time with the Wileys. He very kindly invited me to visit him at Phoenix. With best wishes to you and Margaret and lbooking forward to hear-ing from you at your convenience,I am

Yours Sincerely,

Horton

This letter from Horton Smith to golf instructor Alex Morrison was written while in Springfield on January 19, 1948. Smith writes about his dissatisfaction with the way Detroit Golf Club is treating him as the head professional. He also gives details of his knee operation one month earlier.

HORTON SMITH

GOLF

CONSULTANT
WALTER HAGEN, GOLF
DIVISION OF
WILSON SPORTING GOODS CO.

PROFESSIONAL
DETROIT GOLF CLUB
DETROIT 3, MICHIGAN
PHONE UNIVERSITY 36120

4-26-51.

Dear Alex:

I thought you might be interested in the enclosed photo.

I chatted only briefly with Frank at Augusta and did not play with him - he conformed pretty well to your pattern and seemed pleased despite the "ragging" from the gang.

He reprimanded me for not having made a better effort in the direction of your teaching and expressed confidence in himself. He also paid you nice compliments.

Bob Ross seems to please the members and perhaps his manner and easy going style will fill the bill.

After maneuvering,I finally got our Clubcleaning rates back to the original level of $ 12.00 per season which is still not high everything considered.

Just returned from Oakmont in Pittsburgh where the PGA will be played in June - just a rally and inspection trip.

Presume you will come on for the Open June 14-16 and if so you should think about accommodations etc.

Will be glad to hear from you. With best wishes to you and Margaret.

Yours Sincerely,

Horton

This letter to Alex Morrison from Horton Smith was written April 26, 1951. In the preceding letter, Smith pointed out his displeasure with his treatment from Detroit Golf Club. In this letter, he acknowledges that the club was raising fees for services to the membership that will in turn help him earn more money.

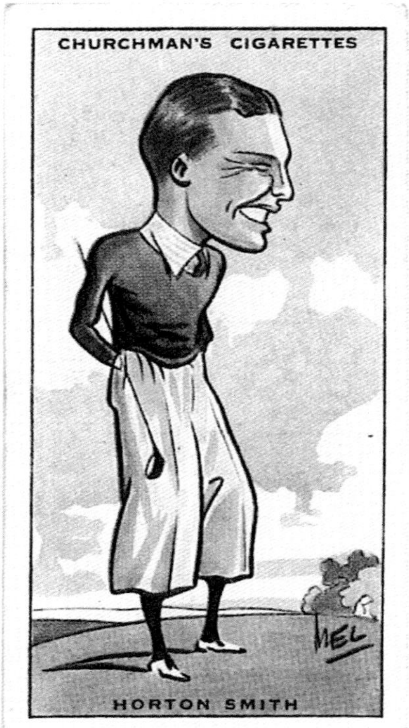

This vintage golf card is from the series Prominent Golfers produced by W. A. and A. C. Churchman tobacco company in Great Britain in 1927. Smith made quite an impression upon European golfers when he won the French Open in 1929. The French Open was only his second tournament on the European circuit.

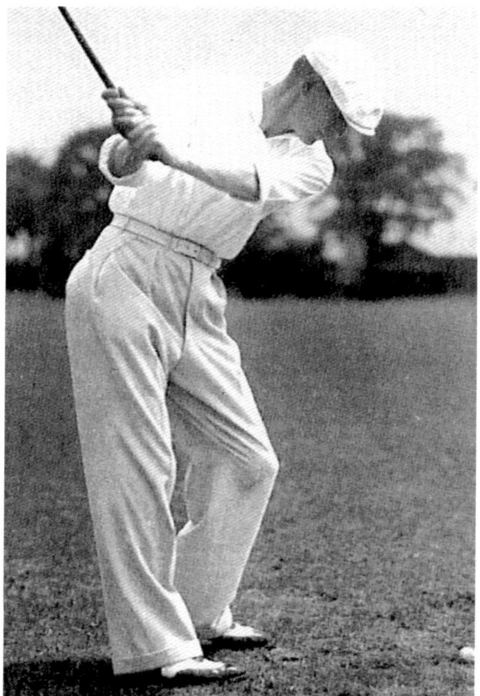

Horton Smith is pictured here in 1931 at the top of his back swing. This fundamentally sound swing helped Smith to 19 professional wins. In July 2000, *Golf Digest* named Smith the 38th greatest player of all time.

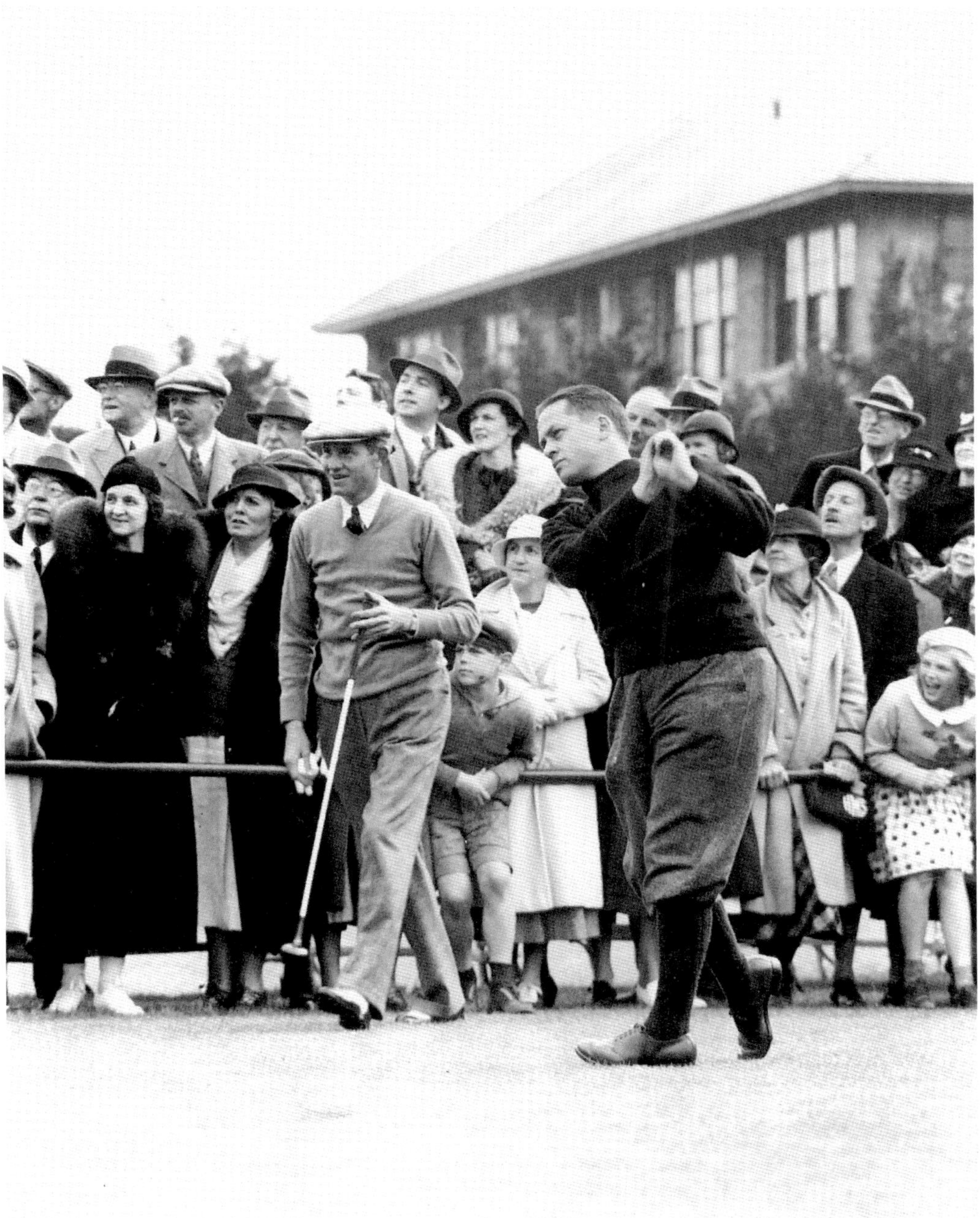

Horton Smith (left) is pictured here with Bobby Jones (right). The two would become friends just before Jones started his tournament, the Masters, in 1934. After Smith's win at the inaugural tournament, he and Jones would travel together to play in exhibitions to promote the game of golf.

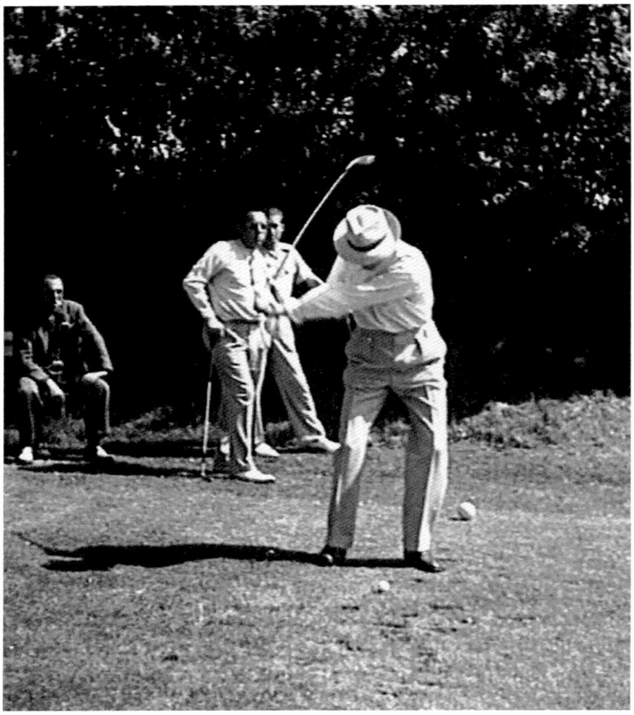

Horton Smith (swinging) and Walter Hagen (left) would meet in 1923 at an exhibition golf match in Joplin, Missouri. At the time, Smith was 15 and caddied for Hagen's playing partner Joe Kirkwood. Eventually, Smith would join this same group to travel America in exhibition matches as photographed here.

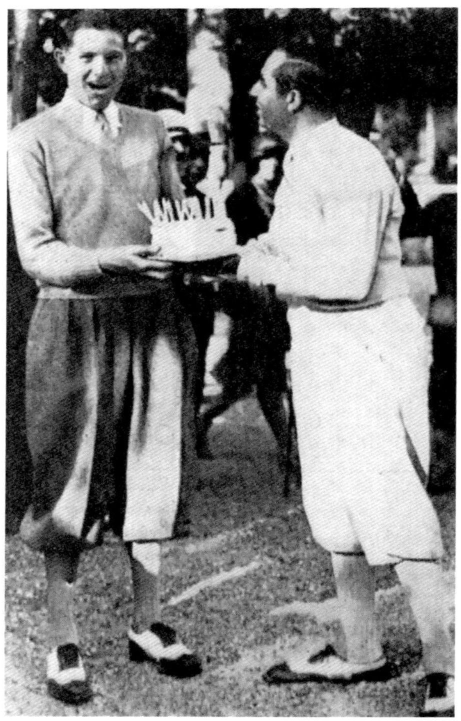

Horton Smith and Walter Hagen's friendship was never more apparent than in 1929 at the French Open, when Hagen presented Smith with a cake for his 21st birthday. As Smith came to the 18th green, Hagen was waiting with cake in hand.

This photograph taken by Alex Morrison depicts Horton Smith's fluid golf stroke. This photograph shows Smith in his back swing. (Courtesy of Photos From the Fairway.)

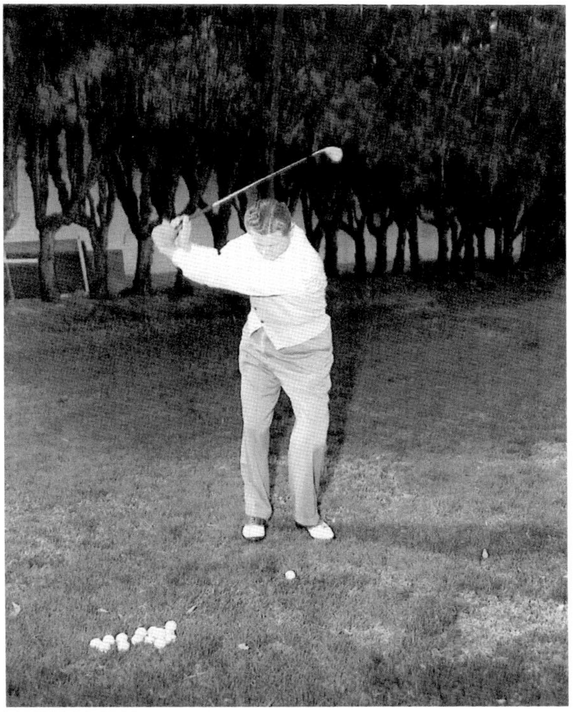

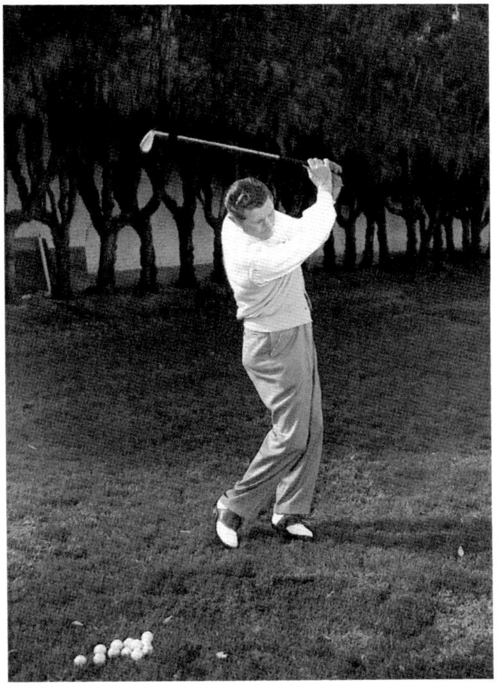

This photograph taken just seconds later by Alex Morrison shows how Horton Smith would maintain the same fluid swing through the finish. (Courtesy of Photos From the Fairway.)

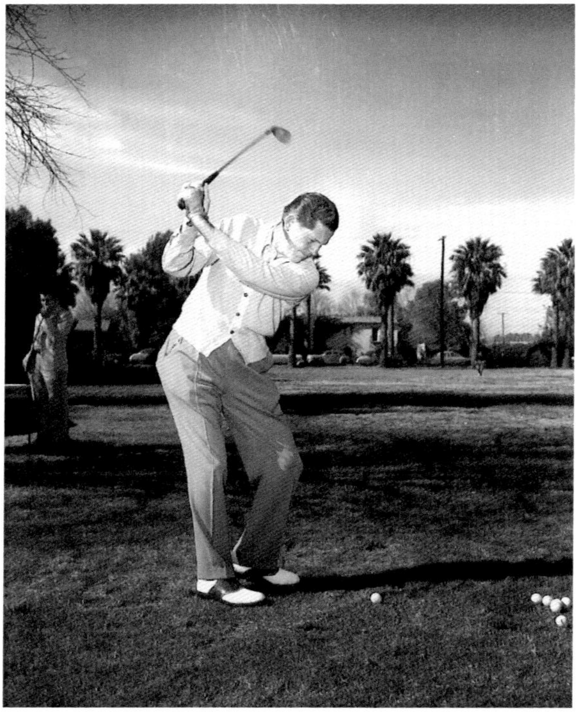

Horton Smith can be seen here hitting to a vintage driving range. This photograph was taken by Smith's golf coach Alex Morrison. (Courtesy of Photos From the Fairway.)

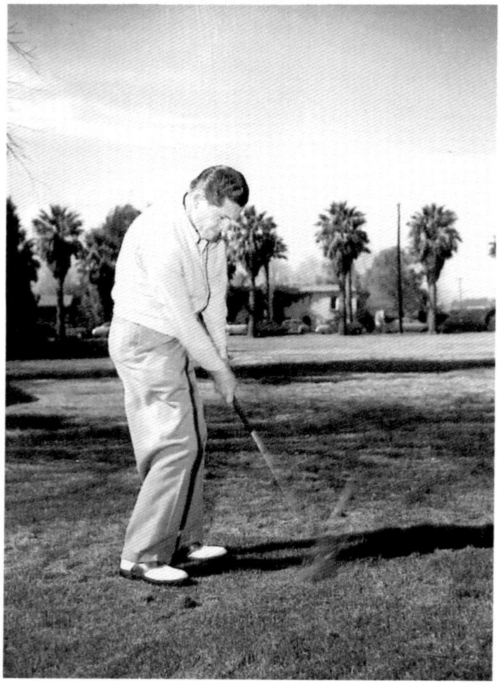

Alex Morrison, Horton Smith's golf coach, would use photographs like these to make even the slightest changes to Smith's swing while on tour. Smith felt being able to see exactly what Morrison was looking at would help him understand the need for change. (Courtesy of Photos From the Fairway.)

Horton Smith was often overlooked when it came to power and length on the golf course. As documented by this photograph, Smith indeed did have a powerful move through the ball at impact. (Courtesy of Photos From the Fairway.)

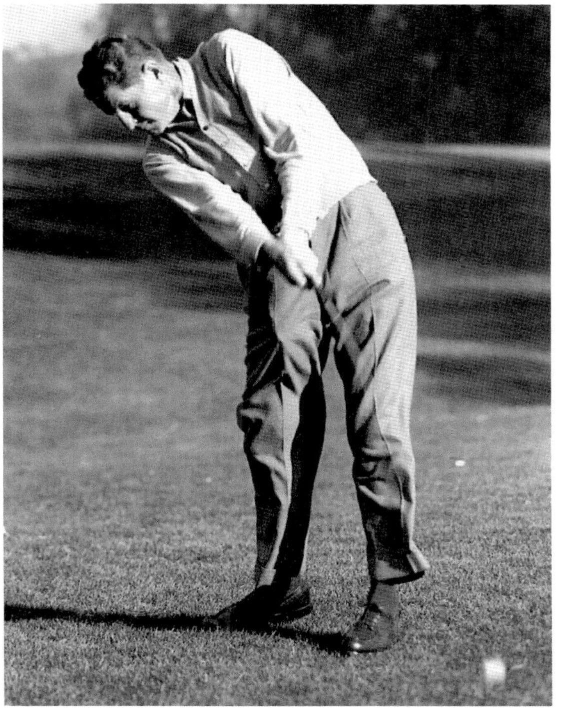

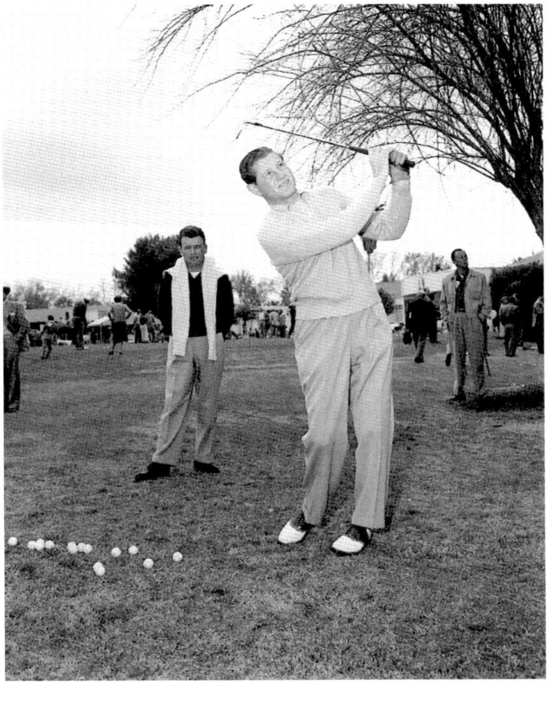

This photograph taken by Alex Morrison shows Jackie Burke Jr. as an onlooker of Horton Smith's swing. Burke won 17 times on the PGA Tour, including the Masters and PGA Championship in 1956. (Courtesy of Photos From the Fairway.)

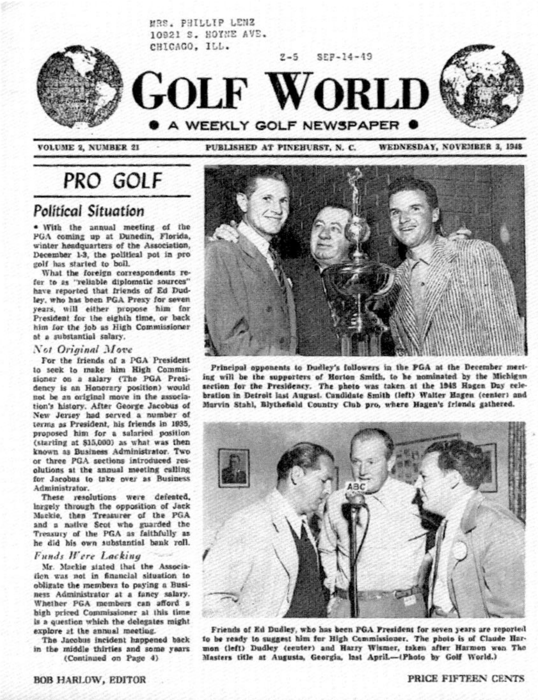

MRS. PHILLIP LENZ
10821 S. HOYNE AVE.
CHICAGO, ILL.
2-5 SEP-14-49

GOLF WORLD

• A WEEKLY GOLF NEWSPAPER •

VOLUME 2, NUMBER 21 — PUBLISHED AT PINEHURST, N. C. — WEDNESDAY, NOVEMBER 3, 1948

PRO GOLF

Political Situation

• With the annual meeting of the PGA coming up at Dunedin, Florida, winter headquarters of the Association, December 1-3, the political pot in pro golf has started to boil.

What the foreign correspondents refer to as "reliable diplomatic sources" have reported that friends of Ed Dudley, who has been PGA Prexy for seven years, will either propose him for President for the eighth time, or back him for the job as High Commissioner at a substantial salary.

Not Original Move

For the friends of a PGA President to seek to make him High Commissioner on a salary (The PGA Presidency is an Honorary position) would not be an original move in the association's history. After George Jacobus of New Jersey had served a number of terms as President, his friends in 1935, proposed him for a salaried position (starting at $15,000) as what was then known as Business Administrator. Two or three PGA sections introduced resolutions at the annual meeting calling for Jacobus to take over as Business Administrator.

These resolutions were defeated, largely through the opposition of Jack Mackie, then Treasurer of the PGA and a native Scot who guarded the Treasury of the PGA as faithfully as he did his own substantial bank roll.

Funds Were Lacking

Mr. Mackie stated that the Association was not in financial situation to obligate the members to paying a Business Administrator at a fancy salary. Whether PGA members can afford a high priced Commissioner at this time is a question which the delegates might explore at the annual meeting.

The Jacobus incident happened back in the middle thirties and some years

(Continued on Page 4)

Principal opponents to Dudley's followers in the PGA at the December meeting will be the supporters of Horton Smith, to be nominated by the Michigan section for the Presidency. The photo was taken at the 1948 Hagen Day celebration in Detroit last August. Candidate Smith (left) Walter Hagen (center) and Marvin Stahl, Blythefield Country Club pro, where Hagen's friends gathered.

Friends of Ed Dudley, who has been PGA President for seven years are reported to be ready to suggest him for High Commissioner. The photo is of Claude Harmon (left) Dudley (center) and Harry Wismer, taken after Harmon won The Masters title at Augusta, Georgia, last April.—(Photo by Golf World.)

BOB HARLOW, EDITOR

PRICE FIFTEEN CENTS

This cover of *Golf World* from November 3, 1948, shows both Horton Smith and Ed Dudley. Smith was pictured with his supporters, (top) Walter Hagen and Marvin Stahl, to become the next president of the PGA. Dudley, president for the last seven years, is pictured with Claude Harmon and Harry Wismer (bottom), his supporters for presidency.

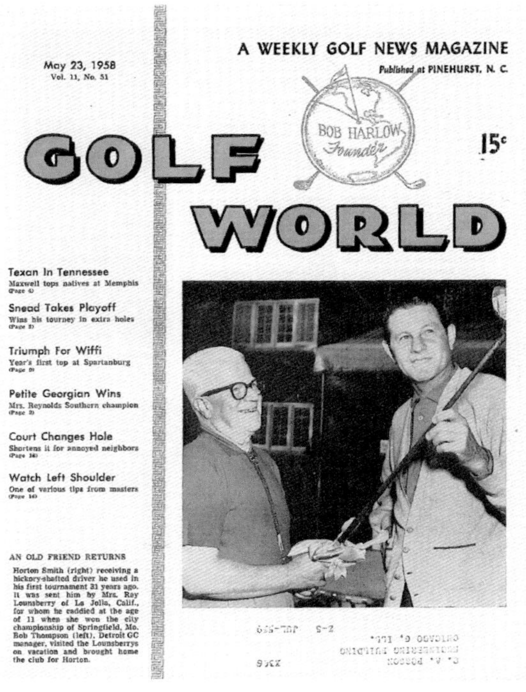

May 23, 1958
Vol. 11, No. 51

A WEEKLY GOLF NEWS MAGAZINE
Published at PINEHURST, N. C.

BOB HARLOW
Founder

15¢

GOLF WORLD

Texan In Tennessee
Maxwell tops natives at Memphis
(Page 4)

Snead Takes Playoff
Wins his tourney in extra holes
(Page 5)

Triumph For Wiffi
Year's first top at Spartanburg
(Page 9)

Petite Georgian Wins
Mrs. Reynolds Southern champion
(Page 3)

Court Changes Hole
Shortens it for annoyed neighbors
(Page 16)

Watch Left Shoulder
One of various tips from masters
(Page 14)

AN OLD FRIEND RETURNS

Horton Smith (right) receiving a hickory-shafted driver he used in his first tournament 31 years ago. It was sent him by Mrs. Ray Lounsberry of La Jolla, Calif., for whom he caddied at the age of 11 when she won the city championship of Springfield, Mo. Bob Thompson (left), Detroit GC manager, visited the Lounsberrys on vacation and brought home the club for Horton.

On the cover of *Golf World* from May 28, 1958, Bob Thompson (left) presents Horton Smith with a driver Smith used in his first tournament 31 years earlier. Mrs. Ray Lounsberry sent him the club; Smith caddied for her at the age of 11 when she won the Springfield City Championship.

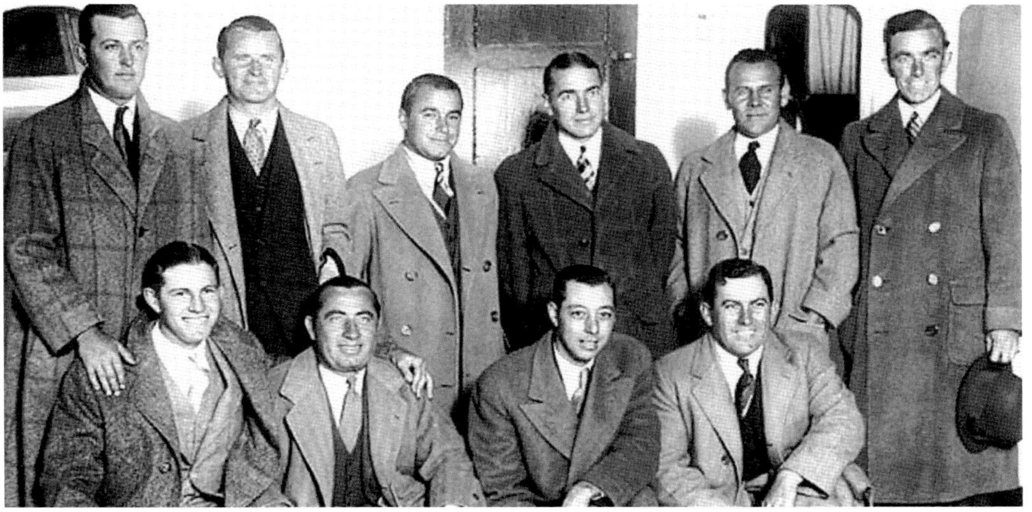

The 1929 Ryder Cup team, captained by Walter Hagen, was Horton Smith's (bottom row, far left) first appearance on the team. Although Smith beat Fred Robson from Great Britain four and two, the team lost to the Europeans seven to five. The U.S. team included Ed Dudley (back row, far left), Johnny Golden, Johnny Farrell, Walter Hagen, Leo Diegel, Gene Sarazen, Jim Turnesa, Horton Smith, Al Watrous, and Al Espinosa.

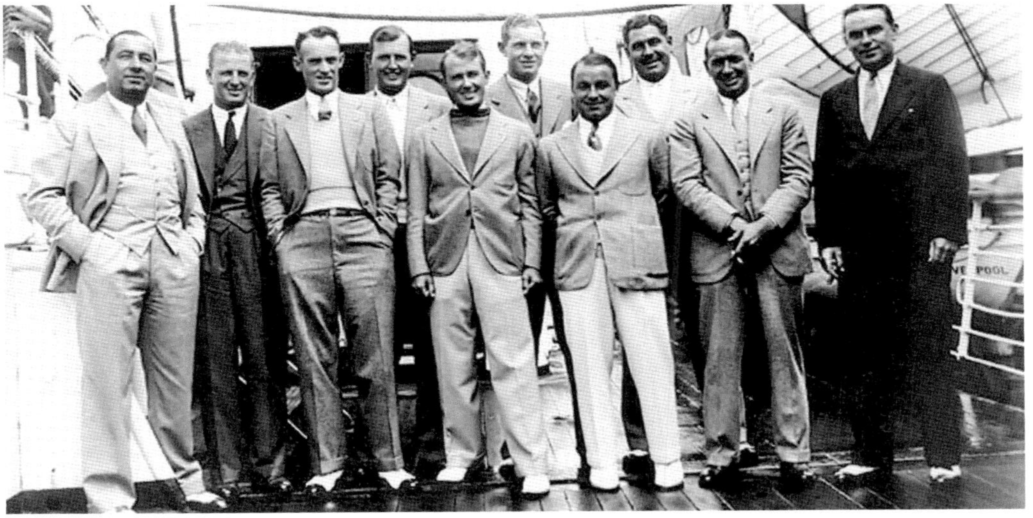

Smith's second appearance on the Ryder Cup team took place in 1933. Again Walter Hagen was the captain and again the U.S. team would lose to the European team. The players on the U.S. squad included Gene Sarazen, Walter Hagen, Olin Dutra, Denny Shute, Craig Wood, Paul Runyan, Ed Dudley (fourth from left), Billy Burke, Horton Smith (sixth from left), and Leo Diegel. Smith would beat Charles Whitcombe 2 and 1 in his match.

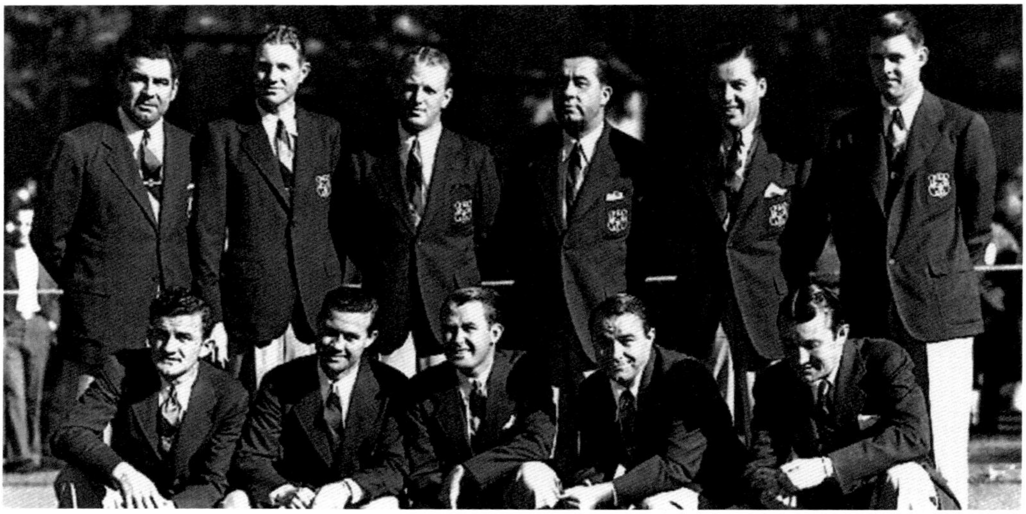

The 1935 Ryder Cup would be Smith's last appearance despite being chosen three more times. The U.S. team would win this event nine to three over Great Britain. Horton would win his 4-ball match with Paul Runyan over Bill Cox and Edward Jarman nine and eight. Smith would also halve his individual match against Bill Cox. The team included Captain Walter Hagen, Gene Sarazen, Henry Picard, Johnny Revolta, Paul Runyan, Horton Smith, Olin Dutra, Ky Laffoon, Craig Wood, and Sam Parks Jr.

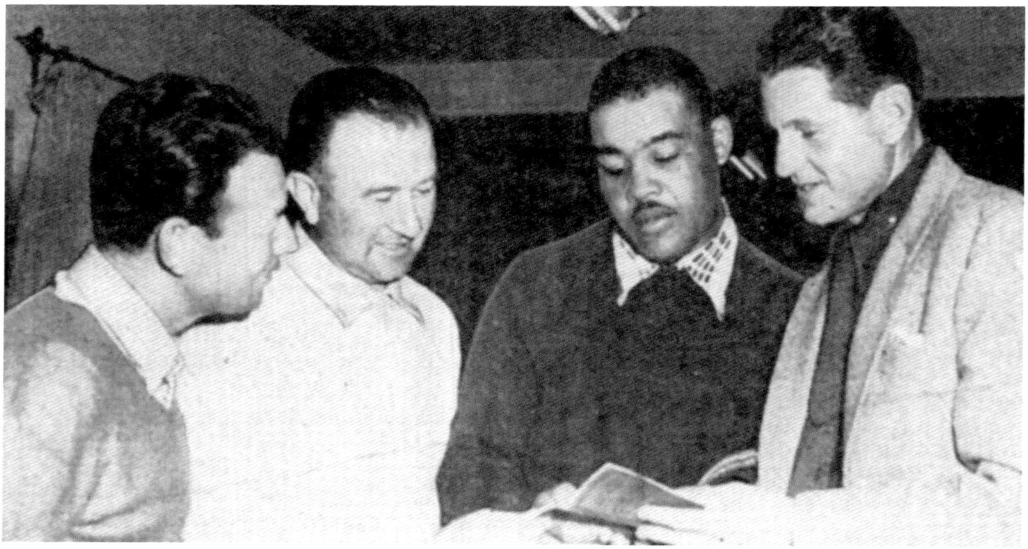

From left to right, Chuck Dupree, Joe Brown, Joe Louis, and Horton Smith are pictured here at the 1952 San Diego Open. Smith was the president of the PGA during the first tournament that allowed an African American golfer, famous boxer Joe Louis, to participate in a professional tournament.

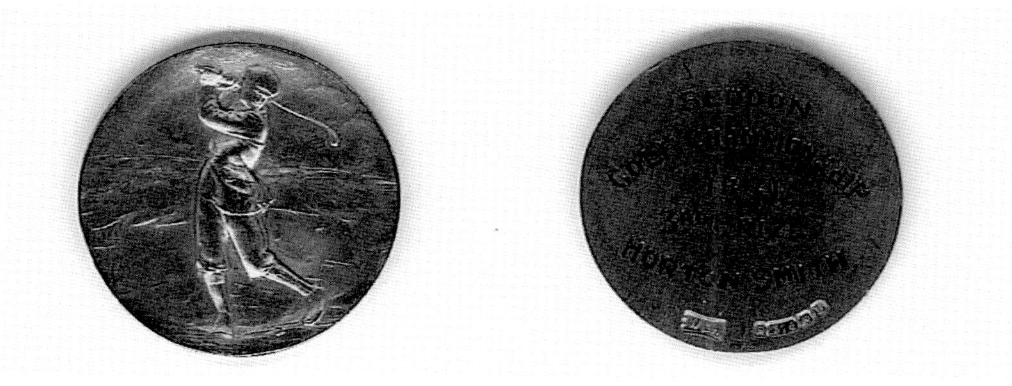

This award was given to Horton Smith in 1931 at the Seddon Golf Championship for finishing in third place. Smith played the Seddon tournament during one of many trips to Europe when he would play several tournaments in preparation for, and after, playing in the British Open. (Courtesy of Ozarks Fairways.)

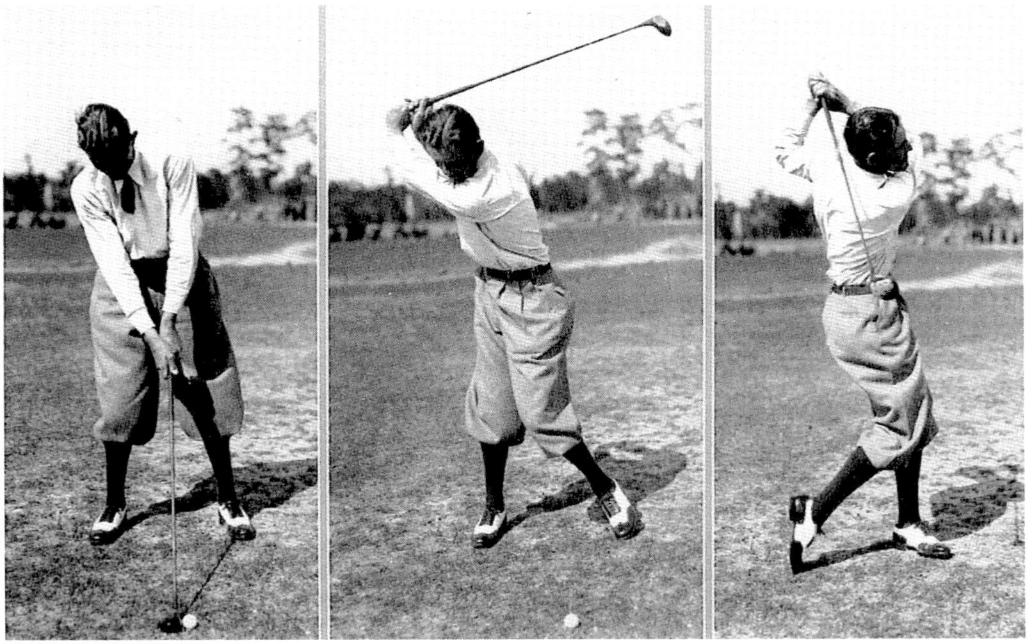

This photograph by John Hemmer was taken in 1930 and was published in the *American Golfer* magazine that same year. This photograph is an excellent study of Smith's swing. As pictured, Smith would shift most of his weight well to the right side.

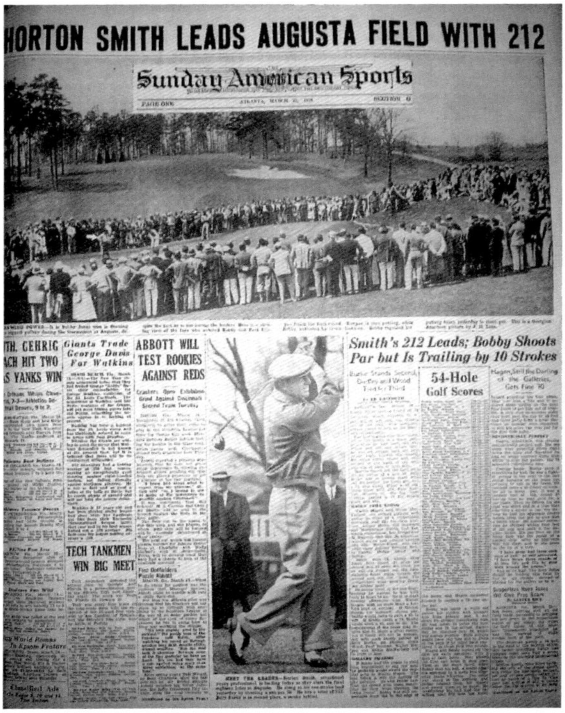

HORTON SMITH LEADS AUGUSTA FIELD WITH 212

Sunday American Sports

Giants Trade George Davis For Watkins

ABBOTT WILL TEST ROOKIES AGAINST REDS

Smith's 212 Leads; Bobby Shoots Par but Is Trailing by 10 Strokes

54-Hole Golf Scores

TECH TANKMEN WIN BIG MEET

The *Atlanta American* March 25, 1934, shows Horton Smith in the lead going into the final round of the Masters held in nearby Augusta, Georgia. The top photograph shows that Bobby Jones's gallery was the largest even though Smith had a one shot lead over Billy Burke.

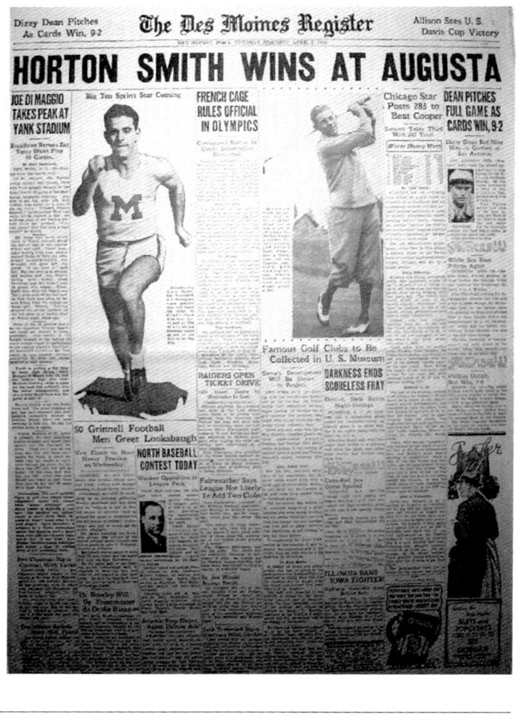

Dizzy Dean Pitches As Cards Win, 9-2

The Des Moines Register

Allison Sees U. S. Davis Cup Victory

HORTON SMITH WINS AT AUGUSTA

JOE DI MAGGIO TAKES PEAK AT YANK STADIUM

Big Ten Sprint Star Coming

FRENCH CAGE RULES OFFICIAL IN OLYMPICS

Chicago Star Posts 285 to Beat Cooper

DEAN PITCHES FULL GAME AS CARDS WIN, 9-2

Famous Golf Clubs to Be Collected in U. S. Museum

RAIDERS OPEN TICKET DRIVE

DARKNESS ENDS SCORELESS FRAY

50 Grinnell Football Men Greet Lookabaugh

NORTH BASEBALL CONTEST TODAY

Fairweather Says League Not Likely To Add Two Clubs

This April 7, 1936, copy of the *Des Moines Register* says it all. "Horton Smith Wins at Augusta." Smith would top Harry "Lighthorse" Cooper for the victory with a total score of 285. The rain-soaked tournament took five days to complete.

Pictured here is the awards ceremony at the 1937 Western Open that Ralph Guldahl (left) would win in a playoff with Horton Smith (right). Smith would present Guldahl with the first-place trophy, a task usually given to the preceding year's winner, but Guldahl had won the preceding two years.

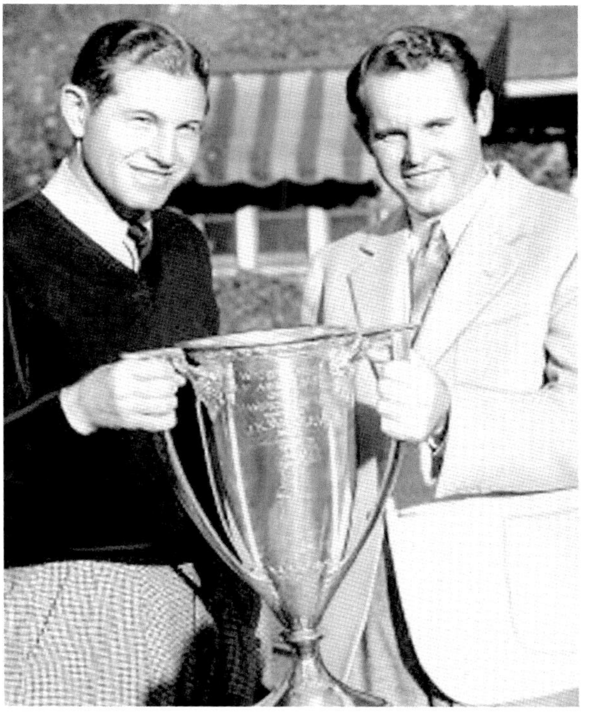

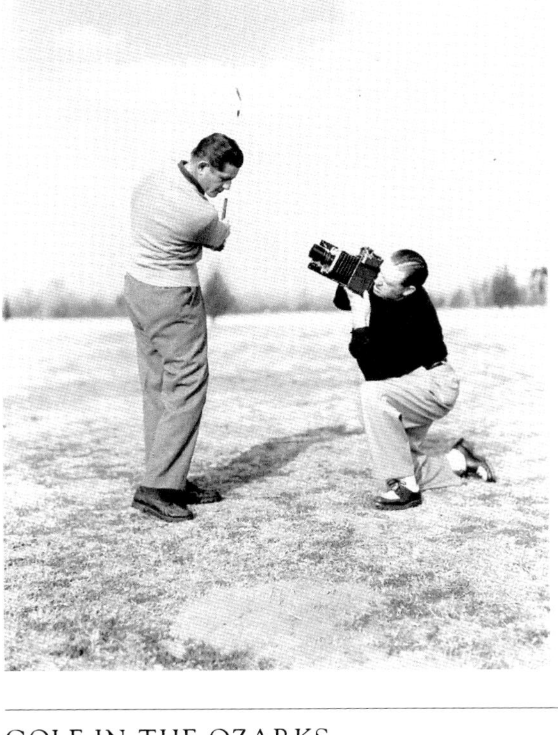

Alex Morrison can be seen in action photographing Horton Smith's swing. Morrison would take thousands of photographs of not only Smith but also other greats like Ben Hogan, Sam Snead, Jack Nicklaus, and Arnold Palmer. (Courtesy of Photos From the Fairway.)

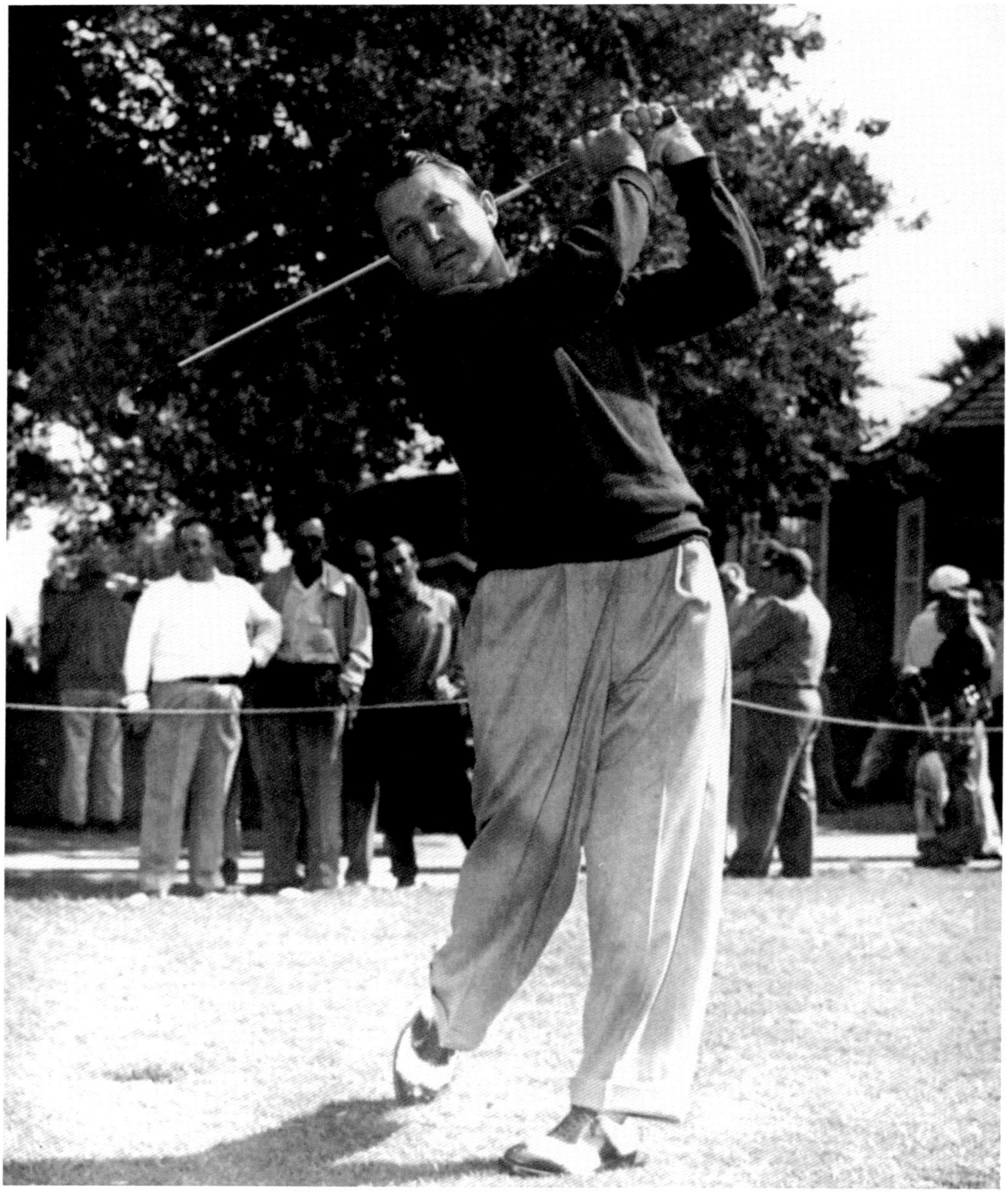

Very few pictures remain of one of the most charismatic golfers in history. Ky Laffoon would regularly play in tour events but was also known for his gambling on the golf course. Laffoon would rarely pose for photographs.

2

CHIEF

Ky Laffoon was one of the most charismatic golfers of all time. Laffoon was born in Zinc, Arkansas, on December 23, 1908. Laffoon spent a large portion of his life growing up in the neighboring state of Oklahoma. He turned professional in 1931 and amassed 10 tournament wins over his 21-year career. Despite his obvious talent for scoring, it was his unbelievable personality that carries his name past his years.

One of the earliest stories of Laffoon was how he earned his nickname "Chief". A reporter made an association with Laffoon's dark complexion and Oklahoma address, and concluded that Laffoon was Native American. Laffoon thought it sounded like a good story, so he created a Cherokee heritage for himself. Reporters started to call him Chief and it stuck.

The most commonly told story of Laffoon was when, after a poor round of three putting, Laffoon tied his putter to the bumper of his car and dragged it all the way to the next tour stop. A police officer pulled Laffoon over for the sparks he noticed coming from behind his car. Laffoon reportedly told the officer that he was punishing the putter for its poor round. This story was more likely derived from a story once told by Ben Hogan, that while he was napping in Laffoon's car he awoke to a car with no driver. Laffoon had his head out the window while grinding down his sand wedge on the road with one hand, and steering with the other.

Another true putter story took place while playing a round during the off-season in Orlando, Florida. According to Judge Jim Bryrd, Ky Laffoon missed a putt on the 18th hole. Laffoon raced to his trunk and pulled out a pistol. He then shot the putter three times while shouting, "Take that you SOB! That's the last time you three-putt on me!" As far as Laffoon's golf career went, it was always overshadowed by his wild antics. In 1933, he won the Nebraska Open. The same year he finished second in the "World's Longest Driver Contest" at the Chicago World's Fair.

During 1934, Laffoon won the Atlanta Open, the Eastern, the Hershey Open, and the Glen Falls tournaments. This phenomenal year placed Laffoon on the 1935 Ryder Cup team, along with earning him the Radix Cup, now known as the Vardon Trophy. The cup was given to the lowest average scorer for the year. The following year, Laffoon kept on winning. He would win the Phoenix Open in 1935. In 1936, he and Walter Hagen won the Inverness Four-Ball Championship together. Back on top of his game in 1938, he and Dick Metz won the Miami Four-Ball, and later that year, he won the Cleveland Open thanks to a wild turn of events. While Ky and Sam Snead were battling it out for first place, the unbelievable happened to Snead. On the 18th hole, Snead hooked his second shot towards the locker room. As the ball approached, someone opened the door and the ball flew into the locker room. The shot cost Snead two strokes and the championship.

While all of this took place on the PGA Tour, Ky Laffoon's best round of golf was at Schifferdecker Golf Course in Joplin, with a round of 61. In 1937, Laffoon shot a course record of 65 at Oak Hill in Joplin, beating the record 66 held by Horton Smith. Laffoon spent many years in the Ozarks regularly playing in pro-ams in Joplin and Carthage.

As was common for professional golfers of the time, Ky would have associations with more than one country club. Over the years, he would be the head professional at Rockdale Country Club in Miami, Oklahoma, now known as Miami Golf and Country Club, then at Oak Hill in Joplin, Missouri, now known as Twin Hills Country Club. He was also a club professional at Northmoor Country Club and Ravinia in Chicago, Meadowbrook Country Club in St. Louis, and Green Gables Country Club in Denver. During his time as a club professional, he was known to give over 600 lessons a year.

During the 1950s to early 1980s, Ky Laffoon would spend most of his time in Springfield. In 1982, Laffoon was diagnosed with cancer. On March 16, 1984, Ky Laffoon was found in his home dead from a self-inflicted gunshot wound.

Career Victories

1933 Nebraska Open
1934 Atlantic Open
1934 Eastern Open
1934 Hershey Open
1934 Glen Falls Open
1934 Tied Western Open
1934 Tied St. Paul Open
1935 Phoenix Open
1936 Inverness Four Ball with Walter Hagen
1938 International Four with Dick Metz
1938 Cleveland Open
1946 Montgomery Invitational

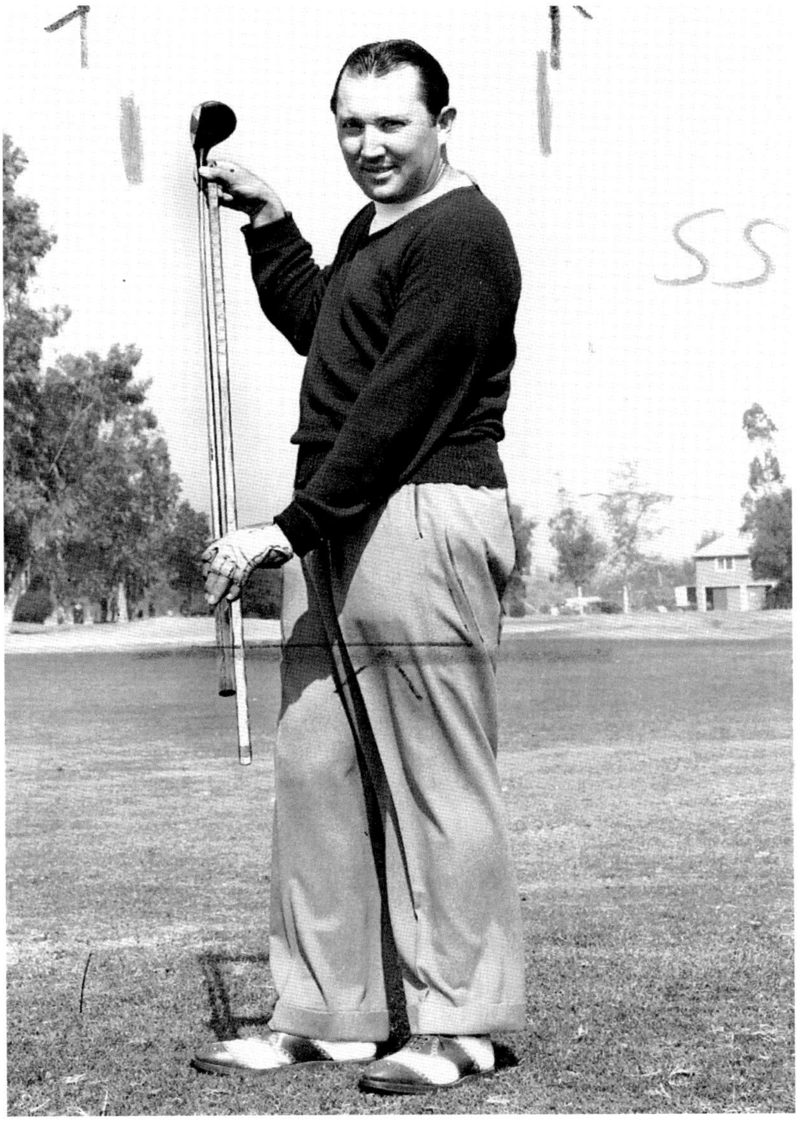

Shown here with one of his bent shafted clubs, Ky Laffoon believed that a bend in the shaft of his driver improved his shots. Laffoon's shaft shows a gradual bend measuring nearly one inch in the middle. As can be seen by the crop markings, this was the actual photograph used by Alex Morrison for a magazine article he wrote.

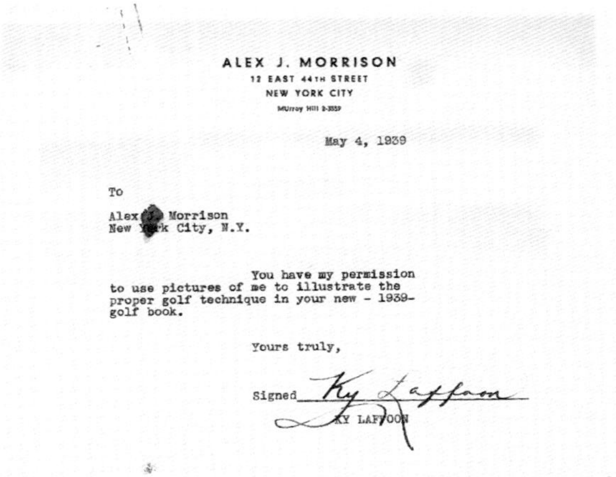

ALEX J. MORRISON
12 EAST 44TH STREET
NEW YORK CITY
MUrray Hill 2-3559

May 4, 1939

To

Alex J. Morrison
New York City, N.Y.

You have my permission to use pictures of me to illustrate the proper golf technique in your new - 1939- golf book.

Yours truly,

Signed Ky Laffoon
KY LAFFOON

Ky Laffoon would send his authorization of the use of his photograph to his golf writer Alex Morrison. Only because of their close relationship would Laffoon allow the use of his image. According to golf reporter Clair Goodwin, Laffoon felt reporters were not there for him when he needed them and he did not feel like he owed them any favors. (Courtesy of Ozarks Fairways.)

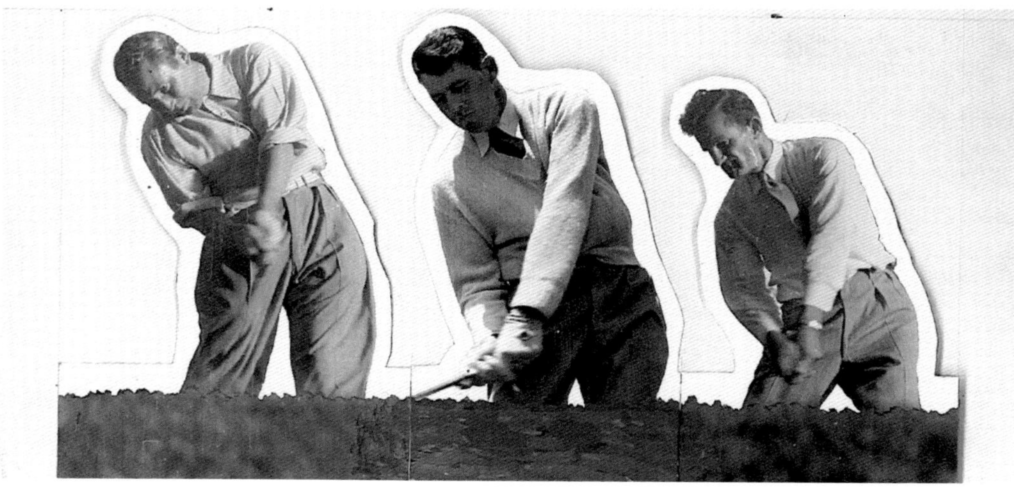

This is the actual photo-board Alex Morrison would use in his book *Better Golf Without Practice*. The photograph depicts golfers just before impact. The golfers include (left to right) Ky Laffoon, Dick Metz, and Johnny Revolta. (Courtesy of Ozarks Fairways.)

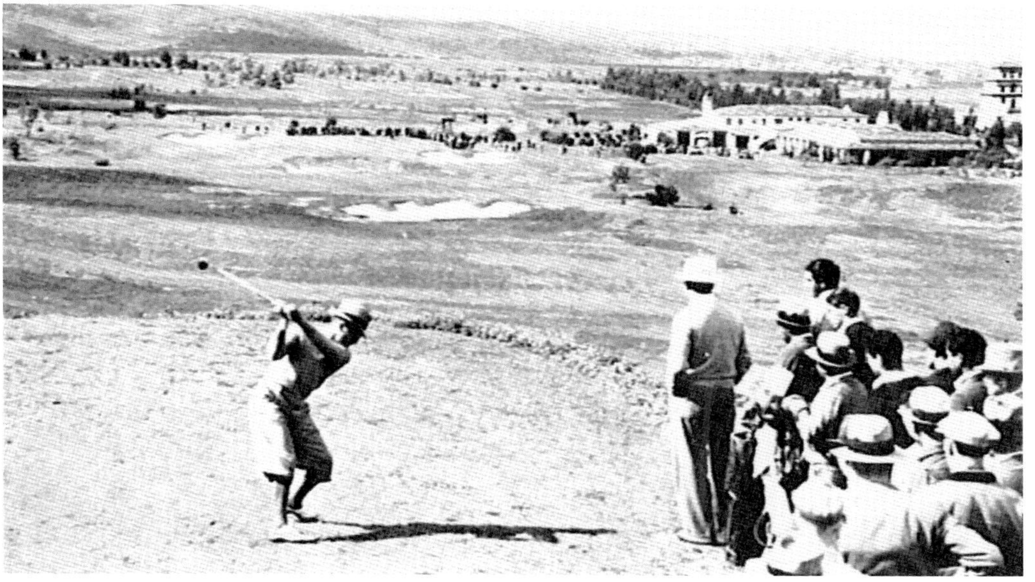

Ky Laffoon is pictured here at the 1934 U.S. Open at Merion Golf Club in Ardmore, Pennsylvania, where he finished in 23rd place behind winner Olin Dutra. Laffoon's best finish in the U.S. Open would be in 1936 when he finished fifth at Baltusrol Golf Club in Springfield, New York.

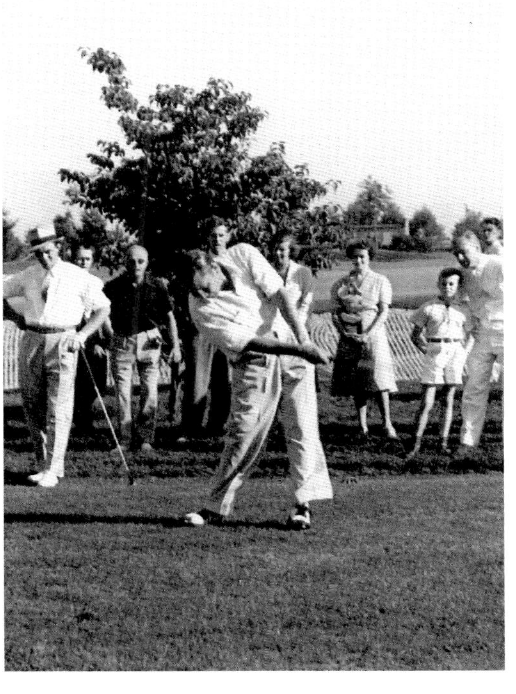

Ky Laffoon (right) would regularly tour the country to play in exhibition matches with the likes of Sam Snead (left). Laffoon's traveling to exhibitions would allow him the opportunity to gamble golfers all across the country. (Courtesy of Ozarks Fairways.)

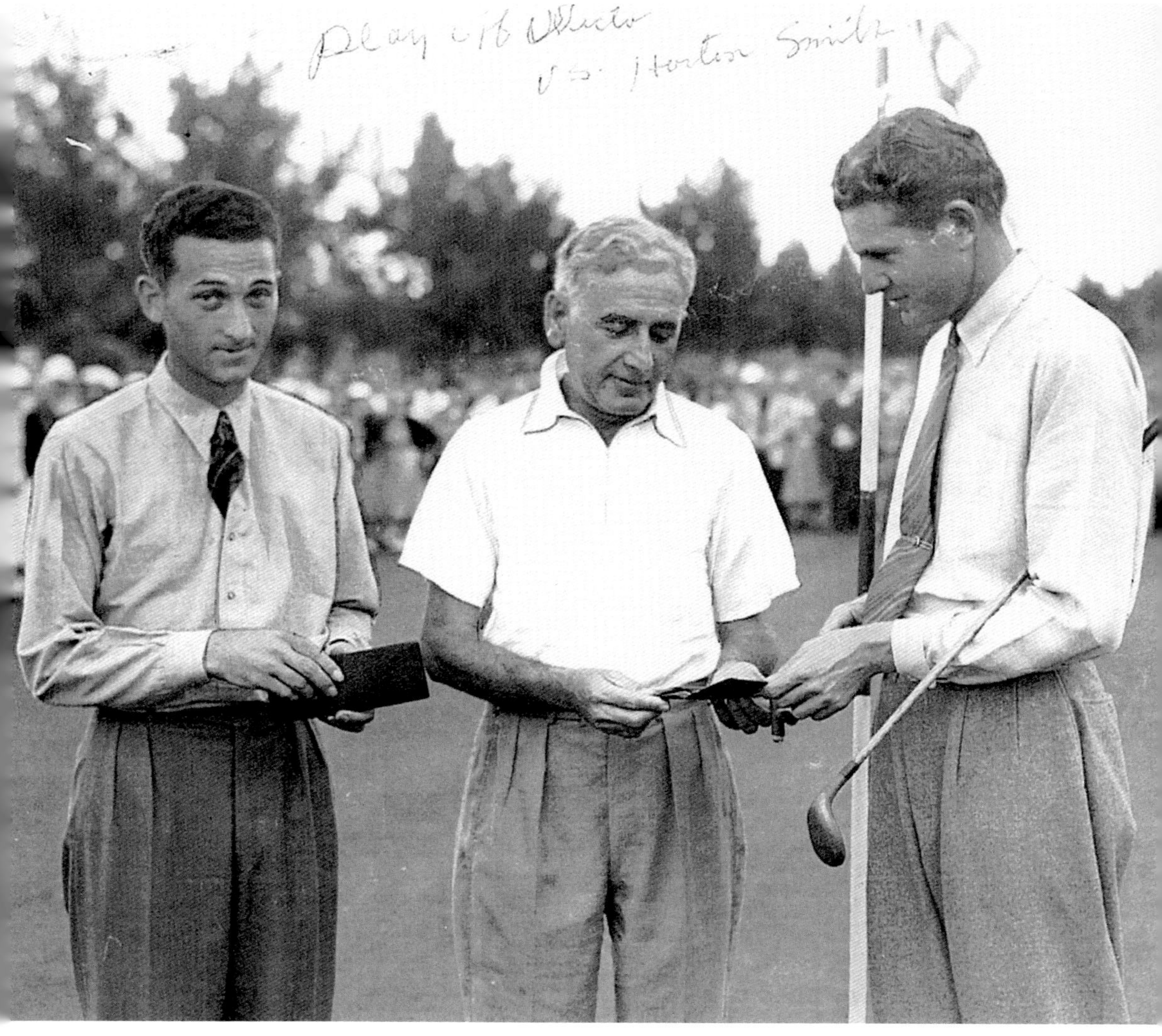

Leonard Dodson (left) won the all-Springfield playoff in the 1939 Hollywood Open against Horton Smith (far right) by three strokes. The payoff was in cash, $750 went to Dodson for his first place finish with $500 going to Smith for second place. (Courtesy of Perry Leslie.)

3

The Best No One Remembers

Leonard Dodson is the best golfer that no one remembers from Ozarks. Due to the crowd he ran with and his storied wagering exploits, the historians in the conservative area he called home tend to have forgotten everything he did right at his craft. Dodson's life, both on and off the course, is most similar to that of the film character "Tin Cup." Surely some of the ideas for the story came from stories told about Dodson, Ky Laffoon, and old running mate Titanic Thompson.

Leonard Dodson was born in Mumford, Missouri, in 1914, one of four boys. It did not take the 150-pound self-confident golf pro and hustler long to make a name for himself nationwide. When growing up in the Springfield area, he learned golf from Horton Smith. Growing up he learned the art of golf and more importantly, the hustle. According to Dodson, "ridge-runners around Springfield didn't believe in the ethics of golf. There was no such thing as a conceded putt. If your opponent had a five footer for the match and you didn't try to talk him out of it, you were either crazy or you weren't a ridge-runner."

During his time in Springfield, he set the course record at Hickory Hills Country Club with a score of 64. At the time, the course was a par 73. During the round, he had an eagle and seven birdies. The day after Dodson shot the course record, a few famous golfers in their own right gave the course a try. The players were Horton Smith, Lawson Little, Harry Cooper, and Jimmy Thompson. The low score was a 67 posted by Little. Dodson won three Springfield City Championships; two of which were back to back with a win over Herman Keiser in extra holes.

Horton Smith helped Dodson get his first pro job in Pembina, Wisconsin. Dodson would later move closer to home to be the head professional at the Old Mission Club in Kansas City and eventually at the Kansas City County Club. In 1941, Dodson was voted Kansas City's King of Sports. He quickly became known in the golf community as quite the storyteller and quite the gambler. An example of Dodson's gambling exploits was when he made a bet with two well-known Jacksonville, Florida, amateurs John Fletcher and Sam Hooper. One day during a winter pro-am, he told them "I will bet you $500 I can beat both of you, and I will play on one foot." Fletcher and Hooper jumped at the chance. Both golfers regularly shot in the 70s. The Jacksonville team had a best ball of 73 due to high winds that day. Dodson beat them three up with two to go. What they did not know was Dodson's ability to hit the ball from his knees, one leg, and even blindfolded. According to Dodson, hitting off his knees was the hardest.

Leonard's gambling exploits were not exclusive to the golf course. One of Dodson's running mates was Titanic Thompson. Thompson was in the Arnold Rothstein clique. Rothstein was the gambler behind the famous "Black Sox scandal," where members of the White Sox were paid to throw the World Series in 1919. One day he and Thompson were at the Busy Bee, a

Tallahassee Café where Dodson was bragging to Thompson about how he was good at guessing peoples' weight. He bet Thompson $1,000 he could guess the weight of all the waitresses in the diner together, closer than Titanic could. He had the manager weigh the waitresses. When they made their guesses, Thompson was within three pounds. Dodson guessed the weight right on the nose. What Thompson did not realize was that the night before Dodson had paid the manager $50 to weigh all of the waitresses. According to Dodson, "I didn't plan to come that close, but I had to because Titanic just missed it and I had to do my best to win."

Dodson was equally impressive with his golf game as with his gambling successes. In 1937, he won the Philadelphia Open, the Iowa Open, and the Western Missouri-Eastern Kansas tournament for entry into the national PGA Championship. But the most important win took place at the Hollywood Florida Open in 1939. Horton Smith and Dodson finished in a tie for first place. As the 18-hole playoff was about to begin, Dodson approached Smith and said, "Lets play for both first and second place money, all the dough to the winner. You know you can't beat me." Smith refused, and later was glad he did. Dodson won.

In 1938, while playing in the Bing Crosby Tournament in Rancho Santa Fe, California, Leonard Dodson found himself in a unique position. The PGA had just implemented a new rule that the golfer was only able to carry 14 clubs in his bag. After a good first round, Dodson discovered a trick collapsible putter that an admirer had given to him years ago, folded up in the pocket of his bag. Dodson became the first professional golfer to be disqualified for carrying more than 14 clubs in his bag.

One of Dodson's biggest victories came in 1941. While playing in the Oakland Open at Sequoia Country Club, Dodson was particularly boisterous that week. One member of the gallery asked Dodson, knowing he was from the Ozarks, if it was true he had not worn shoes until he was 18. Leonard responded "Shucks man, I had to put rocks in my first pair of shoes to get the feel of it." At the end of the tournament Dodson found himself in a tie for the lead with Ben Hogan causing a playoff. During the playoffs, there was standing water on most of the greens due to the daylong rain. At one point, Hogan was able to move his ball on the green because it had landed in casual water. Dodson asked an official to measure the distance from the cup after Hogan had moved his ball. It was discovered Hogan had gained several inches in the move. The resulting fuss unnerved Hogan. He two putted the hole and Dodson went on to win the $1,200 first-place prize money with a score of 71.

Later the same year, Dodson went back to the Crosby Pro-Am in California to redeem himself after the disqualification in 1938. He and his playing partner, an amateur from Kansas City, went on to win the Professional-Amateur portion of the tournament by six strokes. The amateur was Ray Watson, father of golf great Tom Watson.

Leonard Dodson died at the age of 83 in 1997. He was entered into the Ozarks Golf Hall of Fame in 2004.

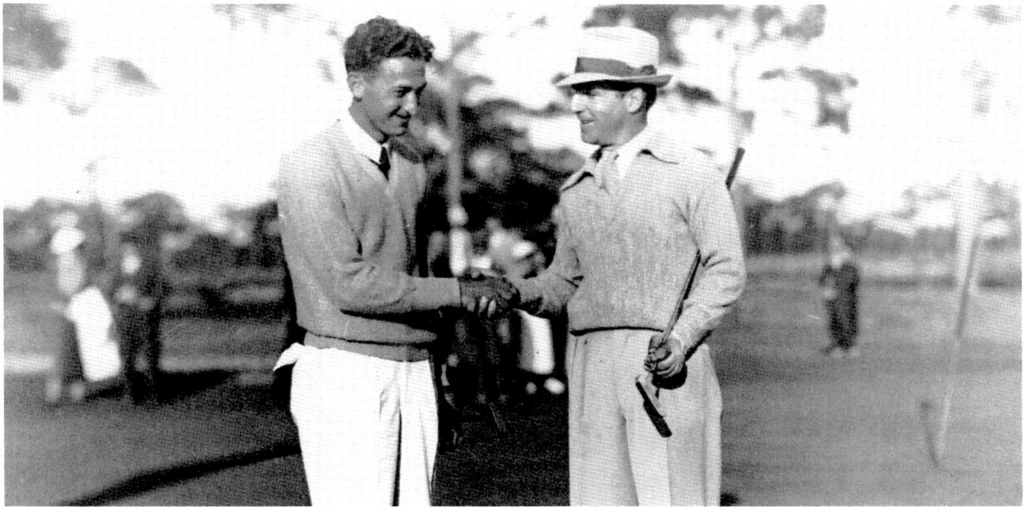

Leonard Dodson (left) and Harry Cooper are pictured here at the 1936 St. Petersburg Open. Dodson would win the tournament beating Cooper in a playoff for the $500 first prize. The tournament was played at the Pasadena Country Club in St. Petersburg, Florida. (Courtesy of Perry Leslie.)

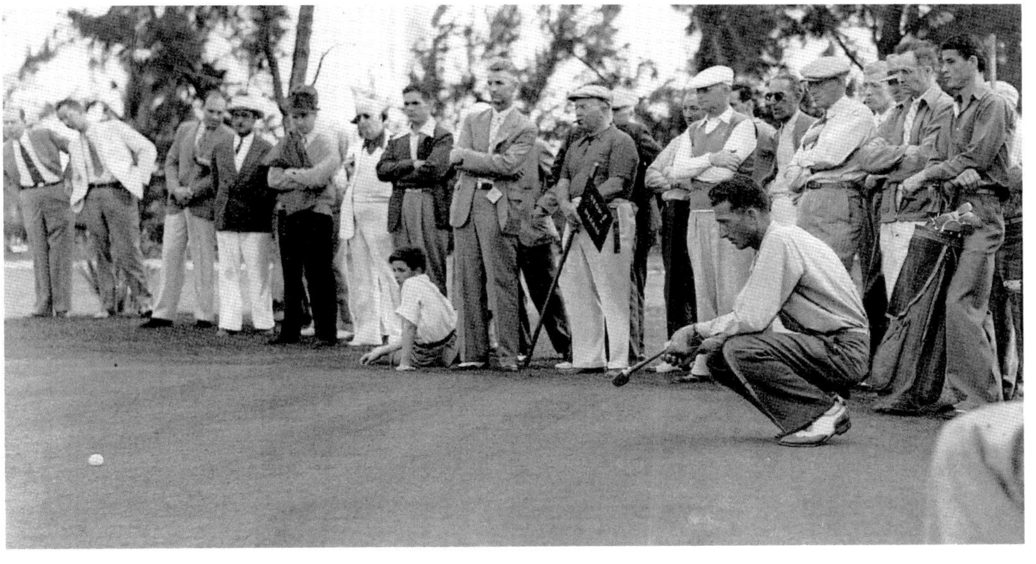

Leonard Dodson lined up his 30-foot putt on the 16th hole in his playoff win over Horton Smith in the 1939 Hollywood Open. Smith was Dodson's golf coach at a young age. Evidently, Smith taught him too well. (Courtesy of Perry Leslie.)

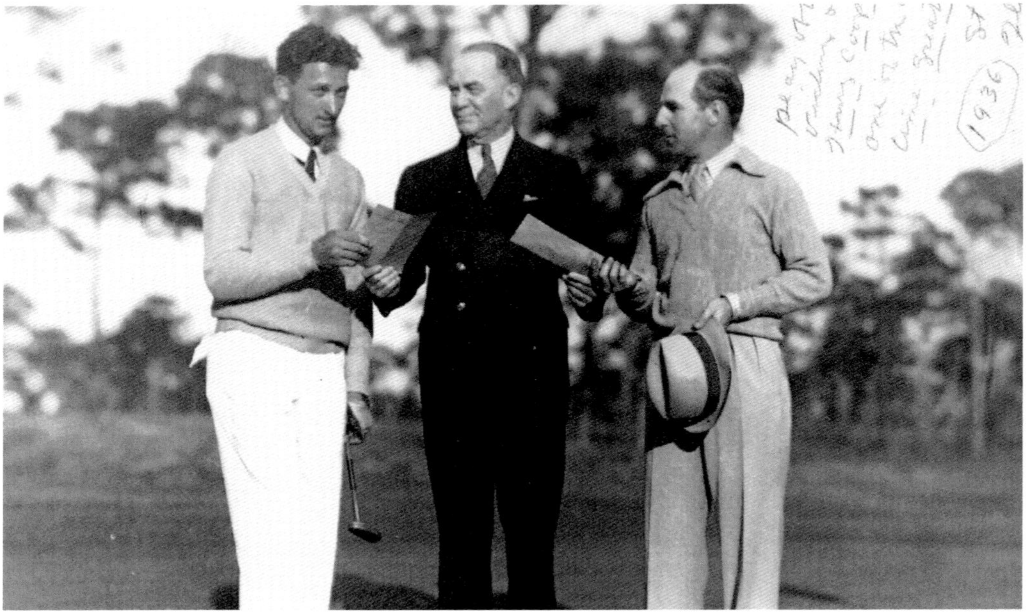

This photograph taken during the 1936 St. Petersburg Open shows winner Leonard Dodson (left) with second-place finisher Harry Cooper (far right). In the final playoff round, Dodson shot a par 72 while Cooper finished with a score of 73. (Courtesy of Perry Leslie.)

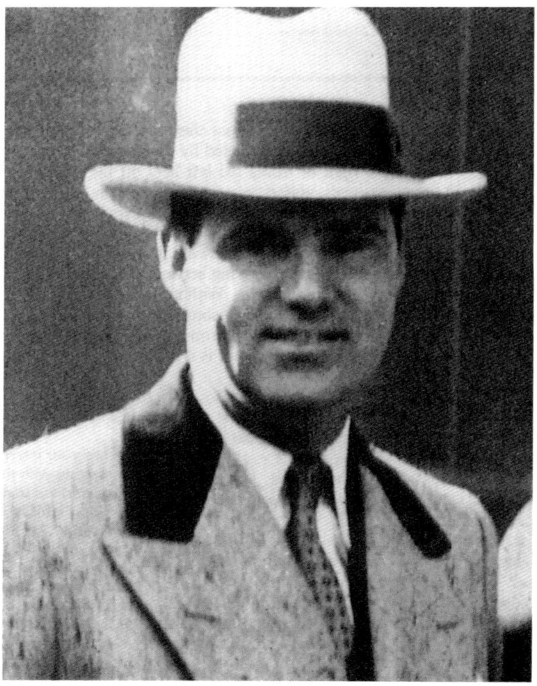

Titanic Thompson was one of golf's greatest hustlers. Leonard Dodson and Titanic Thompson would often travel the country looking for new people to gamble both on and off of the golf course. Thompson would often play someone right-handed and loose only to come back the next day for larger stakes to play them left-handed and win.

Leonard Dodson (left) once wagered a wealthy oilman in San Antonio, Texas, $50 that he could play three holes of the local course in 18 strokes using a six-iron and a tennis ball. Of course, the businessman took the bet. Dodson finished in 16 strokes.

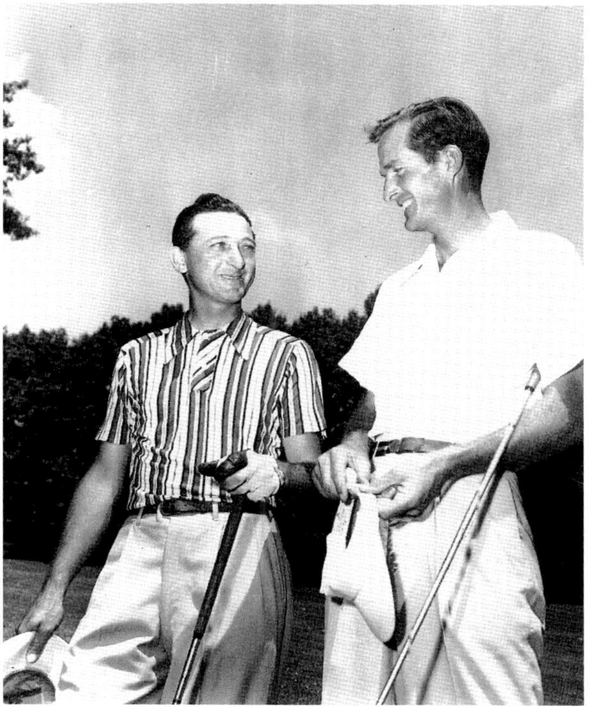

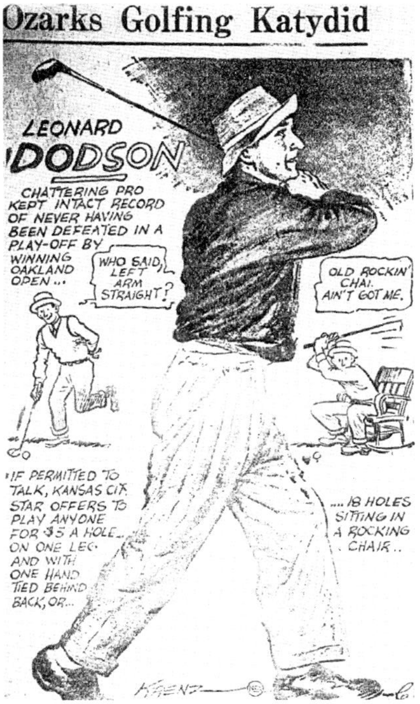

This caricature of Leonard Dodson says it all. This drawing was done for a Springfield newspaper in 1941 and tells the story of Dodson's noted gambling exploits of playing on one leg with one hand behind his back and playing 18 holes while sitting in a rocking chair.

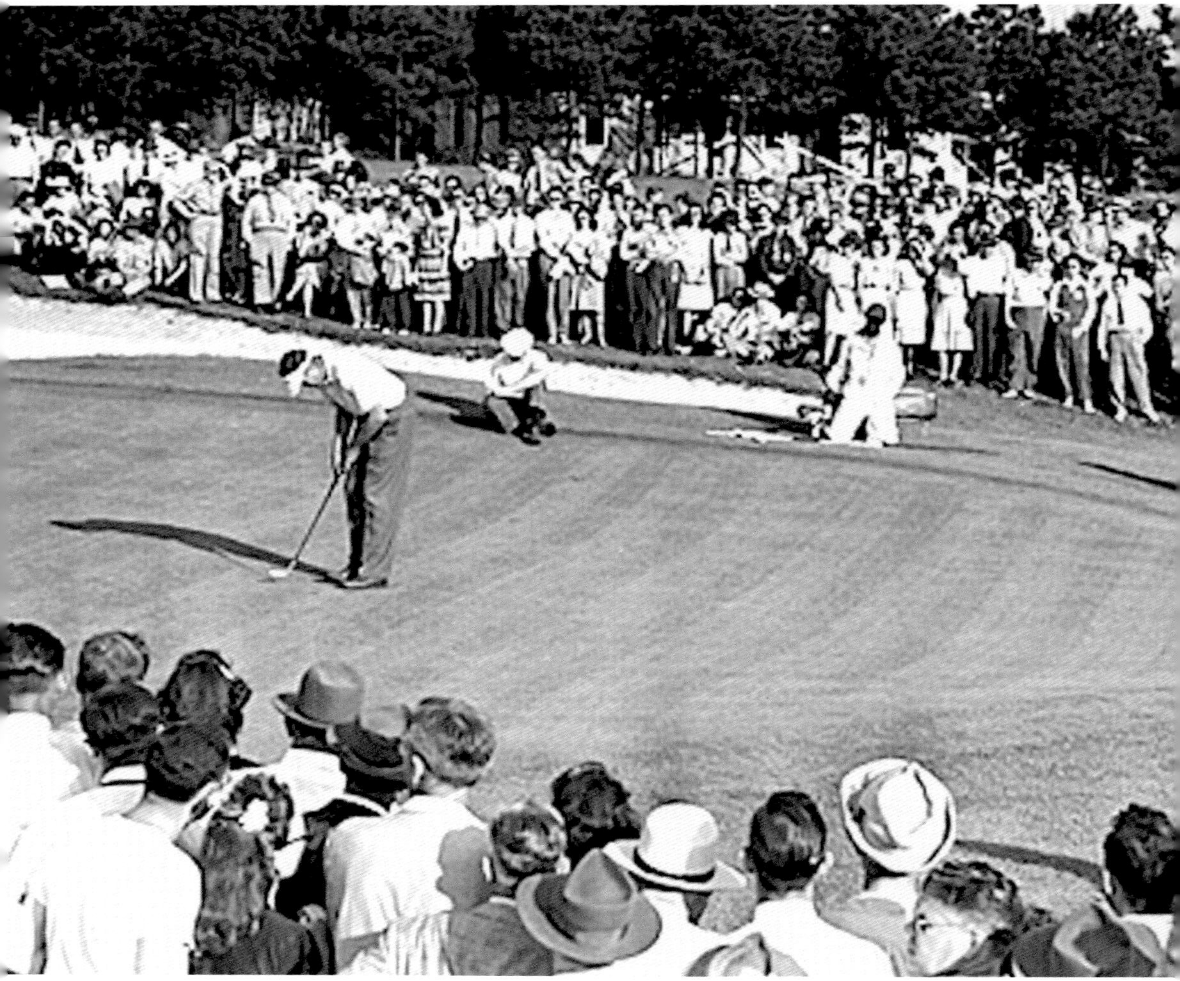

Herman Keiser can be seen here sinking his last putt on the 18th green for a final round 74 to win the 1946 Masters. Keiser's 72-hole total of 282 was one shot ahead of Ben Hogan. The 1946 Masters was the first since 1942 due to World War II.

4

Against All Odds

Herman Keiser had only been out of the navy for a year when he won the Masters in 1946. For three years, Herman would take his clubs aboard the USS *Cincinnati* for the brief opportunities at port when he could fit in a round before heading back to the Atlantic. Thanks to legendary golfer Paul Runyan, Keiser was able to get out of the navy several months early. All he had to do was help a higher-ranking officer with his slice.

Keiser, nicknamed the Missouri Mortician, was born on October 7, 1914, in Springfield, Missouri. He was introduced to golf when two brothers were hitting balls into the field near his home at the corner of Division Street and Perry Avenue. After a while, the boys came to Keiser looking for some of the balls that had landed close to his house. When they arrived, Keiser asked them what the balls were. They explained to him what golf was and let him hit a few balls. That is when Keiser was hooked. He would often go to nearby Springfield Country Club at four in the morning with friends to hit balls to the dew-soaked greens. During the summer, Keiser caddied under caddy master Horton Smith. Smith would have a huge influence on Keiser's golfing career. At the age of 19, Keiser won five local golf tournaments including the Heart of the Ozarks held at the Springfield Country Club, the Mid-Ozarks title in Monett, the All-Ozarks Championship at Hickory Hills Country Club, the Mountain Grove Championship, and finally the Tri-State Championship held in Joplin.

In the late 1930s, Herman put up a driving range across from the Glenstone golf course where he could give lessons and work on his game. In April 1940, Horton Smith found Keiser a pro position in Akron, Ohio, at Portage Country Club under Al Espinosa. The next year, Herman moved over to the storied Firestone Country Club in Akron.

Already known in the late 1930s and 1940s as a good golfer, Keiser became nationally recognized when he beat favorite Ben Hogan by one stroke in the 1946 Masters. According to Keiser, this victory was literally against the odds. Stories began to spread during the tournament that some members of the Augusta National Golf Club had placed large bets on Ben Hogan. Over time, the reported numbers have changed from $50,000 at four to one odds, to $100,000 at 10 to 1 odds. Regardless, these members were obviously pulling for Hogan.

After leading the tournament for the first two days, Keiser felt there were efforts to sabotage his play. Just before the third round, his tee time was changed causing him to rush to the first tee without even hitting balls. During the same round, they gave him a 13-year-old caddie. After demanding a new caddie with more experience, he was denied. Even after these efforts Keiser still remained atop the leader board.

During the final round, despite being the leader, Keiser was paired with Byron Nelson a few groups in front of Hogan. At one point, Keiser had a five-stroke lead, but Hogan made a run to get to within one stroke. At the final hole, Hogan only needed to make a two-foot par putt to force a playoff, but the putt did not drop. Herman Keiser had just won the 1946 Masters, with the purse for the winner at $2,500. Keiser's seven-iron that he used on his approach shot on the final hole is still on display at Augusta National today.

One might think this event would have caused tension between Hogan and Keiser, but it was not the case. In 1947, Keiser was named to the Ryder Cup team headed by Ben Hogan, which took place at the Portland Golf Club. Just before the beginning of the first round of play, Hogan noticed Keiser looking distracted. Hogan asked if something was troubling him. Keiser responded by telling him that a young lady that he recently "dated" for $20 had found out he was a famous golfer. Her fee was now $1,000 or the "date" was going to be called rape. Hogan took out his wallet took out $1,000 and told Keiser to pay him back when he could. This gesture made the two golfers friends for life.

This friendship would be displayed once again on February 2, 1949. During a trip to the Texas Open, Keiser was driving through the remains of what was a terrible traffic accident. While driving slowly through the wreckage, Keiser recognized Hogan's Cadillac flattened at the side of the road. Keiser and Dutch Harrison drove to El Paso, nearly 120 miles away, where the ambulance had taken Hogan. When Keiser arrived at the hospital, Hogan did not look good. Hogan had a bandage over one eye, the other was nearly swollen shut, and a case enclosed his lower body. Hogan gestured for Keiser to come to him. As Keiser leaned over for his friend to speak, he heard Hogan in a whisper say, "Herman, would you check on my clubs?" Keiser has often said that Hogan was "the finest gentlemen I ever knew."

Herman Keiser played in 26 Masters tournaments. His last round at Augusta was in 1974 at the age of 59. Before his death on December 24, 2003, Keiser lived outside of Akron in Copley, Ohio. He would make a trip every April to Augusta for the Masters champions' dinner. According to Keiser, the reason he made the trip was for the $1,500 check he received for attending the dinner. Keiser was inducted into the Springfield Hall of Fame in April 2000.

Career Victories

1938 Iowa Open
1942 Miami Four Ball Invitation
1946 Masters
1946 Knoxville Invitational
1947 Esmeralda Open

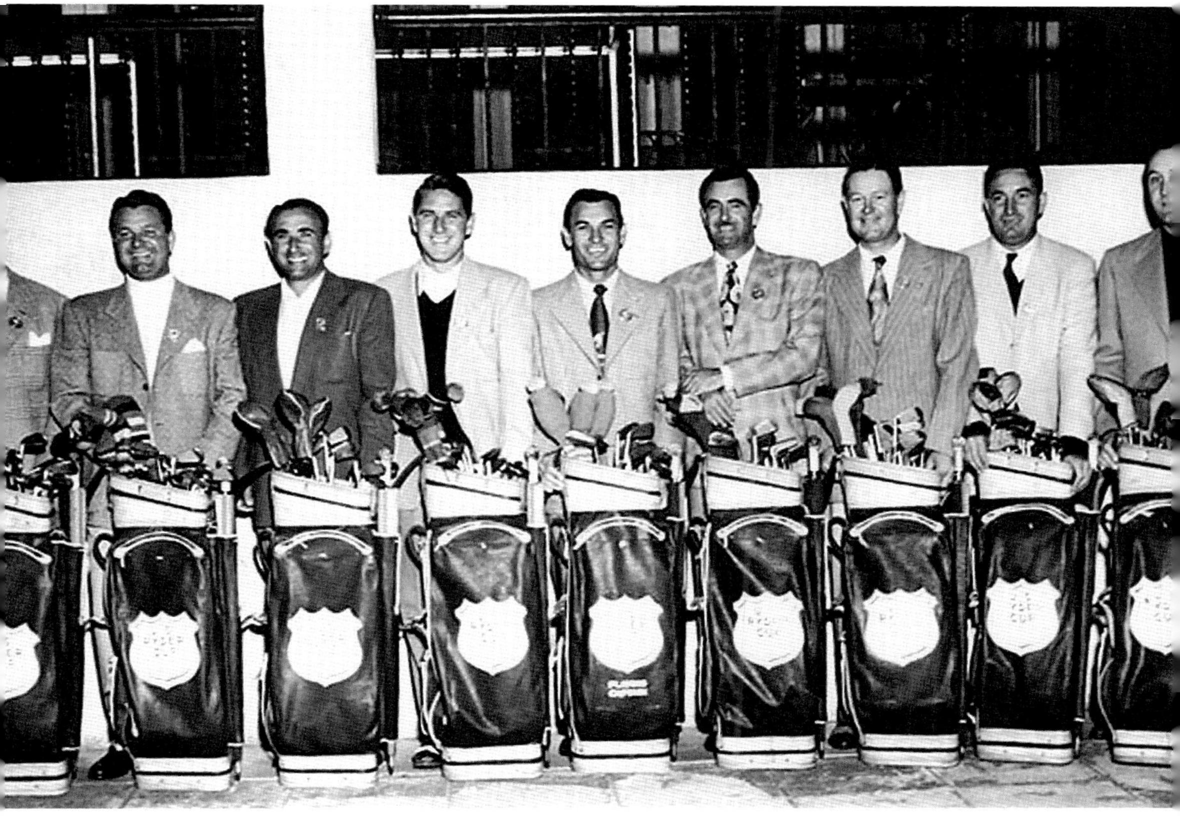

One of the greatest Ryder Cup teams of all time was the 1947 U.S. team that beat the Great Britain squad 11 to 1. The team included Sam Snead, Jimmy Demaret, Ben Hogan, Byron Nelson, and Herman Keiser (far right). Keiser received the team's only loss to Sam King.

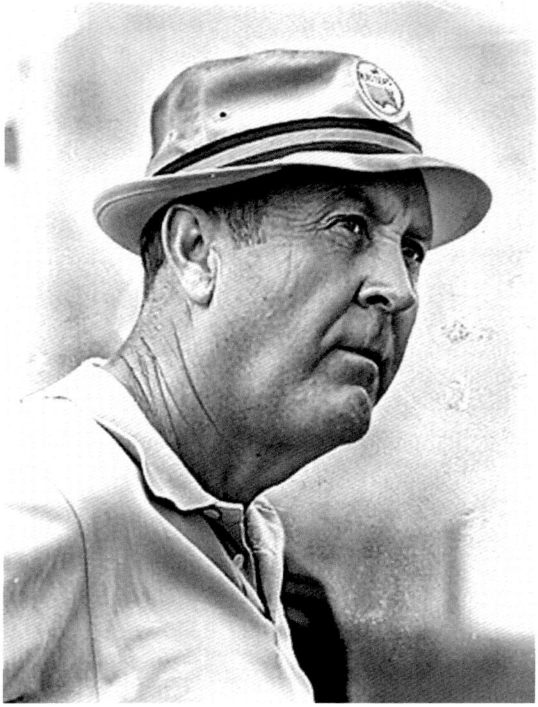

Herman Keiser only played in one Horton Smith Cup match for the Springfield squad. They would win the 1934 competition. That same year, Keiser won the West Plains tournament, the Heart of the Ozarks tournament, Springfield City Amateur Championship, Mountain Grove Invitational, Bolivar Invitational, Aurora District Amateur, and the Ozark Amateur.

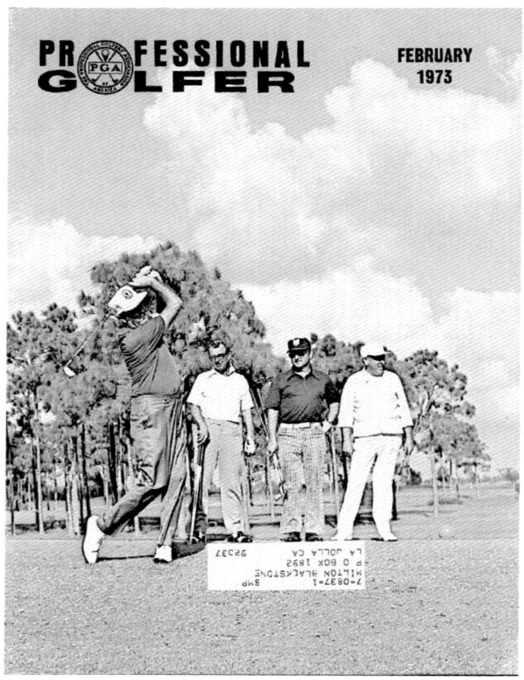

Herman Keiser is pictured here on the cover of the February 1973 *Professional Golfer* magazine. The photograph was taken during the 1973 PGA Stroke Play Championship at the North Course in Palm Beach Gardens in Florida. Also pictured are Loren Krugel, Bill Kowalski, and Hap Malia.

Pictured here at Pine Valley Golf Club in 1946 just after his victory at the Masters, Herman Keiser would put the legendary course to the test. On his first visit to the course, Keiser would shoot a seven over par 77. The course record at the time was 68.

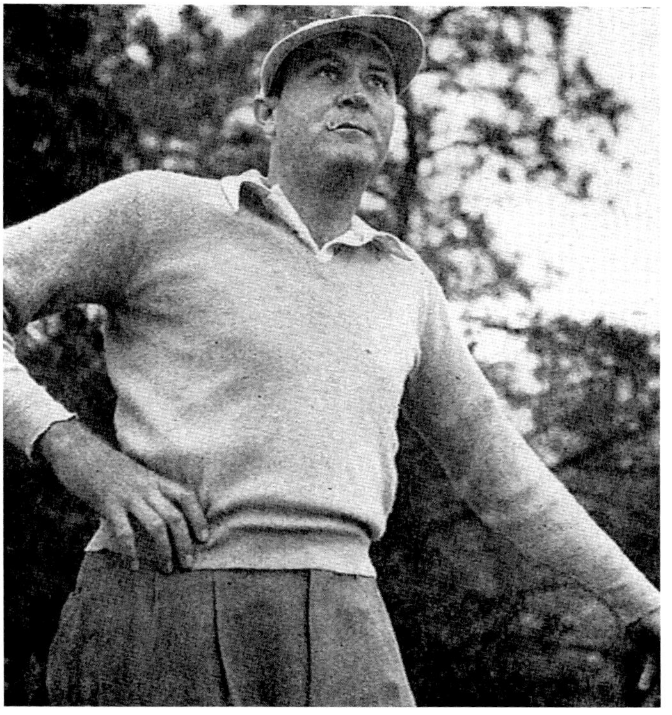

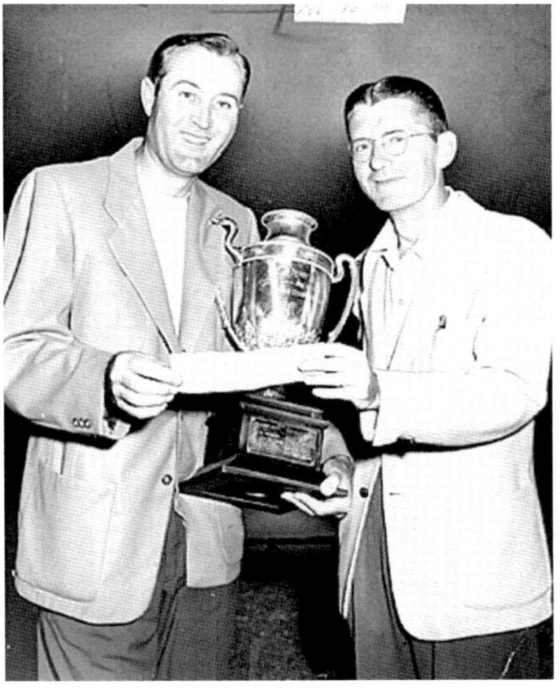

Herman Keiser (left) accepts a championship cup and check from Francis J. Conley for his 1946 Masters win. When reminiscing about his victory at the 1946 Masters, Keiser said, "That was the greatest thing that ever happened to me. I won some other tournaments, but nothing like this one. This was by far the best of them all. There wasn't much money in winning, though [$2,500]."

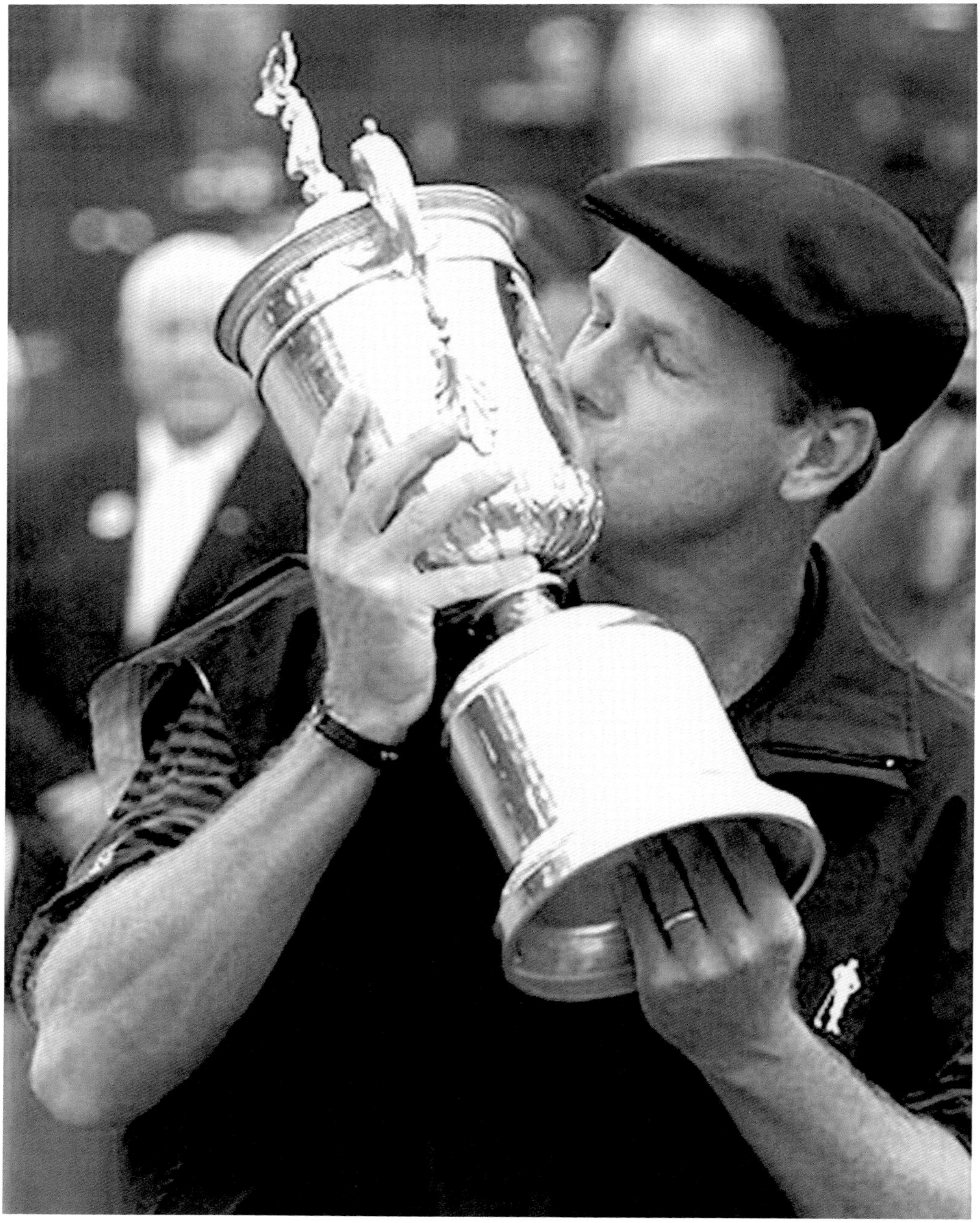

One of the most memorable moments in golf history took place Sunday June 20, 1999, when Payne Stewart won the U.S. Open at Pinehurst No. 2 in Pinehurst, North Carolina. Payne sunk a dramatic 15-foot putt on the final hole to win the championship over Phil Mickelson.

5

William Payne Stewart

Payne Stewart was born on January 30, 1957, in Springfield, Missouri. At the age of three, Payne started hitting the golf course. His mother, Bee, would drop him off at Hickory Hills Country Club, where he would spend the day playing golf and creating havoc at the swimming pool. Payne's father, Bill Stewart, a noted amateur golfer, taught Payne the finer points of the game while club professionals Sam Reynolds and Dorl Sweet would look on. As a child, he was surrounded by golf. His father grew up with Herman Keiser, and often Payne would sit at the foot of the great Ky Laffoon's bed to listen to stories about life on tour in the early days.

Payne Stewart attended Greenwood Laboratory School through Southwest Missouri State University. During his high school years, Payne played football, basketball, and golf. At the beginning of high school golf, Bill Stewart approached Paul Mullins, the golf coach at Greenwood, and got right to the point by saying "Payne knows how to play golf. He doesn't need any help. Please don't mess with his swing." In 1971, during Payne's freshman year, he was a medalist at the SMSU High School Relays. In 1973, he led them to the title of the same event.

Payne Stewart would take his golfing talents on the road to play for Southern Methodist University. In 1977, he tied for 16th place in the Collegiate National Championship. In 1979, he was cochampion of the Southwest Conference along with being voted All-American. College was not just about golf for Payne, as he also obtained a degree in business. In 1979, at the age of 22, Payne won the Missouri State Amateur at Wolf Creek when he beat Jim Holtgrieve eight and seven in the final.

Before obtaining his tour card, Payne played on both the European and Asian tours for two years. He won twice in 1981 at the Indonesian Open and the Indian Open. In 1982, Payne would win his tour card. The same year, he married Tracy Ferguson, whom he met the prior year at a cocktail party while playing in the 1980 Malaysian Open.

In 1982, Bill Stewart would give Payne some important words of advice, "In life you can't blend in with the masses." Soon after, Payne began wearing the knickers and tam o'shanter in which everyone recognized him. The NFL paid Payne to wear the colors of the nearest pro football team in the area of the tournament to help promote the NFL.

In 1982, Payne broke out and won his first tournament at the Quad Cities Open. Payne would say that no other tournament win would be bigger than that one because that was the only one his father would live to see. Bill died of cancer in 1985. Before his first U.S. Open in 1984, Bill told Payne "This is the National Championship. When you send your entry in, you sign your real name William Payne Stewart on the entry form." During Payne's win at Bay Hill in 1987, he donated his winning check of $108,000 to the Florida Hospital's Circle of Friends in Orlando in his father's name.

In 1989, he won the MCI Heritage at Harbor Town, but the biggest win in his young career would come later in the year. During the PGA Championship held at Kemper Lakes, Payne had a first round score of 74 with scores of 66 and 69 during the second and third rounds. During the final holes of the fourth round, there was a seven-stroke swing between the current leader Mike Reid and Payne. Payne would birdie four of the last five holes to shoot a 67 while Reid shot three over on the last three holes. Payne won his first major championship.

Payne prepared for the 1989 U.S. Open at the Olympic Club a little more than normal. The Olympic Club is where his father competed in the 1955 U.S. Open. Payne ended the first round tied for the lead with a 66, but could not keep up the pace. Payne would keep his focus on the Open, which finally paid off in 1991. In the 1991 U.S. Open at Hazeltine National Golf Club, Payne would beat Scott Simpson in a playoff to win his second major championship.

In 1993, Payne would have another personal victory on the golf course. This time he would be able to share this victory with a lifelong friend, Jim Morris, as they won the Pro-Am portion of the AT&T Pebble Beach Pro-Am. They shot a total score of 257 to be the second two-man group to win this tournament from the Springfield area. The first to do so was Leonard Dodson and Ray Watson in 1941. Payne would strike again at Pebble Beach in 1999, winning the professional portion of the rain-shortened Pro-Am tournament.

The most memorable of all of Payne's wins on tour came in 1999 when the U.S. Open was played at Pinehurst No. 2. Before the final round, on Fathers Day, Payne watched a special on NBC that focused on Payne's relationship with his father. Payne did not know they had done the piece. He used the thoughts of his father as motivation to go out and win the tournament.

After arriving at the tournament, Payne headed to the practice range wearing his rain jacket due to chilly weather. While warming up, Payne felt the jacket tugging at his arms. He told his caddy to go and grab some scissors. When he returned, Payne cut the sleeves off of the jacket. Payne's usual attention to looking good was not what he cared about; Payne just wanted to win. On the final hole, Payne sunk a 15-footer to beat Phil Mickelson by one stroke. After the U.S. Open victory, Payne went back to Springfield to celebrate with family and friends with the champion's cup in hand. During the trip, he went to both Hickory Hills and Bill and Payne Stewart golf courses, the latter of which was named in his honor in 1995. At both courses, he talked about the U.S. Open win and gave a clinic to the youth golfers in attendance.

Payne was known as the ultimate patriot, which translated to his love of playing in the Ryder Cup representing his country. Payne was a member of the Ryder Cup in 1987, 1989, 1991, 1993, and 1999. During the memorable Ryder Cup matches in 1999, the U.S. team clinched a win when Justin Leonard hit a clutch putt in his match against Jose Maria Olazabal. The celebration by the U.S. fans was so distracting that during the match between Payne and Colin Montgomerie, Payne would show his sportsmanship and concede Colin's final putt on the 18th green.

In 1999, Hickory Hills Country Club was developing a tribute to the local golf history with Payne being the focus. They wanted a duplicate copy of Payne's U.S. Open trophy for the display. In order to get a copy, Payne would have to ask permission from the United States Golf Association (USGA). The letter would arrive on president David Fay's desk on October 25, 1999. This would be the same day Payne would be traveling from Florida to Texas for a golf tournament. Payne along with five others was aboard a Learjet, which developed mechanical problems and lost cabin pressure soon after take off, causing those aboard to lose consciousness. The plane flew uncontrolled for hours until it ran out of fuel and crashed in Aberdeen, South Dakota. Payne would leave behind his wife, Tracey, and two children, Chelsea and Aaron.

Payne's death shook people, not only in the golf world but also in the Ozarks. Two funerals were held, one in Orlando, where a large contingent of tour players paid their respects, and the other in Springfield at the Second Baptist Church. Payne was inducted into the Missouri Sports Hall of Fame in 1994. On April 19, 1999, he was inducted into Springfield Sports Hall of Fame, the World Golf Hall of Fame in 2001, and the Ozarks Golf Hall of Fame in 2005. *Golf Digest* listed Payne Stewart as the 37th all time greatest golfer.

Career Victories

1981 Indian Open
1981 Indonesian Open
1982 Magnolia Classic
1982 Tweed Heads Classic
1982 Quad Cities Open
1983 Walt Disney Classic
1987 Bay Hill Classic
1989 Heritage Classic
1989 PGA Championship
1990 Byron Nelson Classic
1991 Dutch Open
1991 U.S. Open
1991 Skins Game
1992 King Hassan II
1992 Skins Game
1993 King Hassan II
1993 Skins Game
1995 Houston Open
1999 Pebble Beach Pro-Am
1999 U.S. Open

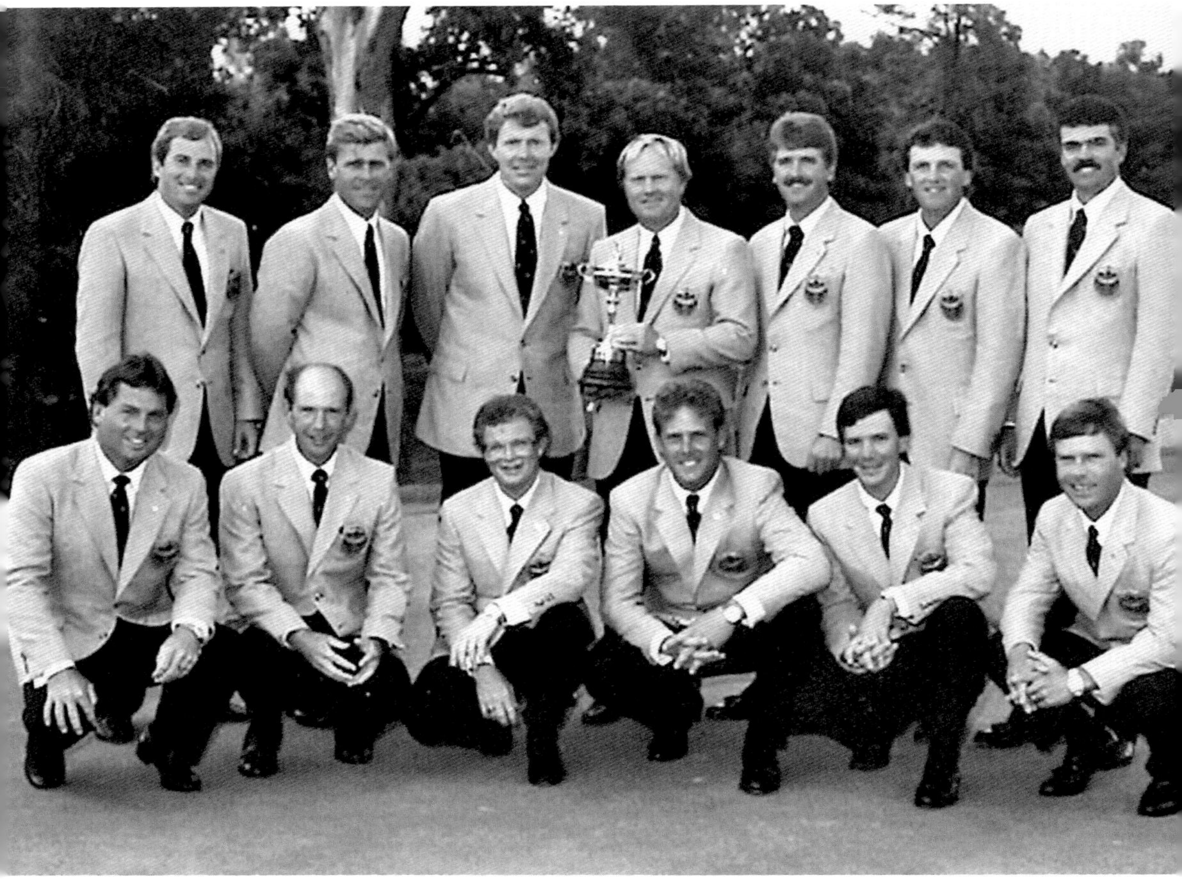

The 1987 Ryder Cup team was Payne Stewart's first. He will always be remembered by representing his country in the cup matches. His record during his Ryder Cup matches was 8–9–2. Stewart is pictured in the bottom row, fourth from the left.

This photograph shows Payne Stewart posing for the golf team photographs while attending Greenwood Laboratory School through Southwest Missouri State University. During his high school years, Stewart would play football, basketball, and golf.

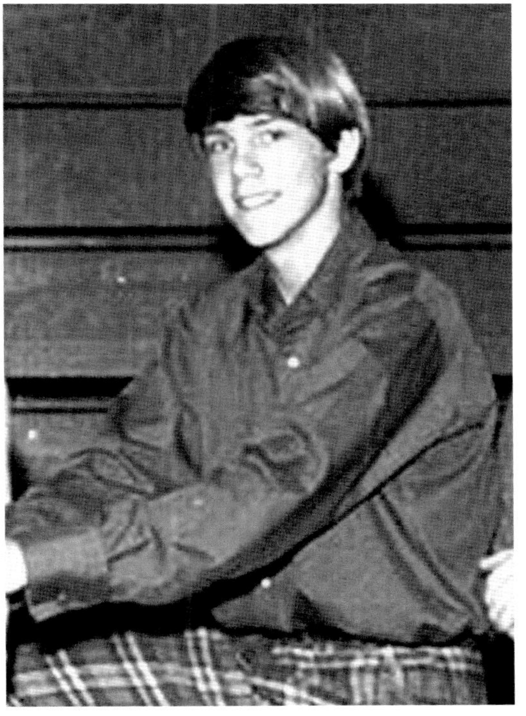

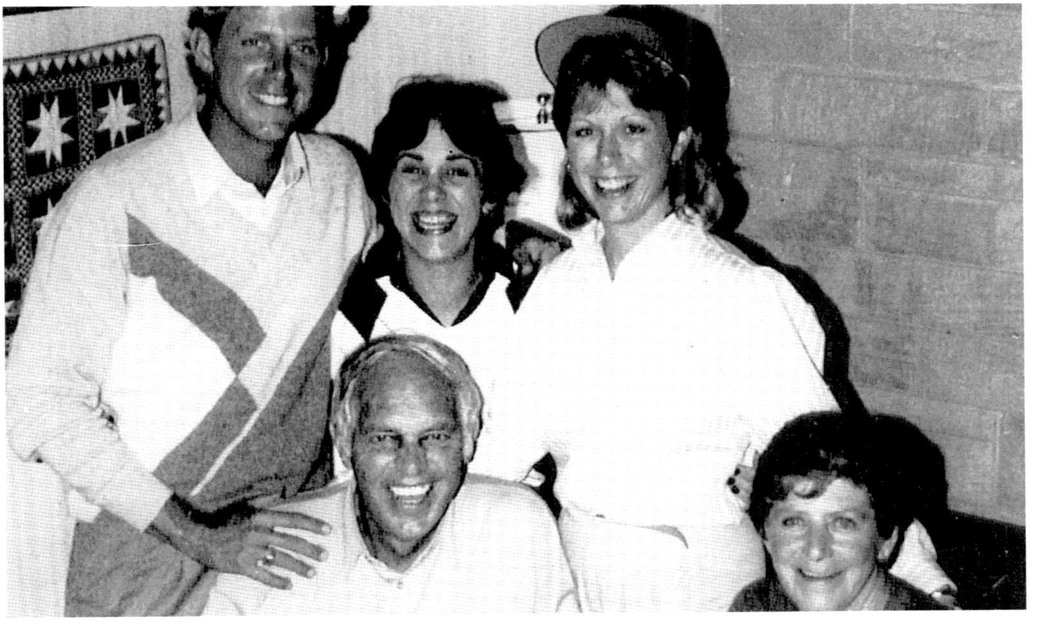

A young Payne Stewart is pictured here with his family in Springfield, Missouri. Pictured is Payne, his sisters Susan and Lora, father Bill, and mother Bee. Payne once said, "Springfield will always be my home. I just happen to live in Florida."

Payne Stewart won the 1991 U.S. Open at Hazeltine National Golf Club over Scott Simpson after Simpson lost a two-stroke lead during the last three holes. This would be Payne's first U.S. Open victory. (Courtesy of Ozarks Fairways.)

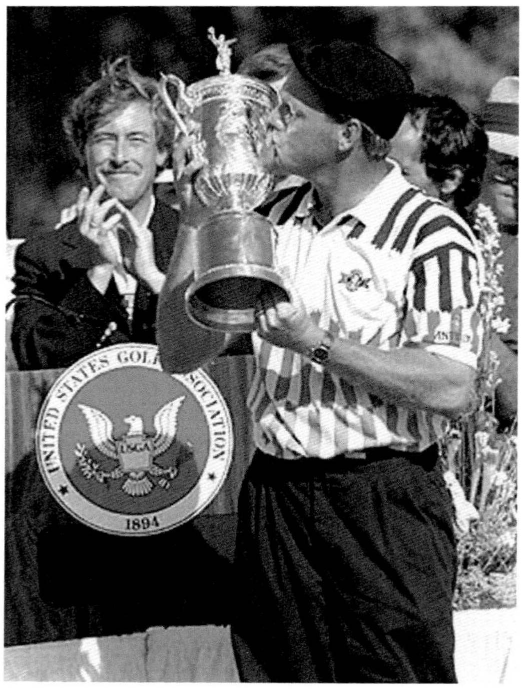

Payne Stewart would have to face Scott Simpson in an 18-hole playoff to decide the 1991 U.S. Open championship. The playoff round was played the day after regulation play. Stewart would shoot a round of 75 while Simpson would finish with a round of 77. (Courtesy of Ozarks Fairways.)

After Payne Stewart made his 15-foot putt on the 18th hole of the 1999 U.S. Open, he could not hide his emotion with his punch into the air. After the tournament, Stewart said, "All I wanted to do was give myself a chance."

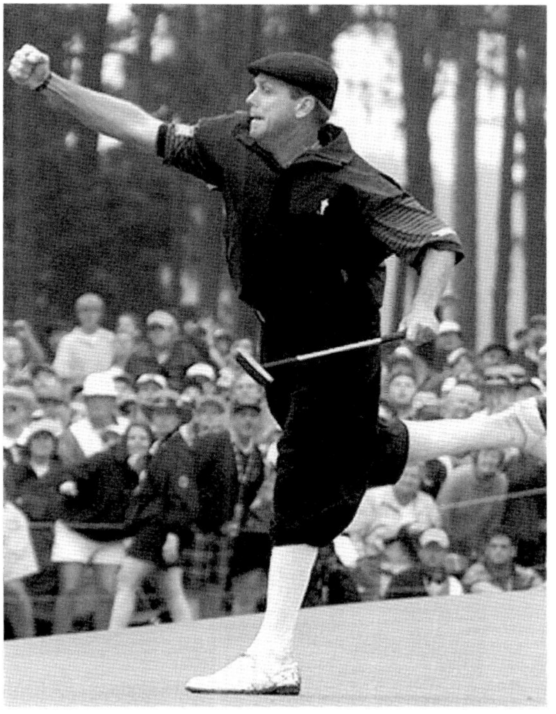

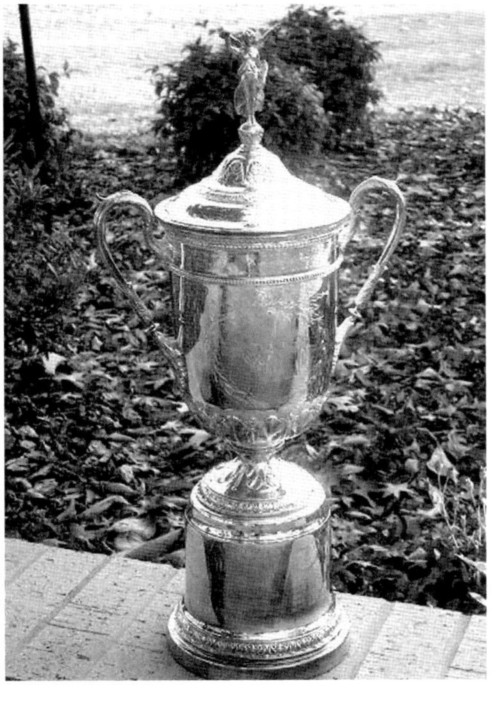

This exact replica of Payne Stewart's 1999 U.S. Open trophy is on display at Hickory Hills Country Club in Springfield, Missouri. USGA president David Fay allowed the club to have a replica made to keep in the clubhouse display case. (Courtesy of Hicory Hills.)

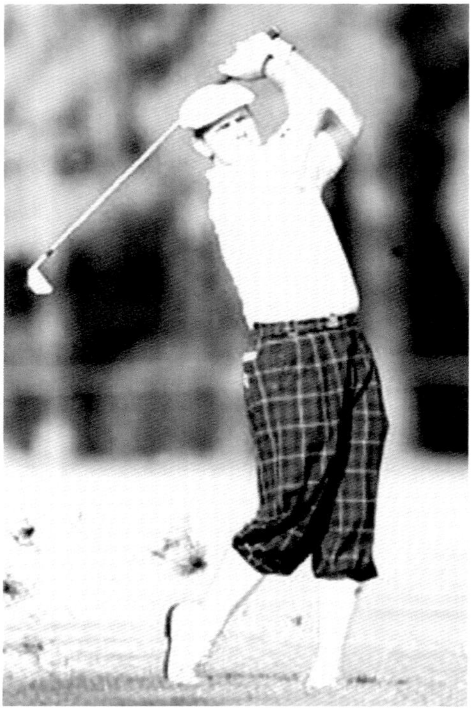

Payne Stewart developed his picturesque swing at an early age. Later in life, Stewart would work with legendary golf coach Chuck Cook, but Cook would do little to alter Stewart's fluid swing.

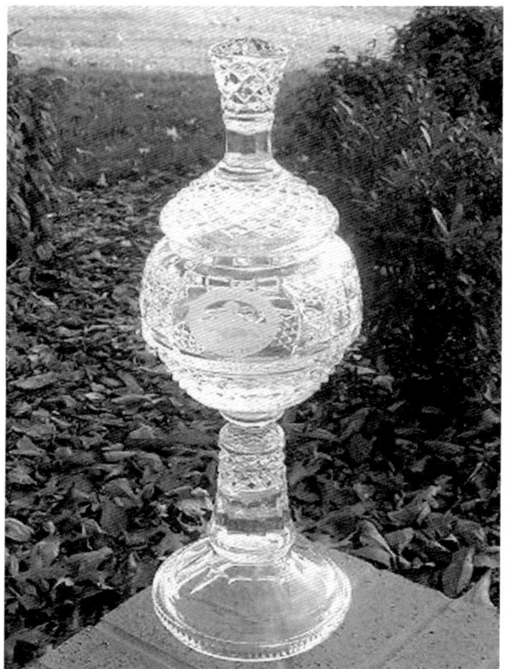

This crystal trophy was given for the victory that Payne Stewart shared with Hickory Hills member and long time friend Jim Morris when they won the Pebble Beach Pro-Am together in 1993. (Courtesy of Hickory Hills.)

During the memorable Ryder Cup matches in 1999, the celebration by fans, for Justin Leonard hitting his winning putt that would allow the U.S. team to win the cup, caused such a distraction that Payne Stewart would show his sportsmanship and concede Colin Montgomerie's final putt on their 18th and deciding hole.

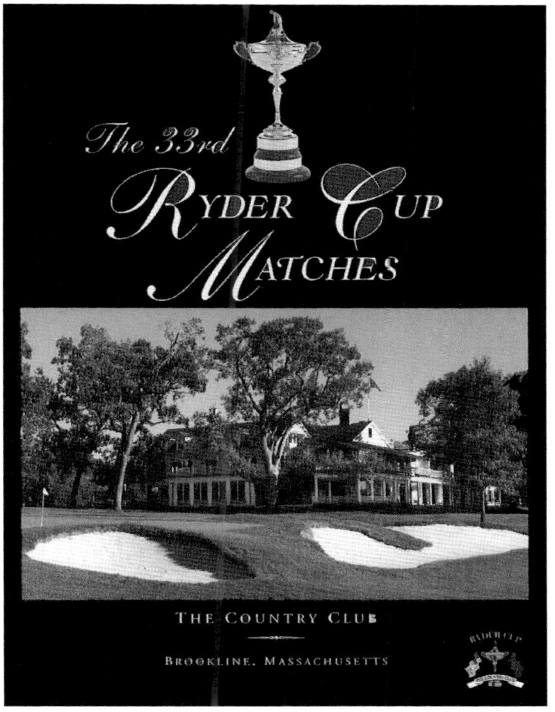

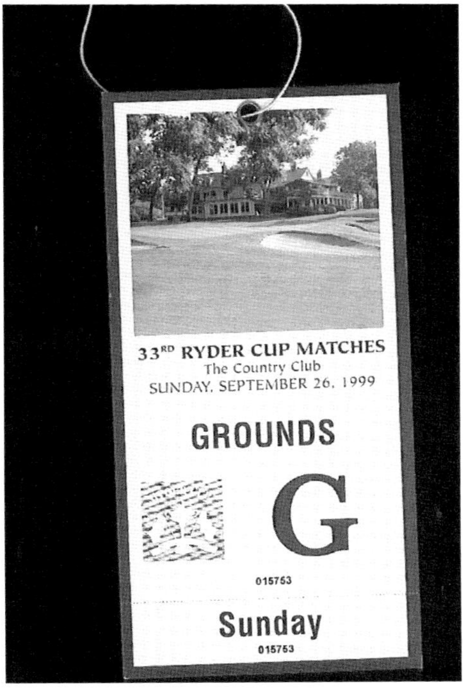

The U.S. Ryder Cup team captained by Ben Crenshaw would win the 1999 Ryder Cup matches over Europe 14½ to 13½ at the Country Club in Brookline, Massachusetts.

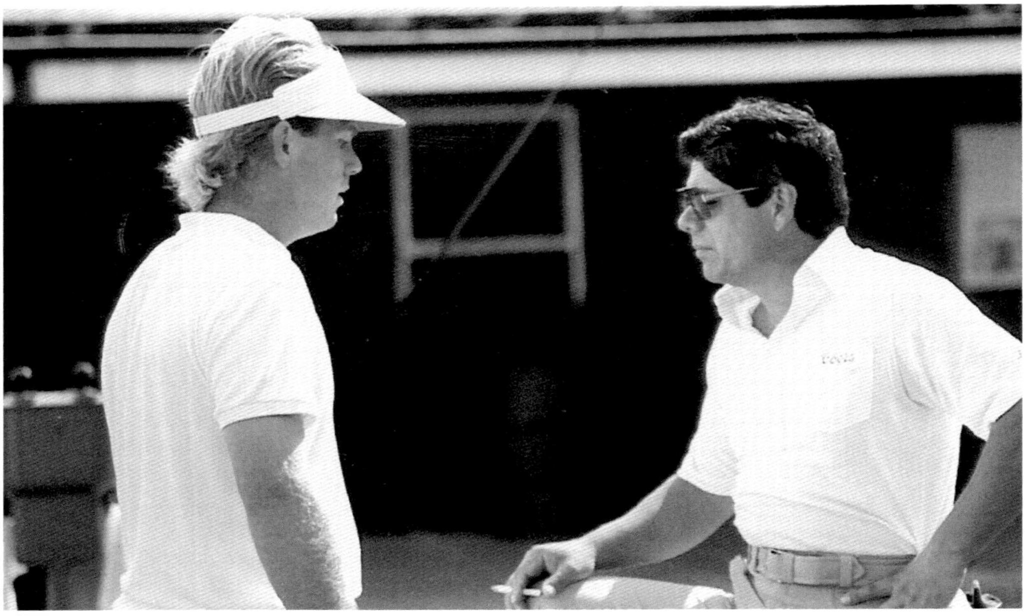

Payne Stewart (left) and golf legend Lee Trevino share a moment while at Hickory Hills Country Club in 1983. Trevino came to Springfield for an exhibition put on by Coors for David Callaway. (Courtesy of Hickory Hills.)

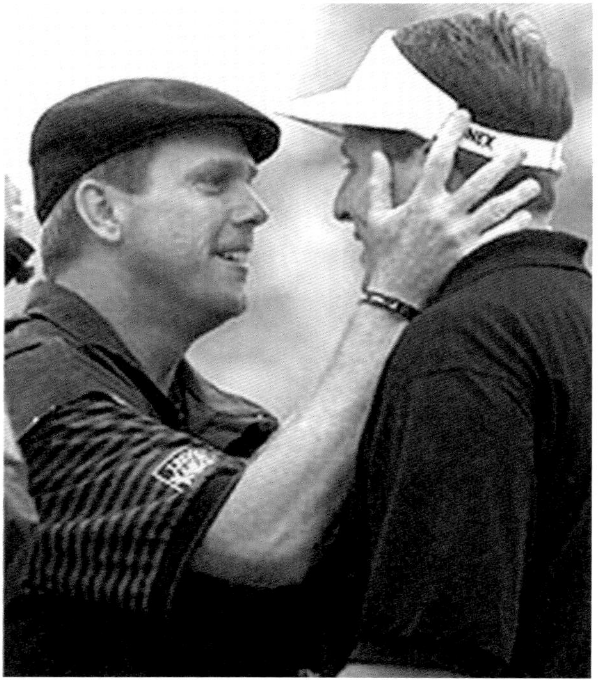

Pictured here is Payne Stewart (left) after his 1999 U.S. Open win over Phil Mickelson (right). During a selfless moment after his final putt, Stewart congratulates Mickelson on his impending fatherhood.

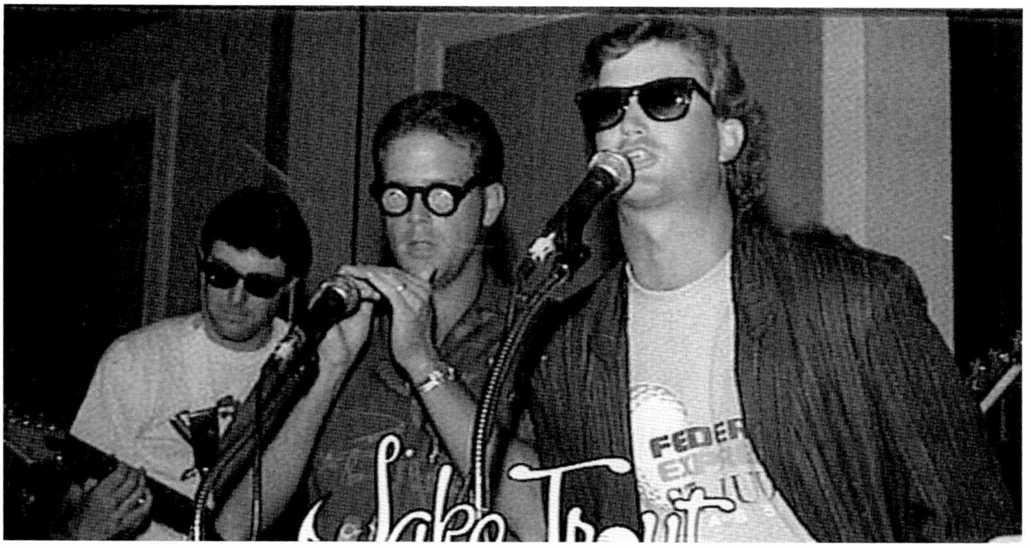

Payne Stewart (middle) loved to get together with his fellow band mates from Jake Trout and the Flounders to jam! Stewart along with Peter Jacobsen (right) and Mark Lye (left) loved to perform old rock and roll hits with a golf twist. They even produced two albums of their songs that included, among others, "I Want a New Glove" and "I Love to Play."

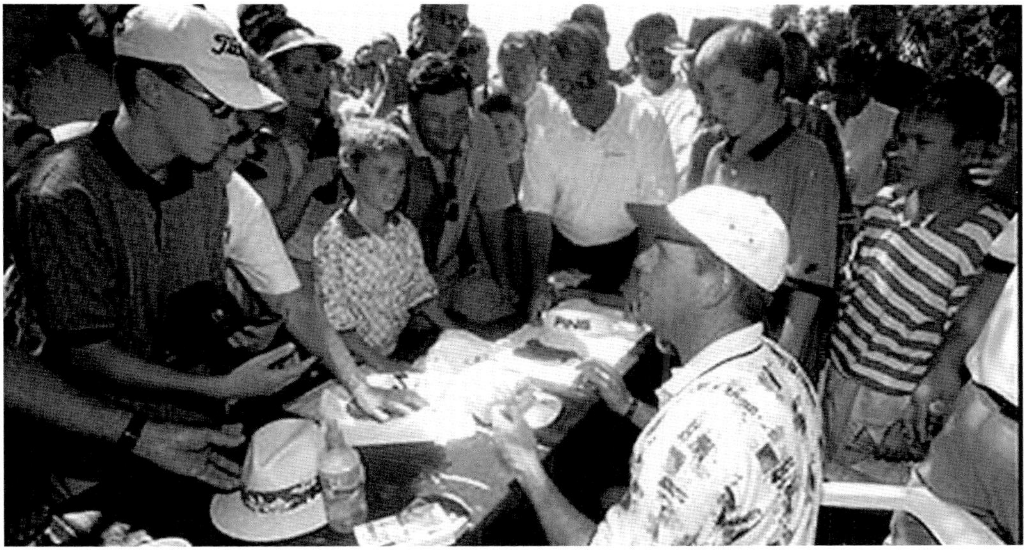

Payne Stewart would come back to Springfield soon after his 1999 U.S. Open victory to give youth golf clinics at Hickory Hills Country Club and Bill and Payne Stewart golf courses. Stewart signed autographs for hours after both clinics.

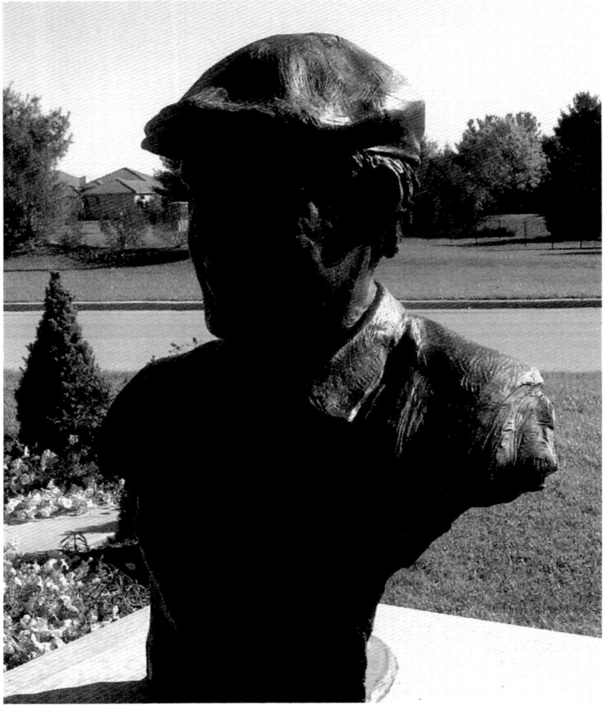

This bust of Payne Stewart was created by Harry Weber and is located at the Missouri Sports Hall of Fame in Springfield, Missouri. The bust is located in the hall's Walk of Fame. Stewart was recognized as a Missouri Sports Legend in 2000.

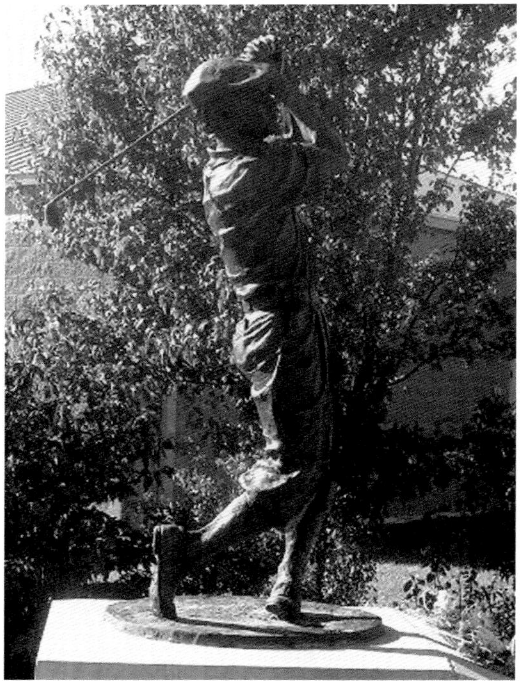

This larger than life statue was created by Harry Weber in 2000 and is located at the Missouri Sports Hall of Fame. It is no coincidence that the statue faces north towards Stewart's golf course.

This statue of Payne Stewart is located behind the 18th green at Pinehurst No. 2 to commemorate his 1999 U.S. Open win there. The statue by Zenos Frudakis captures Stewart's winning moment in detail. (Courtesy of Angela Roberson.)

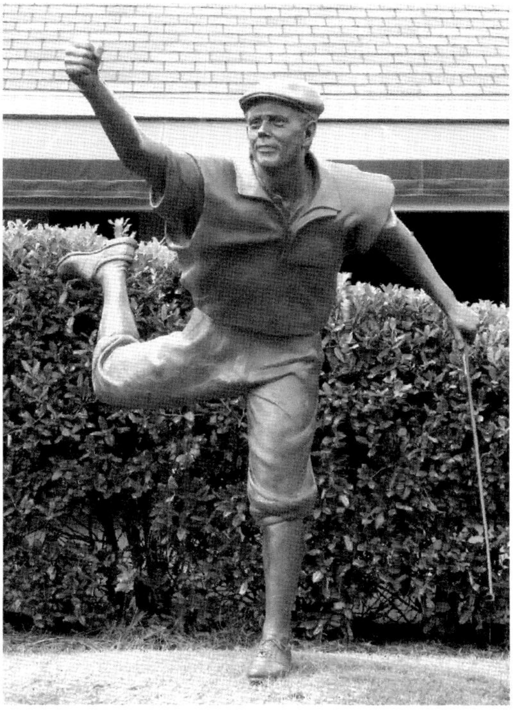

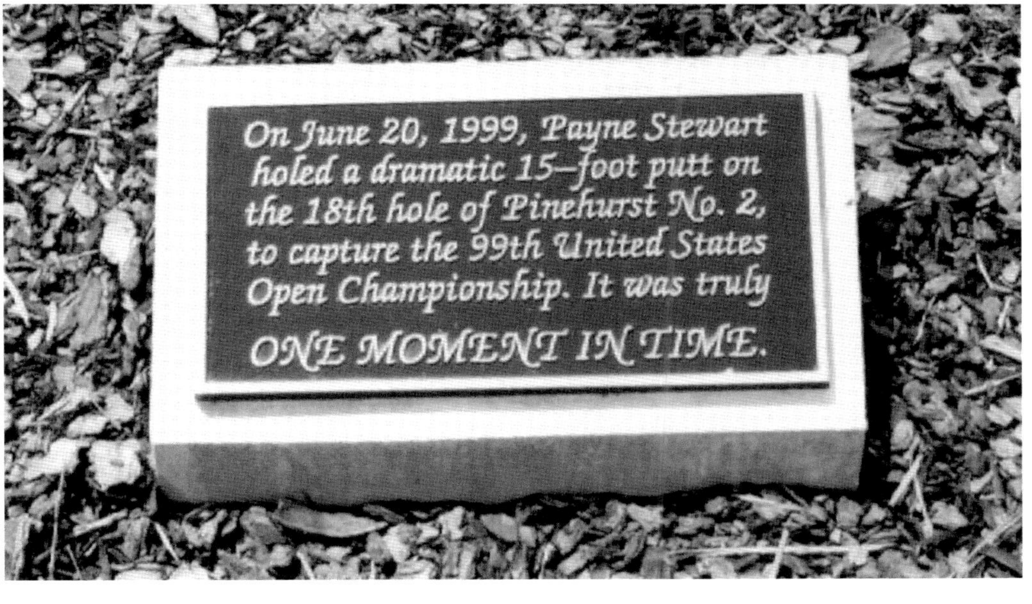

This marker is located with the statue of Payne Stewart at Pinehurst No. 2. The marker notes Stewart's "One Moment in Time," winning the 1999 U.S. Open.

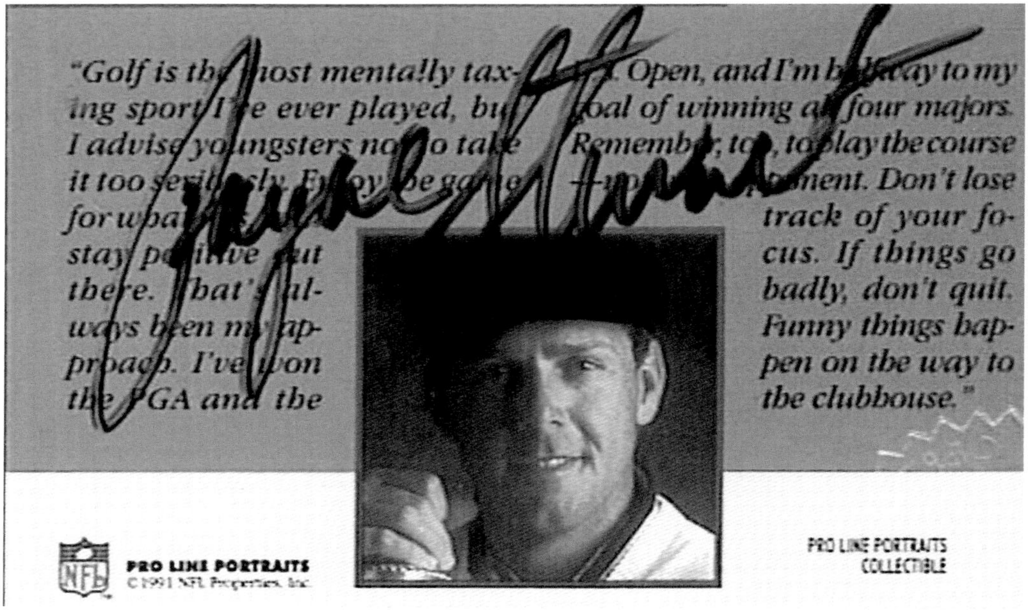

Payne Stewart had a contract with the NFL for several years that he agreed to wear the colors of the nearest NFL team to where the PGA event was being held. They had such a relationship that in 1991, Stewart had a trading card in the Pro Line football card set. (Courtesy of Photos From the Fairway.)

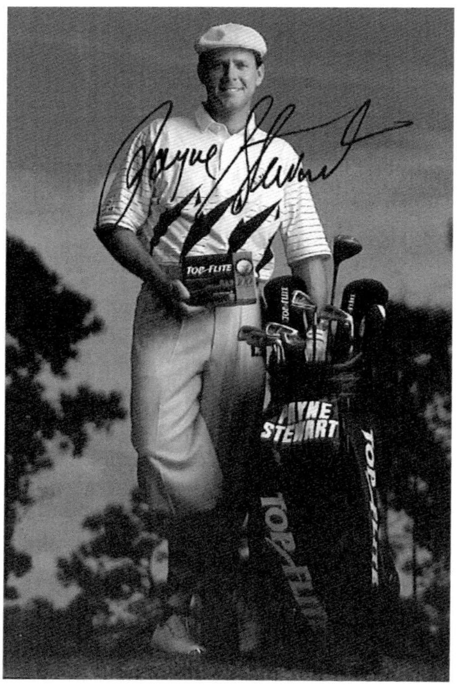

For several years, Payne Stewart would endorse both the NFL and Top-Flight golf balls and clubs. Eventually, Payne would create his own clothing line, which would feature his signature knickers and tam o'shanter hats.

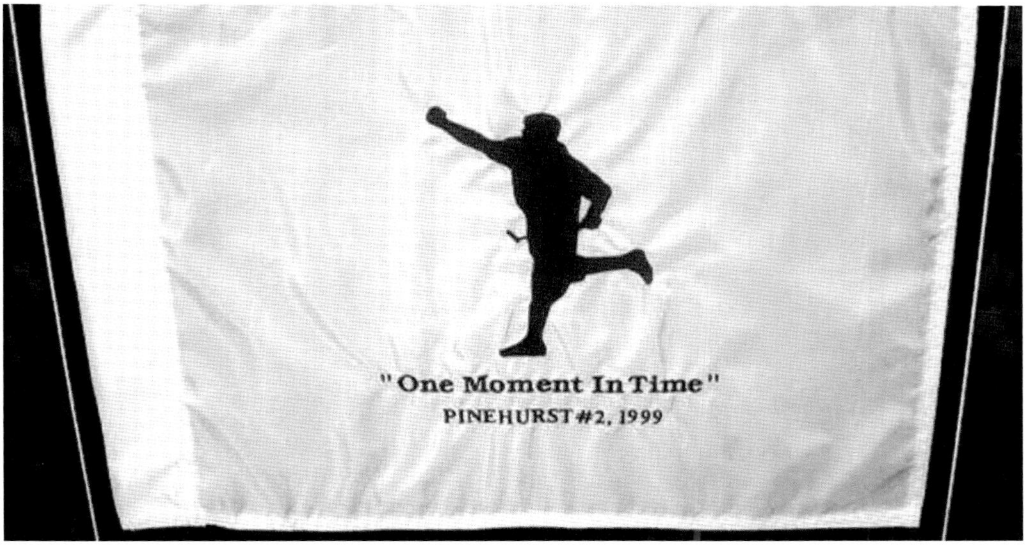

This gift to Hickory Hills Country Club from the USGA, via the Missouri Golf Association, is one of only three flags made to memorialize Payne Stewart's 1999 U.S. Open victory at Pinehurst No. 2. In memory of Stewart's victory, during the 2005 U.S. Open, this 18th hole flag was used during all four competitive rounds. (Courtesy of Hickory Hills)

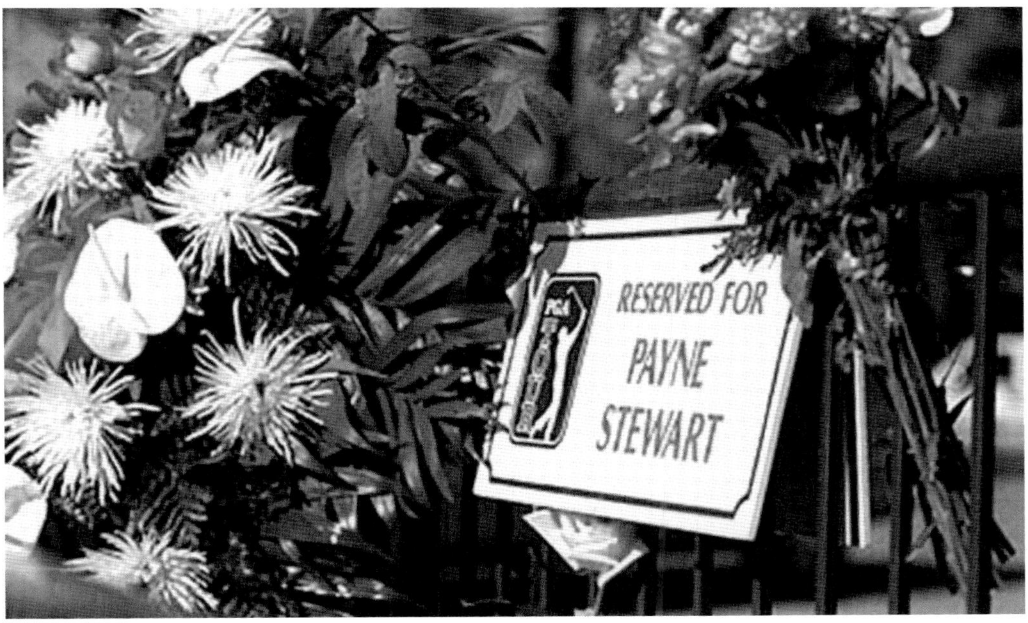

Flowers were placed at Payne Stewart's reserved parking space at the 1999 Tour Championship, where Stewart's plane was headed the day of his fatal crash.

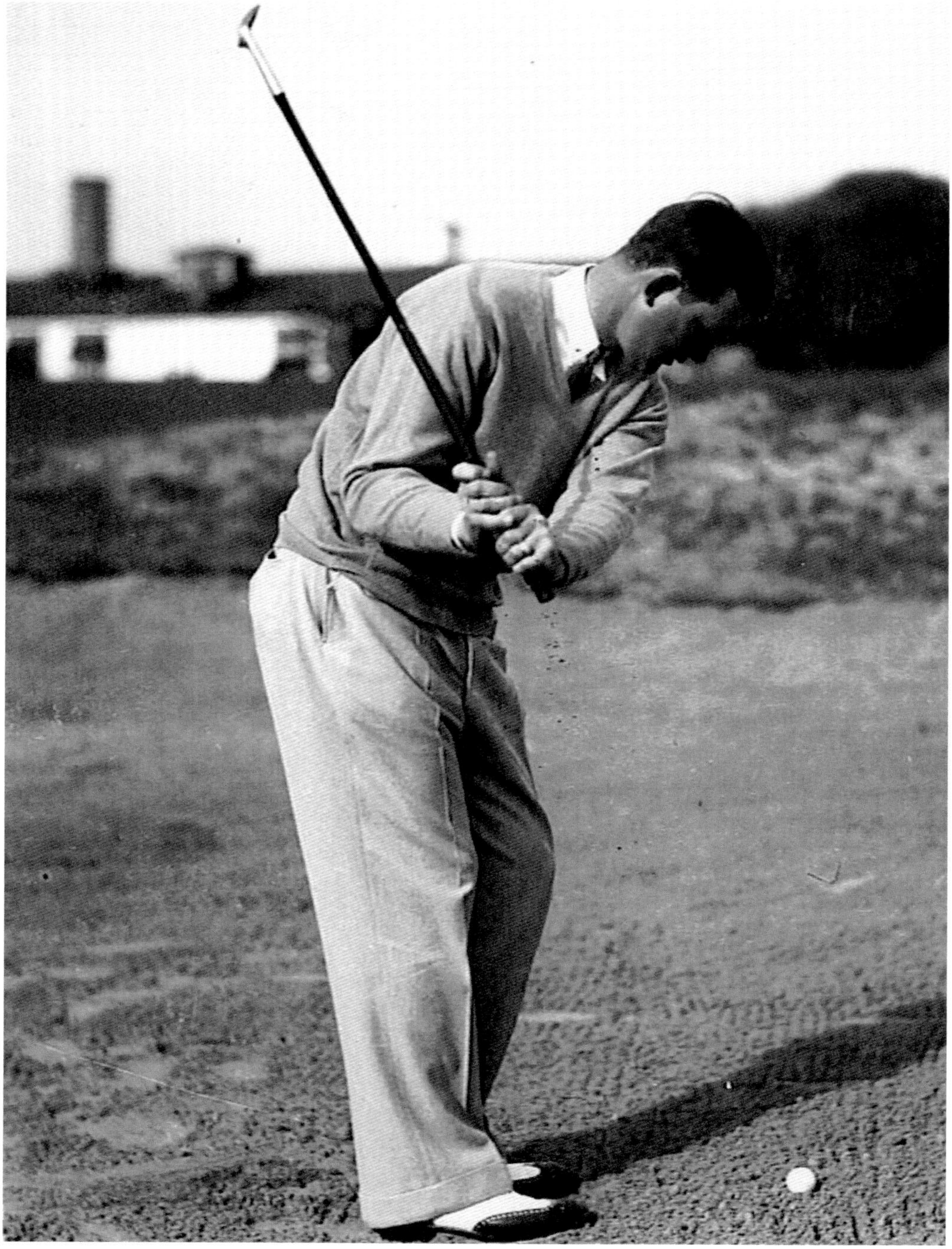

This vintage photograph taken by Alex Morrison shows Ed Dudley swinging out of a fairway bunker. Dudley would work with the legendary coach, Morrison, before taking his skills on tour. (Courtesy of Ozarks Fairways.)

6

THE FIELD

Ed Dudley

Ed Dudley was born in Brunswick, Georgia, on February 10, 1902. He started golf at the early age of 14 years, playing with his uncle. Dudley learned how to play golf from Stewart Maiden, who also taught one of Dudley's childhood friends, Bobby Jones. Dudley found that golf would become his life's work.

Dudley's first job in golf would be as an assistant pro at Rockdale Country Club in Miami, Oklahoma. He soon took the head pro position at the nine-hole Oak Hill Country Club in Joplin during the spring of 1924. A year later, Dudley shot the course record of 29. After two years with Oak Hill, Dudley moved on to become the head professional at Oklahoma City Country Club.

While a club pro, Dudley also found time to compete on tour. His first of 13 tour wins would come at the California Open in 1929, and his final win came at the 1939 Walter Hagen Invitational with Billy Burkes. During his 23-year playing career, Dudley was a three-time member of the Ryder Cup—in 1929, 1933, and 1937. The 1929 team included old playing partner Horton Smith, along with Walter Hagen and Gene Sarazen. In 1929, Bob Harlow, a World Golf Hall of Fame member, was the manager for Walter Hagen, Paul Runyan, Horton Smith, and Ed Dudley. Harlow would book marathon golf exhibitions where the four golfers would play against one another five to six times a week for over a month. The tour traveled throughout the Midwest.

Dudley's relationship with the great Bobby Jones would help land him the head pro position at what would become one of the top golf clubs in the world, Augusta National Golf Club. Jones had started the club in Augusta, Georgia, and in 1932, wanted Dudley to be the club professional. He was the unofficial host pro for all of the Masters tournaments through 1957. Some of his best professional tournaments would take place at Augusta National. In 1937, he finished third behind Byron Nelson and Ralph Guldahl. During the summer months starting in 1941, Dudley served as director of golf at the Broadmoor Golf Club in Colorado Springs.

Dudley was the president of the PGA from 1941 to 1948. Dudley died on October 25, 1963, due to a leg infection he developed while attending the Ryder Cup matches just weeks before his death. While a teaching pro, his students included Bing Crosby, Bob Hope, and Pres. Dwight Eisenhower. Dudley was named to the PGA Hall of Fame in 1964 and has also been inducted into the Georgia and Colorado golf halls of fame.

Career Victories

1929 California Open
1929 California PGA
1930 Shawnee Open
1930 Walter Hagen with Billy Burke
1931 Los Angeles Open
1931 Western Open
1932 International Open with Armour
1932 Pennsylvania Open
1932 Philadelphia Open
1933 Hershey Open

1935 True Temper Open
1936 Shawnee Open
1937 Sacramento Open

John Ferguson

"Horton Wasn't Any Better at Johnny's Age!" was the title of an article from the *Springfield Leader* newspaper in 1931, which said it all. At the age of 15, Ferguson tied the amateur record at Hickory Hills Country Club with a score of 68. The same year, he became a member of the first Horton Smith Cup team for Springfield against rival Joplin. As if that was not enough at such a young age, Ferguson also won the 1931 Springfield City Amateur Championship with an amazing score of ten up with nine holes still to play over Dick Farrington at the Lake Shore Golf Club. He would achieve a second title in 1931 by winning the West Plains golf tournament.

In 1932, Ferguson won the All-Ozarks Golf Championship over Tom Woodruff in a dramatic playoff. Ferguson played golf for Drury College in Springfield. He later transferred to Yale Medical School, where he was unable to play on the school's golf team but did win the annual fall amateur tournament held by the university in 1934. Ferguson returned to Springfield during the summer of 1934 to beat Herman Keiser five up with four holes remaining in the Glenstone Invitational. Ferguson would lead the whole round. The next summer, Ferguson would win the 1935 Glenstone Invitational over Gene Sallee. Ferguson won his second Springfield City Amateur Championship in 1936 over Joe Bill Hogeboom five holes up with four holes left to play. Dr. Ferguson is a member of the Ozarks Golf Hall of Fame.

Tom Talbot

Tom Talbot won the Springfield Junior Championship in 1925 and never looked back. Talbot was a member of Drury College's first golf team in 1928, along with being a star on the school's football team. In 1929, Talbot won the Springfield City Championship and again in 1930. During the 1930 Horton Smith Cup matches at Joplin's Schifferdecker Golf Course, he shot a record round of 65 tying Ed Dudley, Eddie Held, and Ted Longsworth. During the same year, Tom spent the fall with the Chicago Bears until knee injuries ended his football career.

Talbot served as head pro at Glenstone Municipal Golf Course in Springfield for three years, followed by a short stint at the Springfield Country Club. In October 1934, Talbot moved to Hickory Hills Country Club and finally, spent 16 years as the head professional at Grandview Golf Course in Springfield. Talbot started a citywide junior golf clinic while also heading up the first boys Horton Smith Cup team. In 1949, he won the Midwest PGA Championship held in Kansas City. Even after Talbot retired, he would teach golfers the finer points of the game at Fremont Hills and other courses around the Ozarks. Talbot died in 1992. In 1999, Talbot was inducted into the Springfield Hall of Fame.

Gene Sallee

Gene Sallee snuck onto the golf scene in the Ozarks while the focus was on the battles between John Ferguson and Herman Keiser in the mid 1930s. Sallee made his first Horton Smith Cup team in 1935. That same year, he placed second in the Glenstone Invitational tournament in Springfield. He finally won that tournament in a battle with John Ferguson in 1937. The victory would be followed by another win in the 1937 Springfield City Amateur.

In 1953, Sallee won the Tri-State Amateur in Joplin by shooting a two-day total score of 134, which equaled eight under par. Sallee shot an unbelievable 30 on the first nine holes and never looked back. He would win again a year later in the 1954 Springfield City Amateur. Sallee became the first head professional at Twin Oaks Country Club in Springfield and would hold that position for several years.

Bill Stewart

Jack Bill Stewart grew up as a childhood buddy of Herman Keiser. Stewart was the first Springfieldian to win the Missouri Amateur Championship in 1953. The 1957 Missouri Amateur final played at Hickory Hills was one of the most exciting to date. Jim Tom Blair was leading Stewart two up with three holes to go. Stewart birdied the last two holes to force a playoff. Both players birdied the first two playoff holes. On the third playoff hole, number three at the old Hickory Hills course, Stewart would birdie again winning his second state title.

In 1955, Bill Stewart qualified for, and competed in, the U.S. Open held in San Francisco at Olympic Country Club. Par for the course was 70. Jack Fleck was the winner of the Open, while Stewart missed the cut with rounds of 83 and 88. Stewart contended in several national tournaments, such as the U.S. Amateur and Western Amateur. In 1977, he and Bruce Hollowell won the Stephenson Cup at the Trans-Mississippi Amateur.

In 1979, Stewart won the Missouri Senior Amateur the same year his son Payne won the Missouri Amateur. In 1980, Stewart was inducted into the Missouri State University Athletics Hall of Fame for his lettering in golf, football, and basketball. In 1983, he was inducted to the Springfield Sports Hall of Fame. He was the Hickory Hills Club Champion eight times and won the Springfield City Amateur Championship three times. Bill Stewart died in 1985 after his fight with cancer.

Sam Reynolds

Sam Reynolds was born in Wichita Falls, Texas. A caddie in his youth, Reynolds turned golf into a career. Reynolds was an assistant pro at Blue Hills Country Club in Kansas City. In 1957, he and his wife had their first child, Cathy, whose birth prompted the family to move to Springfield, Missouri. Reynolds would take the head professional position at Hickory Hills Country Club. He continued playing in tour events during his time at Hickory Hills. He played in the PGA Championship in 1961, 1964, 1965, and 1966. He also played in the U.S. Open in 1963, finishing in 32nd place. While on tour, Reynolds had a total of five second-place finishes, and he had seven victories in the Midwest Section of the PGA Championships. He would stay at Hickory Hills for 40 years and be elected as the Professional of the Year in 1982 by the Midwest Section of the PGA.

Jim Hatfield

James "Jim" Hatfield was born in Stearns, Kentucky, in 1927. He served in the U.S. Navy during World War II and in the U.S. Army during the Korean Conflict. While serving the military took up the peak years of his golf career, Hatfield would return to form quickly to win the Ozark Amateur championship in 1960 and 1961 at Schifferdecker Golf Course in Joplin. Hatfield made the most of his years on the Senior PGA Tour from 1984 to 1991. In 1990, Hatfield had his best tournament on the senior tour when he finished in 42nd place at the Gatlin Brothers Southwest Classic at Fairway Oaks Country Club in Abilene, Texas. His years on the senior tour put him at number 441 in career earnings with $56,270 earned. Hatfield played in a U.S. Open and three

Senior U.S. Opens. He was inducted into the Joplin Golf Hall of Fame in 1997. During his final years, Hatfield was a teaching professional in and around Bella Vista, Arkansas. Hatfield died on July 1, 2005, in Rogers, Arkansas.

Marshall Smith

Marshall Smith has been a legendary golf instructor for over 50 years. After a competitive amateur golf career, Smith turned his focus to teaching. Smith considered Ky Laffoon his mentor and like Laffoon would help hundreds of golfers each year and shape the golf careers of some of the sport's finest. Smith has worked with Craig Stadler, Chi Chi Rodriquez, Gary Player, and others. Smith is also known for his teaching relationship with Mickey Mantle. Smith headed Mantle's Celebrity Golf Classic at Shangri-La Resort and the Kids Come First tournaments held in the 1980s and 1990s.

Smith currently writes articles for *Golf Tips* magazine and has authored a book titled *Hit the Second Shot First.* His method of teaching implements the "K.I.S.S. Method." Smith currently teaches out of Peoria Ridge golf course in Miami, Oklahoma. Smith was voted into the Joplin Golf Hall of Fame in 1998.

Hale Irwin

Hale Irwin was born on June 3, 1945, in Joplin, Missouri. He grew up learning golf on the local golf courses in Joplin, including Schifferdecker Golf Course. He began attending the University of Colorado in 1965. While at Colorado, Irwin showed his athleticism in both golf and football. He won the 1967 NCAA Championship in golf. He started as quarterback during his sophomore year and made the All Big Eight Conference as a defensive back his last two years. While at the university, he earned his bachelor's degree in marketing.

Irwin joined the PGA Tour in 1968 through qualifying school. His first tour win came in 1971 at the Heritage Classic held at Harbor Town Golf Club. He would come back to win the same tournament two years later in 1973. His third tour win would be among his most memorable. In 1974, Irwin won the U.S. Open at Winged Foot. The Open was coined "Massacre at Winged Foot," due to what was perhaps the most difficult conditions in U.S. Open history. Irwin won with a score of seven over par. He won the U.S. Open twice more in 1979 at Inverness and in 1990 at Medinah. The Open win of 1990 was at the age of 45, making him the oldest person to win the tournament. He would win 20 times on tour and has more than 10 wins abroad. He was a member of the Ryder Cup five times in 1975, 1977, 1979, 1981, and 1991. His lifetime Ryder Cup record was an impressive 13–5–2.

Irwin started work on the Senior PGA in 1995 and was chosen the Senior PGA Rookie of the Year with two wins. In 1998, he was voted Senior PGA Player of the Year due to his seven tour victories. Irwin has had an impressive senior career by winning the Senior U.S. Open twice in 1998 and 2000, and winning the Senior PGA Championship four times. He also is involved in designing golf courses. Irwin was inducted into the World Golf Hall of Fame in 1992. Two years later, in 1994, he was admitted into the Missouri Sports Hall of Fame and in 2001 to the Joplin Golf Hall of Fame.

Career Victories

1971 Sea Pines Heritage Classic
1973 Sea Pines Heritage Classic
1974 U.S. Open
1975 Atlanta Classic
1975 Western Open
1976 Glen Campbell Los Angeles Open
1976 Florida Citrus Open Invitational

1977 Atlanta Classic
1977 Colgate Hall of Fame Golf Classic
1977 San Antonio Texas Open
1979 U.S. Open
1981 Hawaiian Open
1981 Buick Open
1982 Honda Inverrary Classic

1983 Memorial Tournament
1984 Bing Crosby Pro Am
1985 Memorial Tournament
1990 U.S. Open
1990 Buick Classic
1994 MCI Heritage Classic

Bruce Hollowell

Bruce Hollowell is among the all-time greats of Ozarks amateur golf. Hollowell was part of the team at Southwest Missouri State University to win the regional team title in 1962, 1963, and 1964. In his final year, he was the medalist at the Mid-American Intercollegiate Athletics Association meet. In 1969, Hollowell won the Ozark Amateur held at Joplin's Schifferdecker Golf Course, and in 1972, he won the Kansas Amateur at Crestview Country Club. In 1975, Hollowell would win his biggest tournament, the Missouri Amateur, at Indian Hills, over Jim Rollins five and four. Hollowell would win the Missouri State Senior Championship in 1998. He furthered his influence on golf in the area when he started his coaching career by heading the Southwest Missouri State University golf team in 1985. He would lead the team to back-to-back conference championships in 1987 and 1988. He coached the Southwest Missouri State University team for 12 years. Hollowell was inducted into the Southwest Missouri State University Athletic Hall of Fame in 1985 and the Ozarks Golf Hall of Fame in 2004.

Robert Russell

During the early 1990s in Joplin, it felt like Robert Russell won every tournament he played in. Russell has many victories, including the Joplin Globe City Championship in 1991, 1992, and 1994; the Ozark Amateur in 1994 and 1995; the Twin Hills Invitational in 1995 and 1996; and the Briarbrook Invitational 1994, 1995, and 1996. Further, he won the Michelob golfer of the year in 1994, the National Junior College Champion in 1995, and 17 collegiate titles. In 1999, Russell played in the U.S. Open at Pinehurst No. 2. Russell currently plays on the Hooters Tour.

Joyce Mahoney

Joyce Mahoney "is" women's golf in Springfield. In 1975, she was a Missouri State Amateur finalist. Mahoney won her first Springfield Area Women's Golf Association Championship in 1970 and her record 18th at the age of 71 in 2001. She also won the Missouri State Senior Championship in 1980 through 1984 and the Hickory Hills Club Championship 10 times. Other victories include her win at the Tri-State Championship in 1996, as well as the Highland Springs Country Club Championship in 1990. She also placed third in the National Senior Olympics in 1988. Mahoney is equally recognized as an activist for women's sports. Mahoney was a founding inductee to the Ozarks Golf Hall of Fame in 2002.

Joan Thomas

Joan Thomas won the women's Tri-State Classic a record eight times. She was a perennial member of the Joplin Women's Horton Smith Cup team and was medalist of the event 26 times. She was a medalist in the Missouri Amateur Championship and was the runner up of the tournament twice. Victories also include the 1955 Women's Amateur Championship in Puerto Rico, the Southeast Iowa Amateur Championship, and the Club Championship at Twin Hills Country Club a record 29 times. Thomas participated in the 1964 U.S. Amateur at Prairie Dunes in Hutchinson, Kansas.

In 1973, Thomas became the president of the Missouri Women's Golf Association. She was elected to the Joplin Golf Hall of Fame in 1985 and was inducted into the Ozarks Golf Hall of Fame in 2004.

Cathy Reynolds

Cathy Reynolds was born in July 1957 in Kansas City, Missouri. Her father and golf pro, Sam Reynolds, put a golf club in Cathy's hands at the age of five. After years of working with Sam at Hickory Hills Country Club, Cathy went on to win the Missouri State Junior Amateur in 1971, 1972, 1974, and 1975. She qualified for the U.S. Open at the age of 15, which was a record that would be held for several years. In 1976, Cathy won the Missouri State Amateur Championship at Hickory Hills. As Cathy entered Glendale High School, there was no girl's team, so she became a star for the boy's team.

While growing up playing junior golf tournaments, Cathy Reynolds grew close to fellow amateur Nancy Lopez. Both Reynolds and Lopez felt going to the Ladies Professional Golf Association (LPGA) Tour was just around the corner as they were finishing high school. Both found that Tulsa University was building a top rate women's golf team. After heading to Tulsa for college, Reynolds had one of her best years as an amateur. In 1977, she was ranked as the second-best amateur in the country. That year, she would win the Mexican Amateur and the Trans-National at Southern Pines, North Carolina, over Beth Daniel. Reynolds would last at Tulsa three years before deciding to leave to join the LPGA in 1978.

Reynolds won her first tour event during her fourth year on tour in 1981 at the Golden Lights Championship in Greenwich, Connecticut. Reynolds's best year on tour was 1981, finishing 20th on the money list. She played on the LPGA Tour for 17 years and played in 13 U.S. Opens.

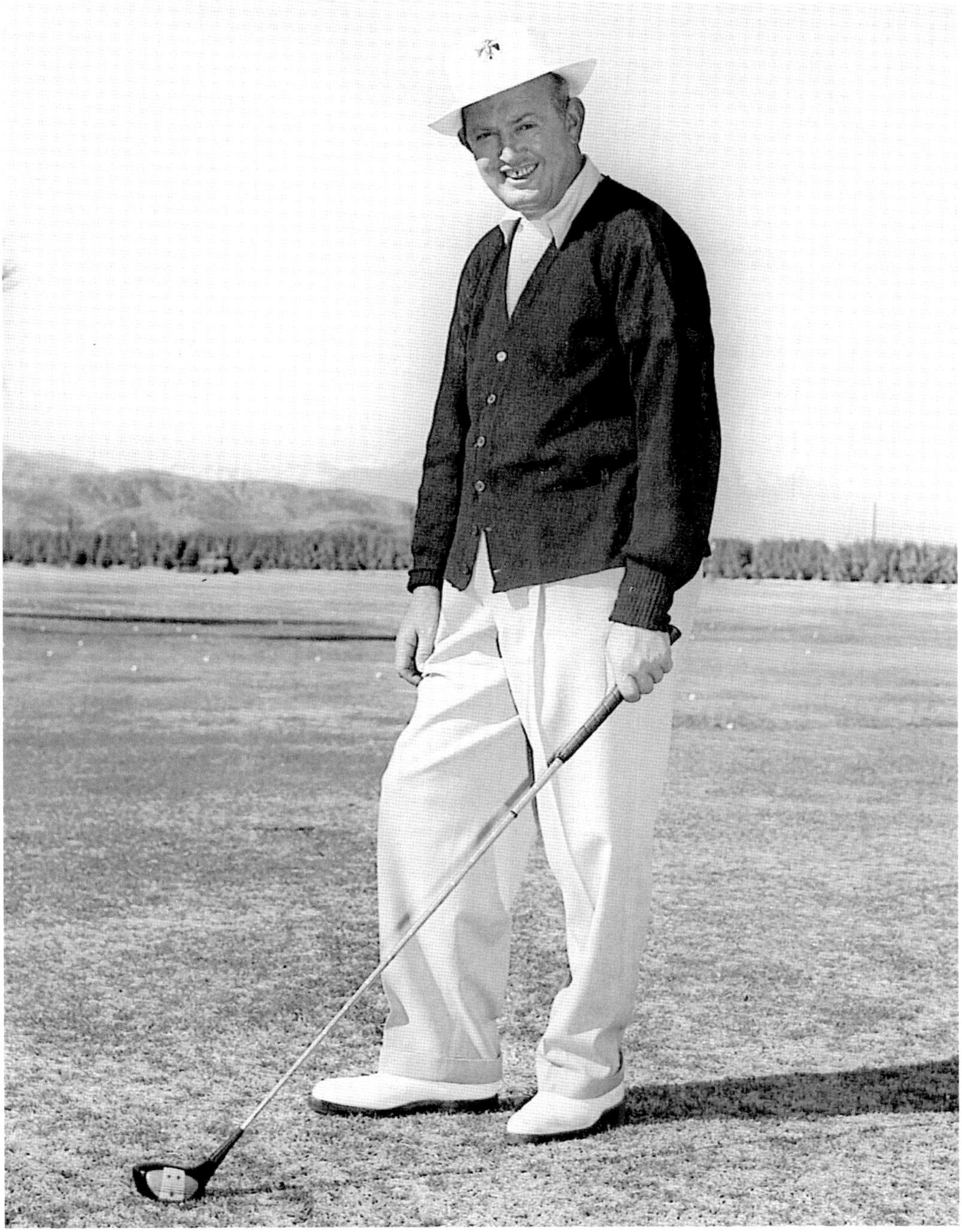

Ed Dudley had the complete golf experience. Dudley won 13 golf tournaments while on the professional tour, resided as the head golf professional at the top golf course in the country, Augusta National, and was the president of the Professional Golf Association. (Courtesy of Photos From the Fairway.)

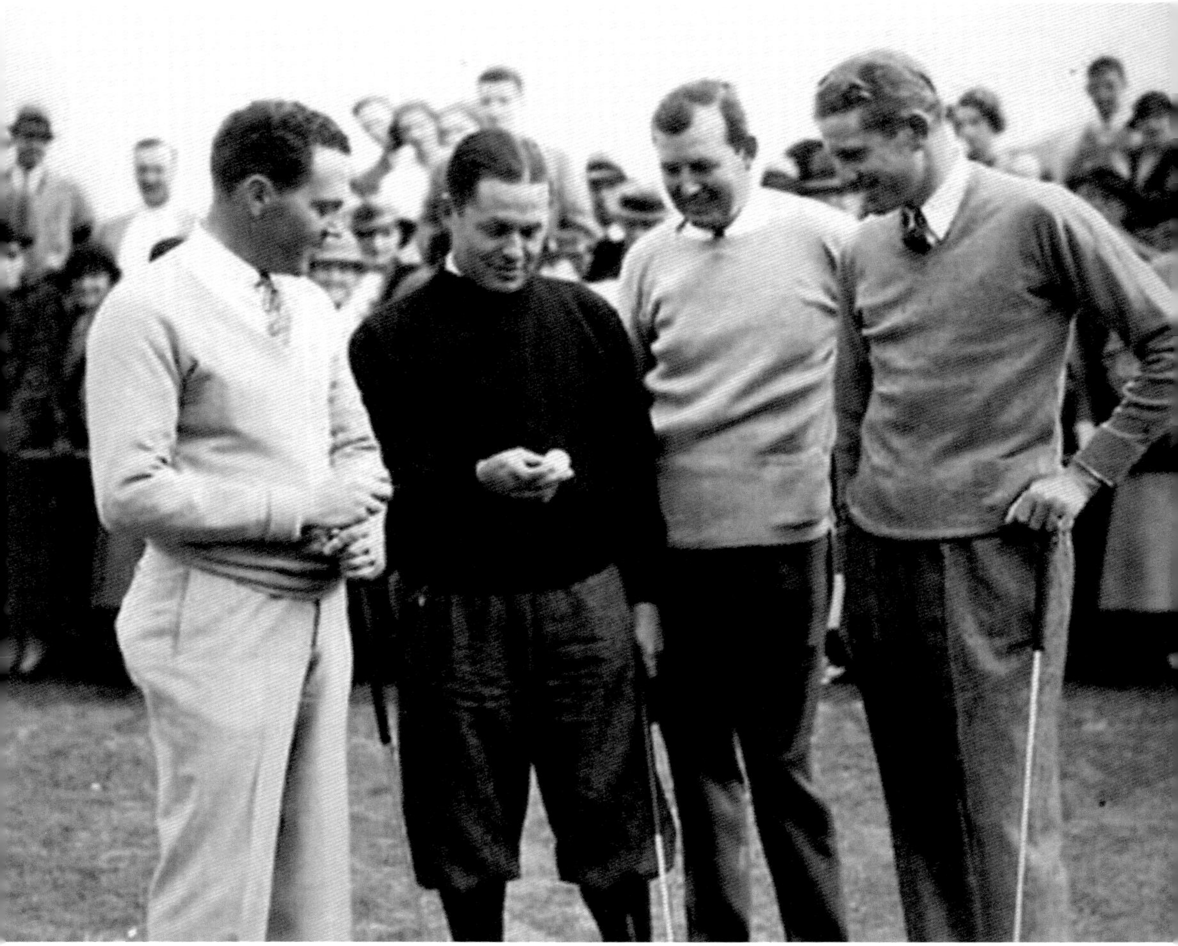

Ed Dudley (second from right) was photographed here in 1934 when two periods of his golf career converged. Dudley is pictured with Bobby Jones (second from left), his new boss at Augusta National, and Horton Smith (far right), his former playing partner from Joplin.

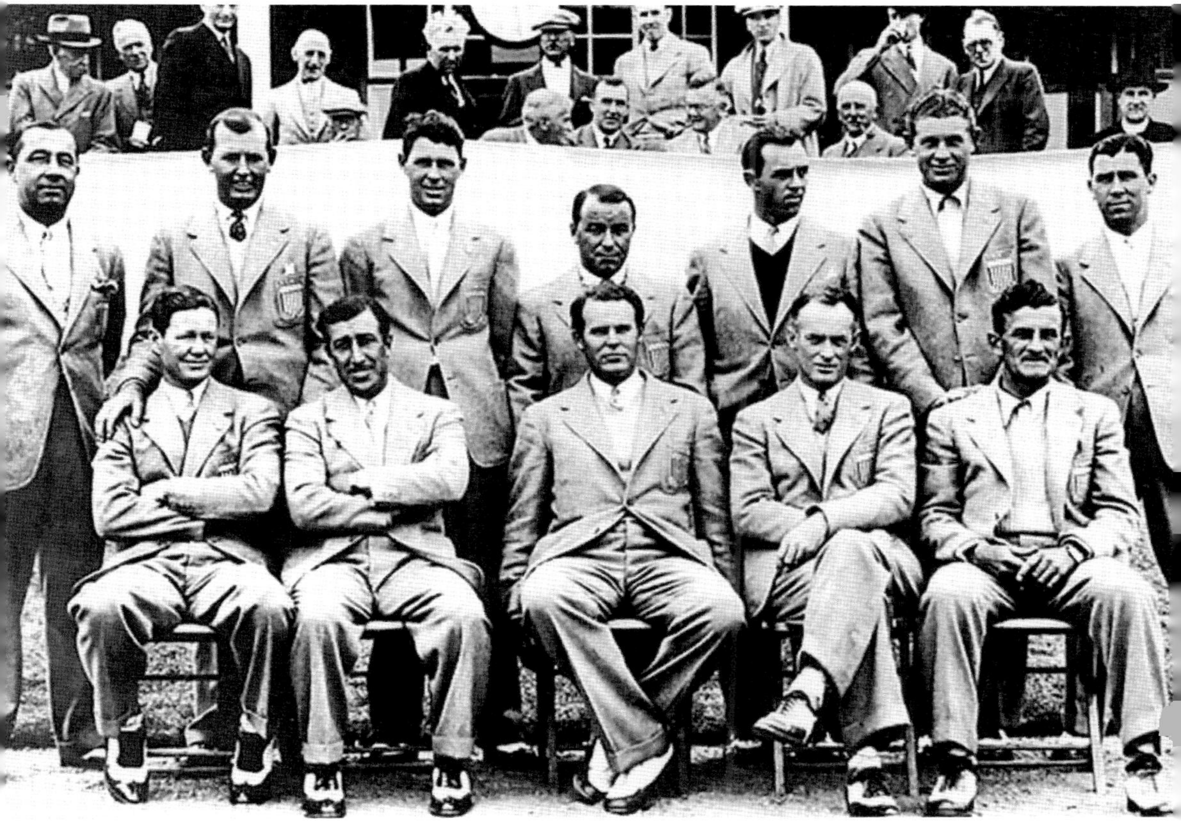

The 1937 American Ryder Cup team defeated Great Britain 8 to 4. The team included captain Walter Hagen, Ed Dudley (back row, second from left), Gene Sarazen, Sam Snead, Horton Smith (back row, second from right), Byron Nelson, Tony Manero, Ralph Guldahl, Deny Shute, Henry Picard, and Johnny Revolta. Ed Dudley would win his singles match over Alf Perry 2 and 1.

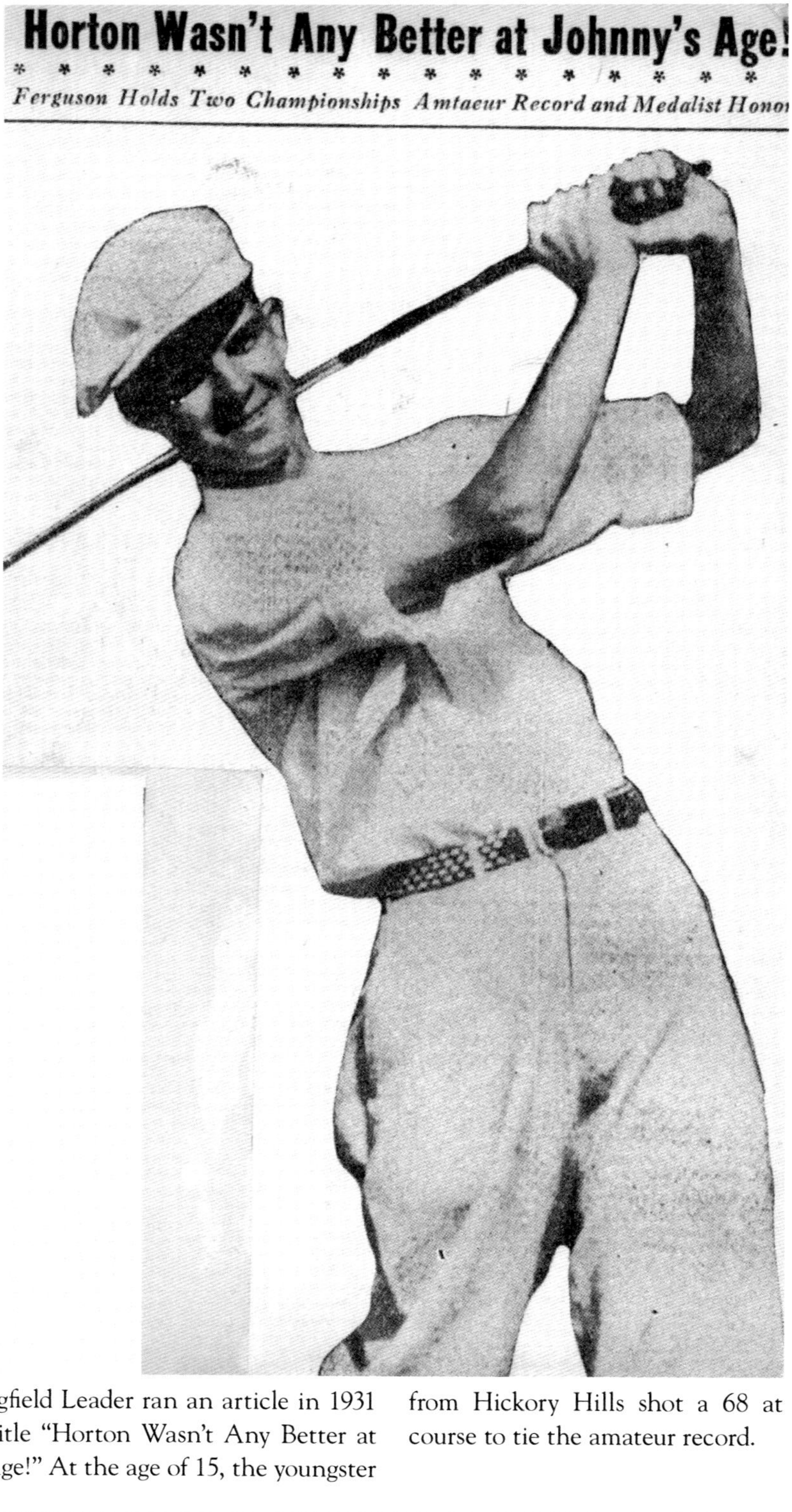

Horton Wasn't Any Better at Johnny's Age!

Ferguson Holds Two Championships Amtaeur Record and Medalist Hono

The Springfield Leader ran an article in 1931 with the title "Horton Wasn't Any Better at Johnny's Age!" At the age of 15, the youngster from Hickory Hills shot a 68 at his home course to tie the amateur record.

A young John Ferguson shows his form. At the age of 14, Ferguson was already shooting in the low 70s at Springfield Country Club. Along with Walter Thomas, Dick Farrington, and Joe Bill Hogeboom, he was considered the future of golf in the Ozarks.

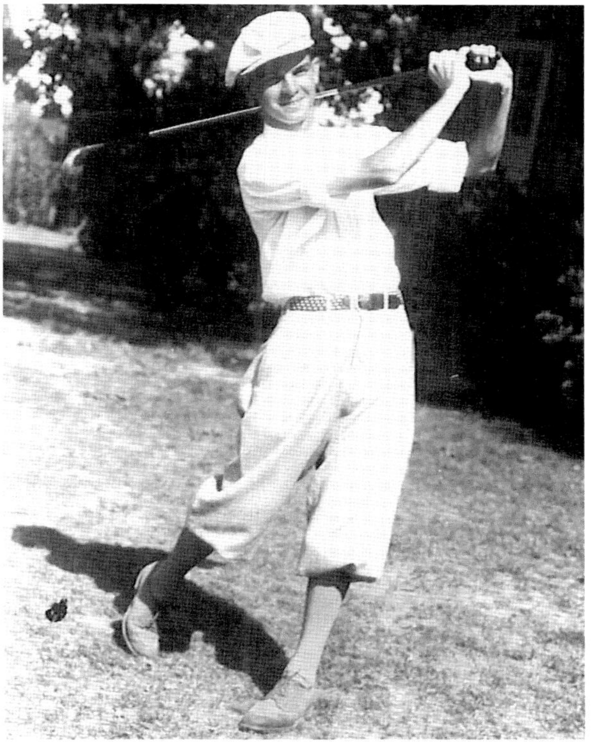

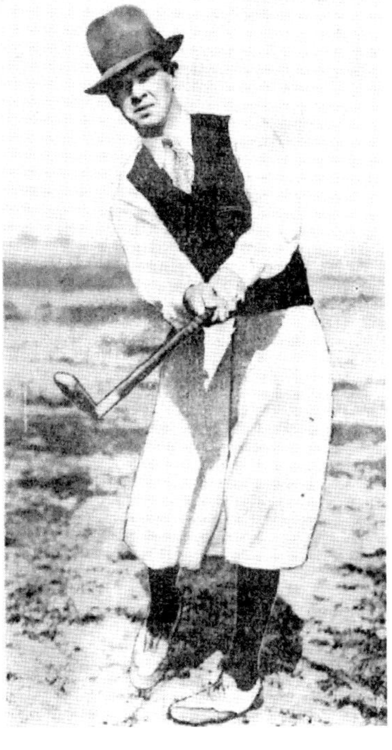

John Ferguson is pictured here in vintage golf attire. He would win the All-Ozarks championship, the District Interscholastic Championship three times, the West Plains Invitational twice, and the City Amateur Championship twice.

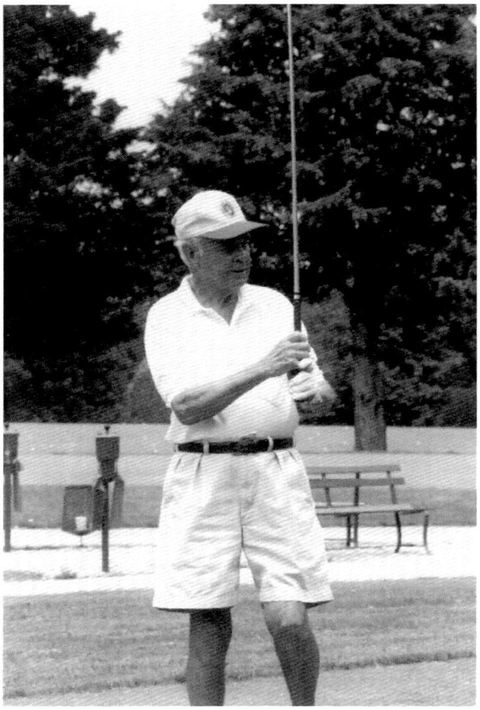

Dr. John Ferguson still plays golf and is an active member at Hickory Hills Country Club in Springfield, Missouri.

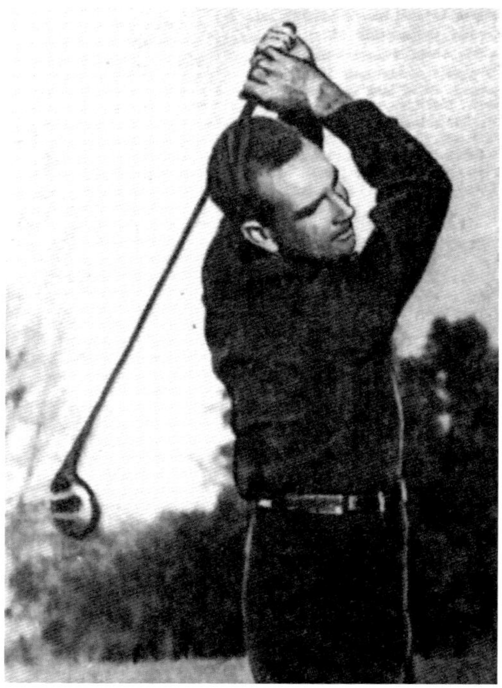

Tom Talbot enjoyed a winning amateur golf career before serving as head golf professional at several Springfield golf courses including Glenstone, Springfield Country Club, Hickory Hills Country Club, and finally Grandview golf course for 16 years.

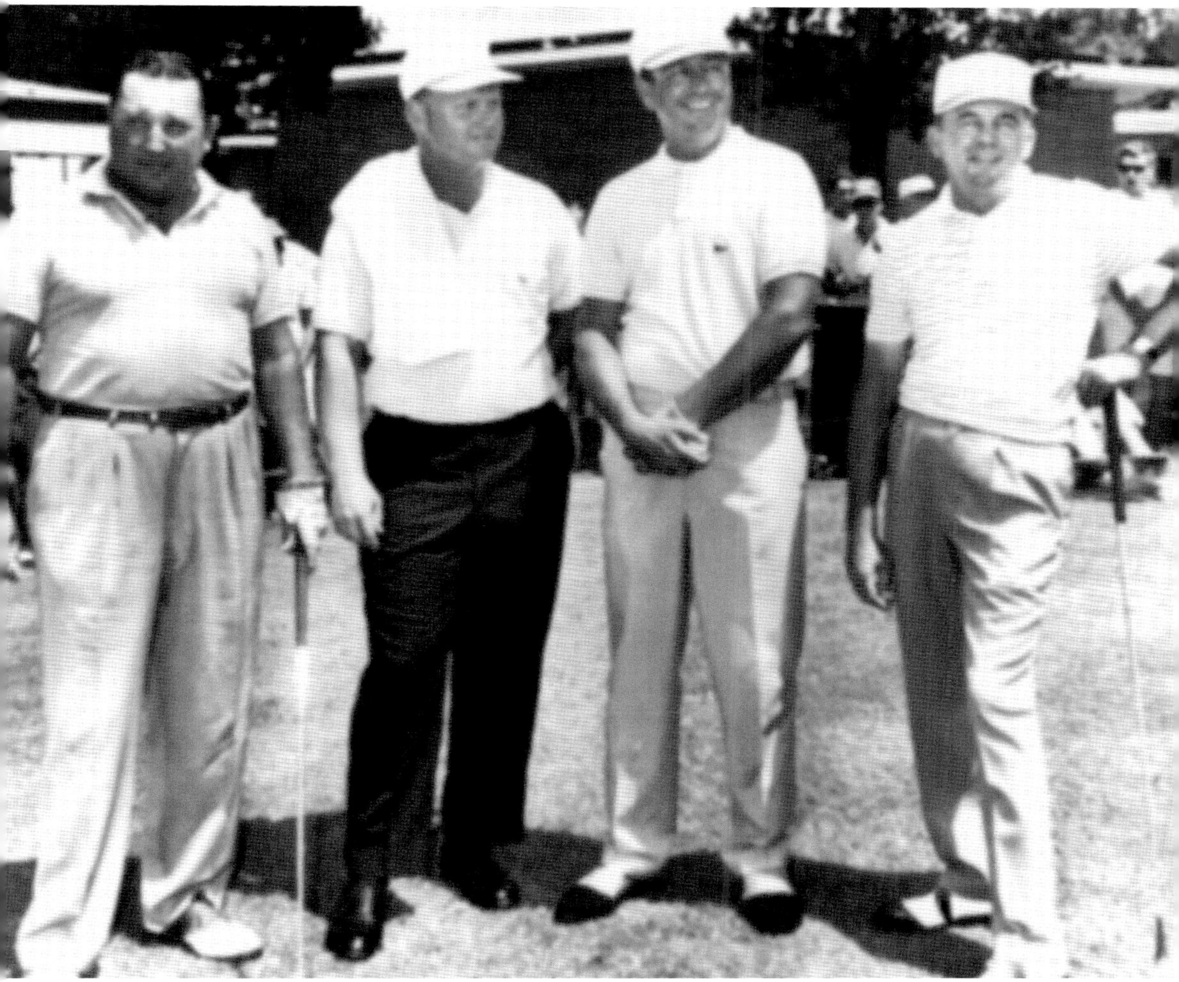

This photograph was taken during a golf exhibition at Hickory Hills in 1964. The professionals pictured from left to right are Ky Laffoon, golf legend Jack Nicklaus, Sam Reynolds, and Gene Sallee. (Courtesy of Hickory Hills.)

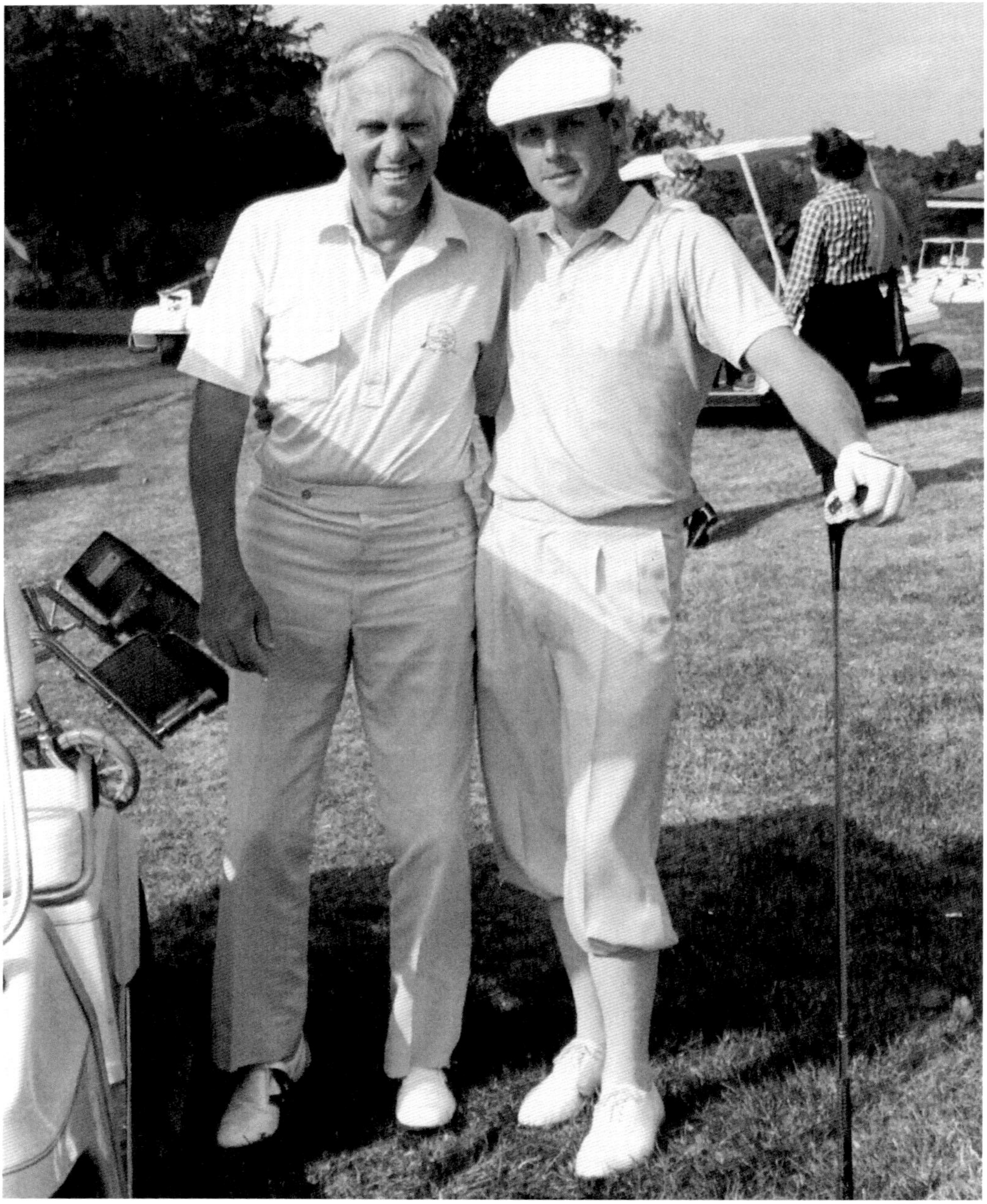

Bill Stewart (left) and son Payne Stewart are the only father-son winners of the Missouri Amateur Championship. Bill won the event twice in 1953 and 1957, while Payne won the event in 1979. (Courtesy of Hickory Hills.)

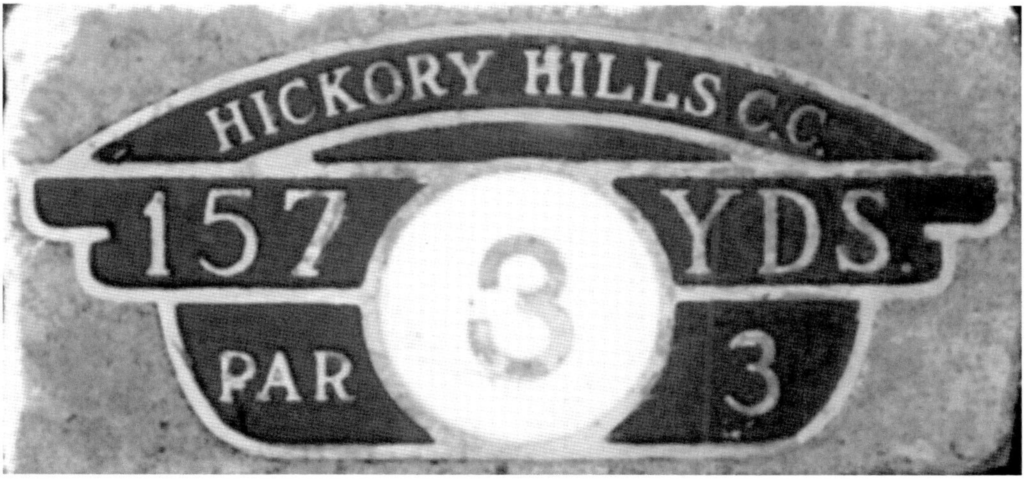

This is the actual tee marker from the third hole at Hickory Hills before the course was redesigned. The third hole is where Bill Stewart birdied the third playoff hole in the 1957 Missouri State Amateur to beat Jim Tom Blair for the championship.

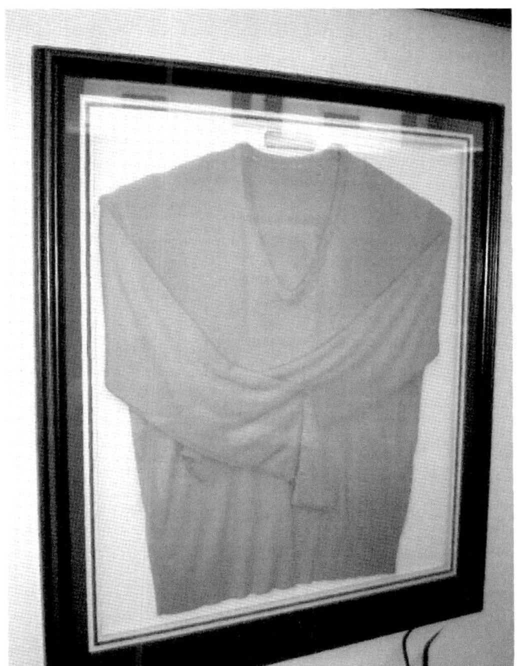

Bill Stewart's security blanket (his sweater) is framed and hanging in the Bill Stewart Library in the pro shop at Hickory Hills. The library is a memorial in tribute to Bill's love for the game of golf. The library was designed to display trophies and recognize important accomplishments in the game.

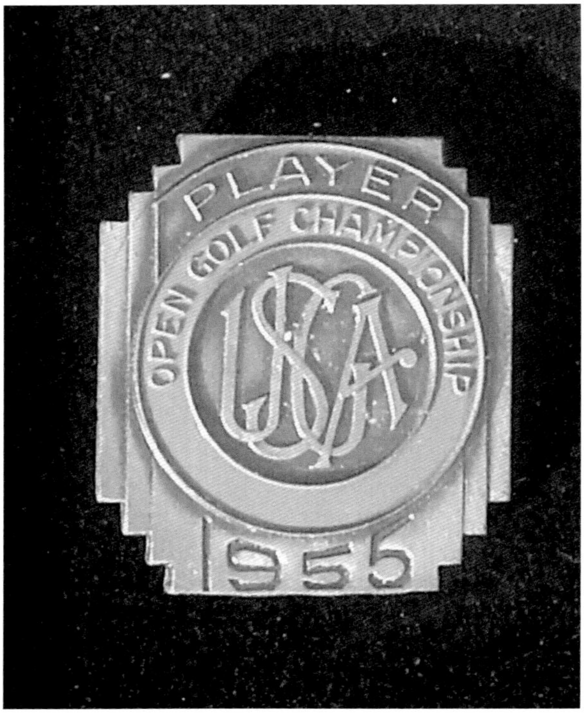

In 1955, Bill Stewart participated in the U.S. Open held in San Francisco at Olympic Country Club. Jack Fleck won the tournament in a dramatic play-off with legend Ben Hogan. Only contestants receive these special clips.

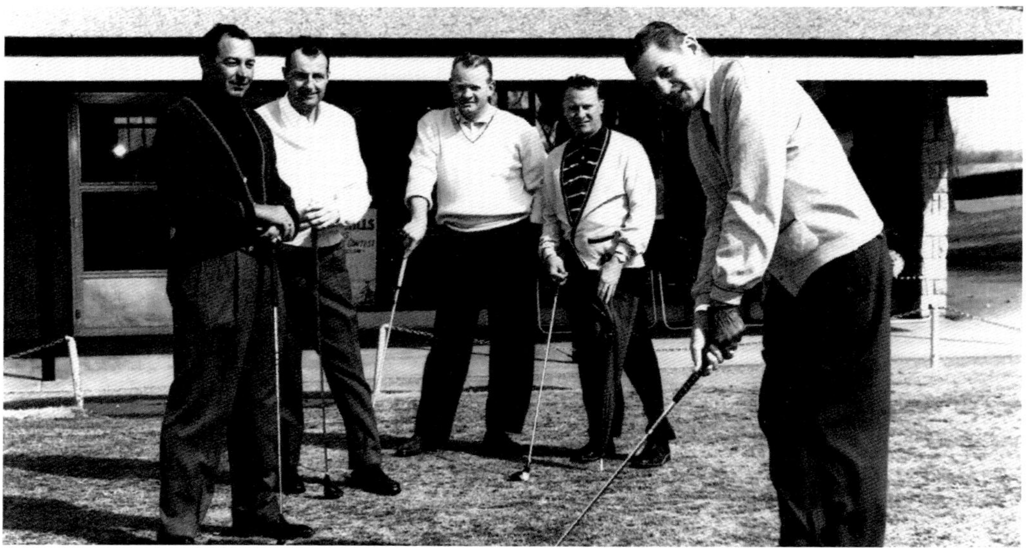

Sam Reynolds (far left) and others look on as Horton Smith poses for a photograph outside the pro shop at Hickory Hills Country Club. While Reynolds was the head professional at Hickory Hills, many golf greats would pass through for a round at the historic course. (Courtesy of Hickory Hills.)

Hale Irwin would learn golf at a young age growing up in Baxter Springs, Kansas. He would regularly make the trip to courses in the Joplin area, including Schifferdecker Golf Course.

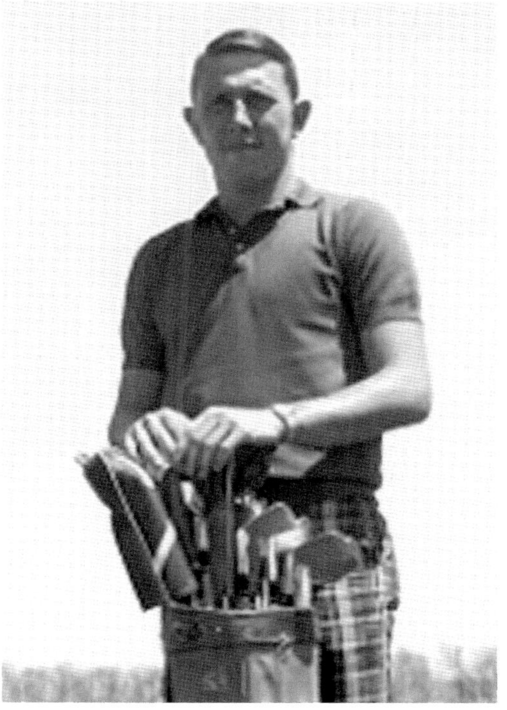

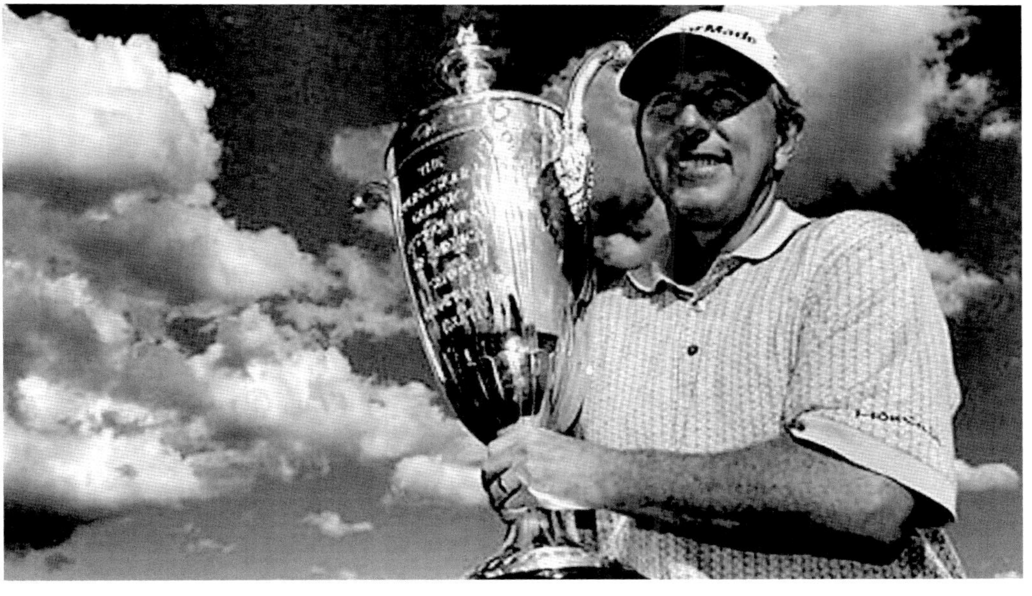

Hale Irwin holds the trophy from his victory at the 2005 Senior PGA Championship at Laurel Valley Golf Club in Ligonier, Pennsylvania. The win would mark his fourth victory of the championship. (Courtesy of Montana Pritchard.)

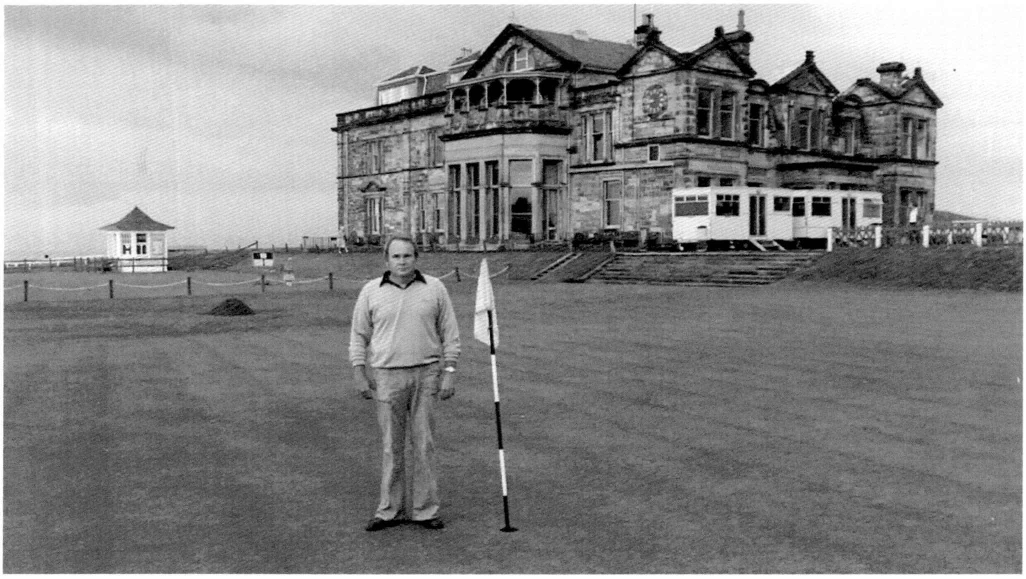

A young Bruce Hollowell poses at the 18th hole on the Old Course at St. Andrews during a golf trip to Scotland. (Courtesy of Hickory Hills.)

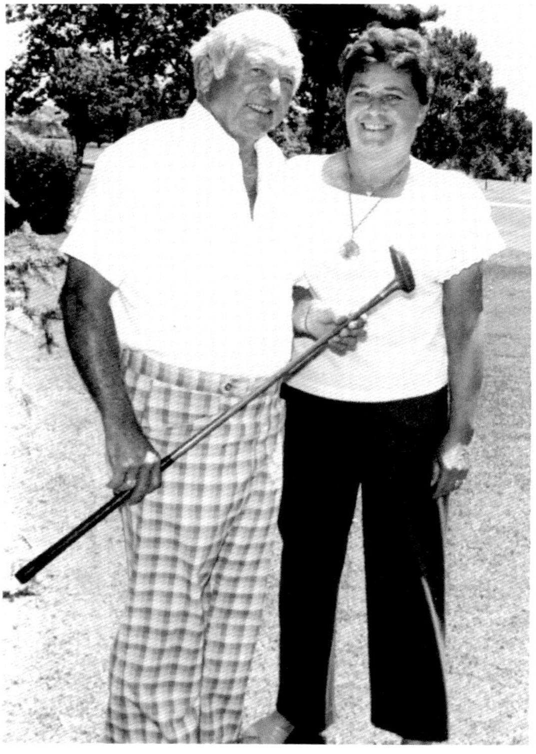

Joplin area standout Joan Thomas is pictured here with her husband Jimmy Thomas, who also was a regional standout golfer. Joan was the perennial women's Club Champion at Twin Hills Country Club in Joplin, Missouri, winning the event a record 29 times. (Courtesy of the *Joplin Globe*.)

Joan Thomas is the only female member of both the Ozarks Golf Hall of Fame and the Joplin Golf Hall of Fame. (Courtesy of the *Joplin Globe*.)

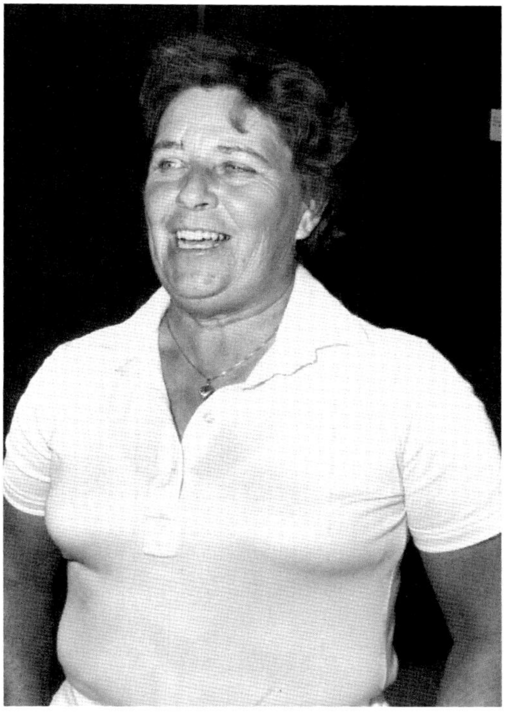

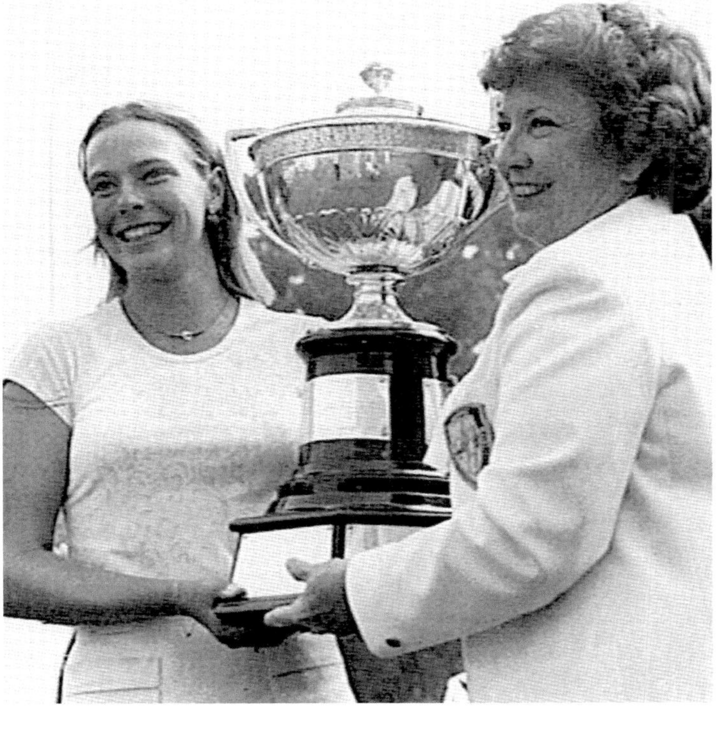

Cathy Reynolds (left) was able to win the 1977 Trans National Golf Association's golf tournament in Southern Pines, North Carolina, over Beth Daniel. Reynolds was also the co-medalist of the tournament with a round of 73. Reynolds turned professional the next year.

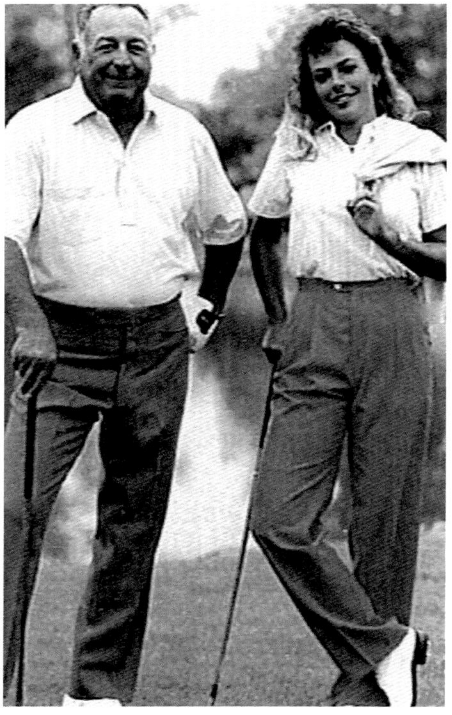

Cathy Reynolds, pictured here with her father, golf professional Sam Reynolds, started playing golf at the age of five. She learned golf under Sam at Hickory Hills Country Club while Sam was the club professional there.

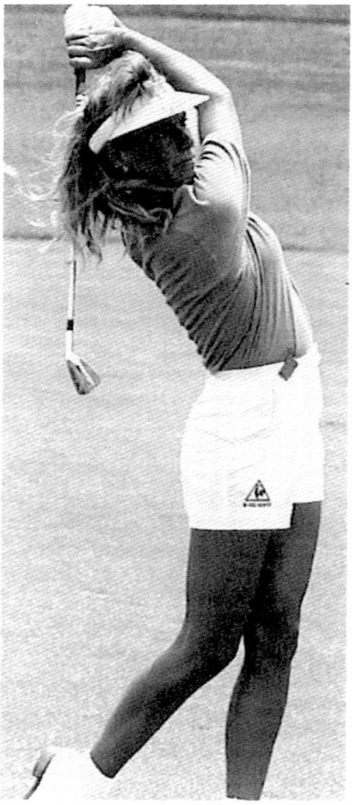

Cathy Reynolds used the fluid swing she developed with her father at Hickory Hills Country Club on the LPGA Tour for 17 years. Her first professional win came at the 1981 Golden Lights Championship in Greenwich, Connecticut.

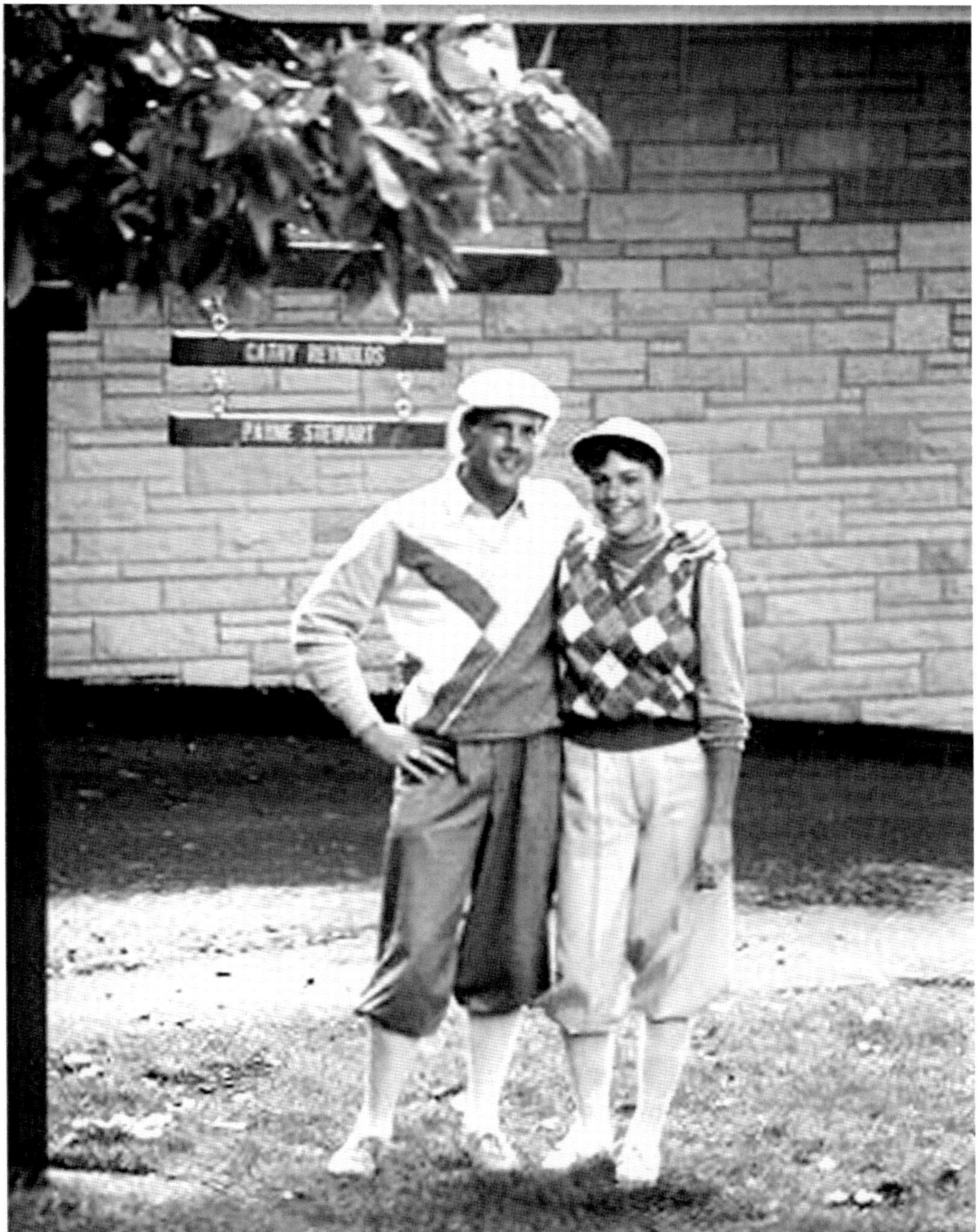

This photograph of Payne Stewart and Cathy Reynolds was taken at Hickory Hills where they grew up playing. Hickory Hills was so proud of their young professionals there was a sign erected near the front of the clubhouse that read "The home of tour professionals Payne Stewart and Cathy Reynolds." (Courtesy of Hickory Hills.)

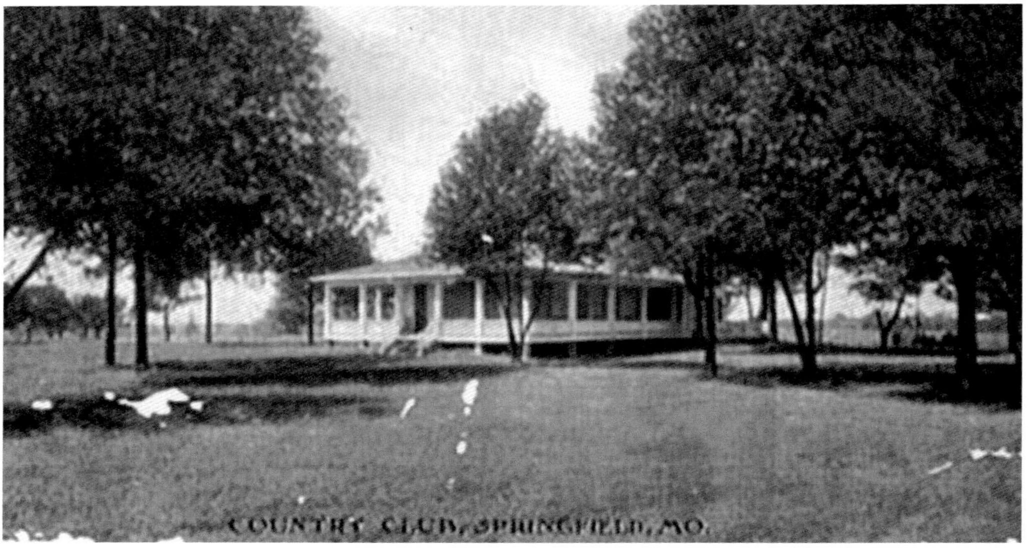

This postcard depicts the clubhouse at the oldest golf club in the Ozarks, Springfield Country Club. The club was built in 1908 on Glenstone between Portland and Meadowmere Streets. The original clubhouse was lost to a fire in 1939. (Courtesy of Springfield-Greene County Library.)

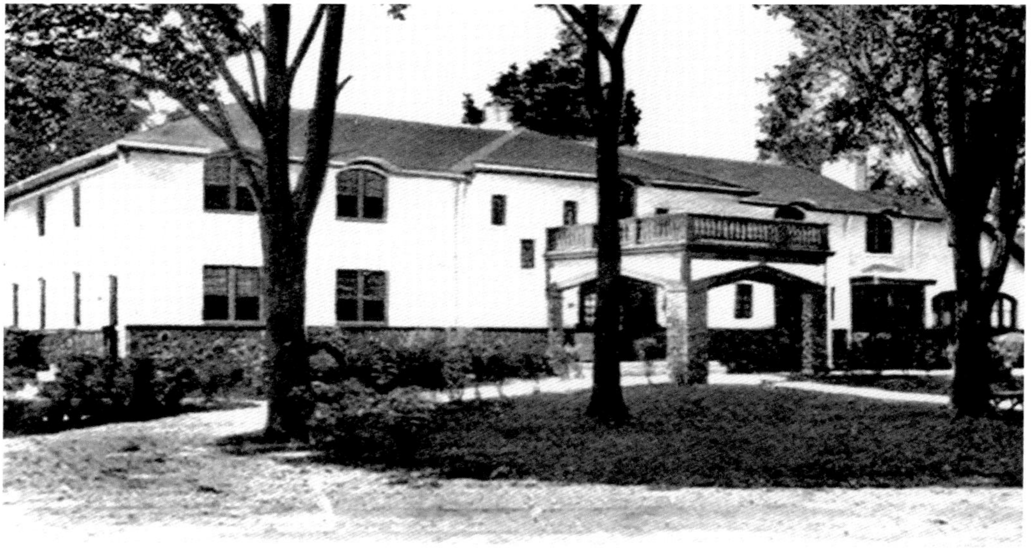

This clubhouse for the Springfield Country Club was erected after the original clubhouse burned down in 1939. After World War II, John Q. Hammons would purchase the property and develop what is now the Country Club Plaza and housing development behind the center.

7

Ozarks Fairways

The first known golf courses in the Ozarks opened at the turn of the 20th century in Springfield. The first courses were the Glenstone Golf Course and Springfield Country Club, built in 1908. In 1911, Joplin, Missouri, received its first golf course, Oak Hill Golf Club on Gus Mattes' property on the west side of town. The original course was designed by John Rodd, who later became the head professional. The sand green nine-hole course would have nine more holes added in 1947, when it became Twin Hills Country Club.

Another course in Joplin, Schifferdecker Golf Course, would be added soon after Oak Hill in 1920. Schifferdecker was built as a nine-hole public course originally, but the city added nine more holes to the course in 1924. Schifferdecker soon became the location of one of the oldest tournaments in the region, the Tri-State Amateur. In 1922, the tournament would be known as the Ozark Amateur. In 1925, Neosho Golf Course would be the final addition for several years to the Joplin area golf courses.

More expansion would take place in Springfield with the addition of Hickory Hills Country Club in 1926 on John Woodruff's farm on the east side of Springfield. Together with Rev. Paul R. Talbot, Woodruff designed a course that was reported to be an almost exact replica of the famous St. Andrews in Scotland. In 1937, Hickory Hills held a historical exhibition that included professional golfers Horton Smith, Harry Cooper, and Lawson Little.

The Lake Shore Golf Club in Springfield opened in 1930. The 6,666-yard course would be one of the first built with grass greens. One year later, Honey Creek golf course was designed by Horton Smith and developed just north of Aurora.

The next course added to the area was built in Carthage in 1937 and was designed by Mike Farlow. Only six years later, Springfield would follow in 1943 with the addition of Grandview, now known as the Bill and Payne Stewart golf course. World War II would mark a pause in the golf course expansion. In fact, in 1941, the property of Glenstone golf course was donated by the city of Springfield to the U.S. Army to build the O'Reilly Hospital, which was located where Evangel University stands now. In 1952, the land that made up the Springfield Country Club was purchased by John Q. Hammons, who developed the Country Club Plaza and the housing development behind it. The property of Lake Shore Golf Course was developed into the United States Federal Medical Prison.

After the war, course development would pick up where it left off with the construction of Twin Oaks in Springfield in 1955. The course was built on the Johnson family farm, where despite the name, there were no oak trees to be found. The course was designed by Floyd Farley of Oklahoma City. Local golf standout Gene Sallee was hired as the first head professional.

In the early 1960s, two additional area courses were built. The first was Springfield's Horton Smith Municipal Golf Course in 1962. Horton Smith himself joined in the inaugural round along with Tom Talbot, Sam Reynolds, and Gene Sallee. The next course added was Briarbrook Country Club in Carl Junction in 1964. The hilly course was designed by Jim Latimer. The 1960s would mark another era of exhibitions in the area by noted golfers. Arnold Palmer would come to Twin Hills in 1963 to play for the crowds of followers. The next year, in 1964, Jack Nicklaus would play a round at Hickory Hills with Ky Laffoon, Sam Reynolds, and Gene Sallee.

Fremont Hills was built and designed in 1971 by noted course designer Press Maxwell. Press was the son of Perry Maxwell, the noted golf course architect that designed Southern Hills in Tulsa, Oklahoma, and Prairie Dunes in Hutcheson, Kansas. In 1980, Loma Linda was built in the same fashion as Fremont Hills in that a large housing development was built around the course itself. Donald Sechrest would design the first of two courses at Loma Linda.

During the late 1980s and early 1990s, Mickey Mantle had a home at Loma Linda Country Club. He helped promote the club, and he held annual charity golf tournaments. Mantle invited friends from his playing days such as Billy Martin, Yogi Berra, Warren Spahn, Fred Patek, and Ralph Terry. The tournament would benefit local charities and Missouri Southern State College athletics.

Highland Springs opened in 1989. This high-end club and housing development was built by John Q. Hammons, and the course was designed by noted golf course architect Robert Trent Jones. Just one year later, the club held its first Hogan Tour Event. Now known as the Buy.com Tour, it is considered the minor league of the PGA Tour. The inaugural event, the Ben Hogan Greater Ozarks Open, was won by now PGA Tour veteran John Cook. Other notable winners include Chris DiMarco, Stewart Cink, and Tommy Tolles. The 2005 winner, Roger Tanbellini, took home $94,500 for his victory.

Two courses were added to the Ozarks in 1996. The Millwood Golf and Racquet club was developed on the southeast edge of Springfield, while the Top of the Rock course was built just outside of Branson. Top of the Rock is a one of the finest par-three golf courses in the country. The course is located at Bass Pro Shop's Big Cedar Lodge. The course was designed by Jack Nicklaus and was the first par-three golf course that he designed. The course is certified by the Audubon Cooperative Sanctuary Program.

Branson would go through a growth in course development to match its growth in tourism. Branson would add Thousand Hills and Ledgestone, but the most noted addition would be Branson Creek, which had its grand opening in the summer of 2000. The course was designed by Tom Fazio and was quickly named by *Golf Magazine* as a "Top 10 Courses you can play" in 2000. In 2004, Branson Creek was listed as the 66th top public course in America.

Rivercut golf course is currently the newest public course in the Ozarks. The upscale public course was designed by Ken Dye in 1998. The course also houses the Ozarks Golf Hall of Fame display and the Connie Morris Learning Center. Next to the learning center is the Betty Allison Golf Course. This special course is designed specifically for youth golfers. The course is funded by the Heart of the Ozarks Junior Golf Foundation.

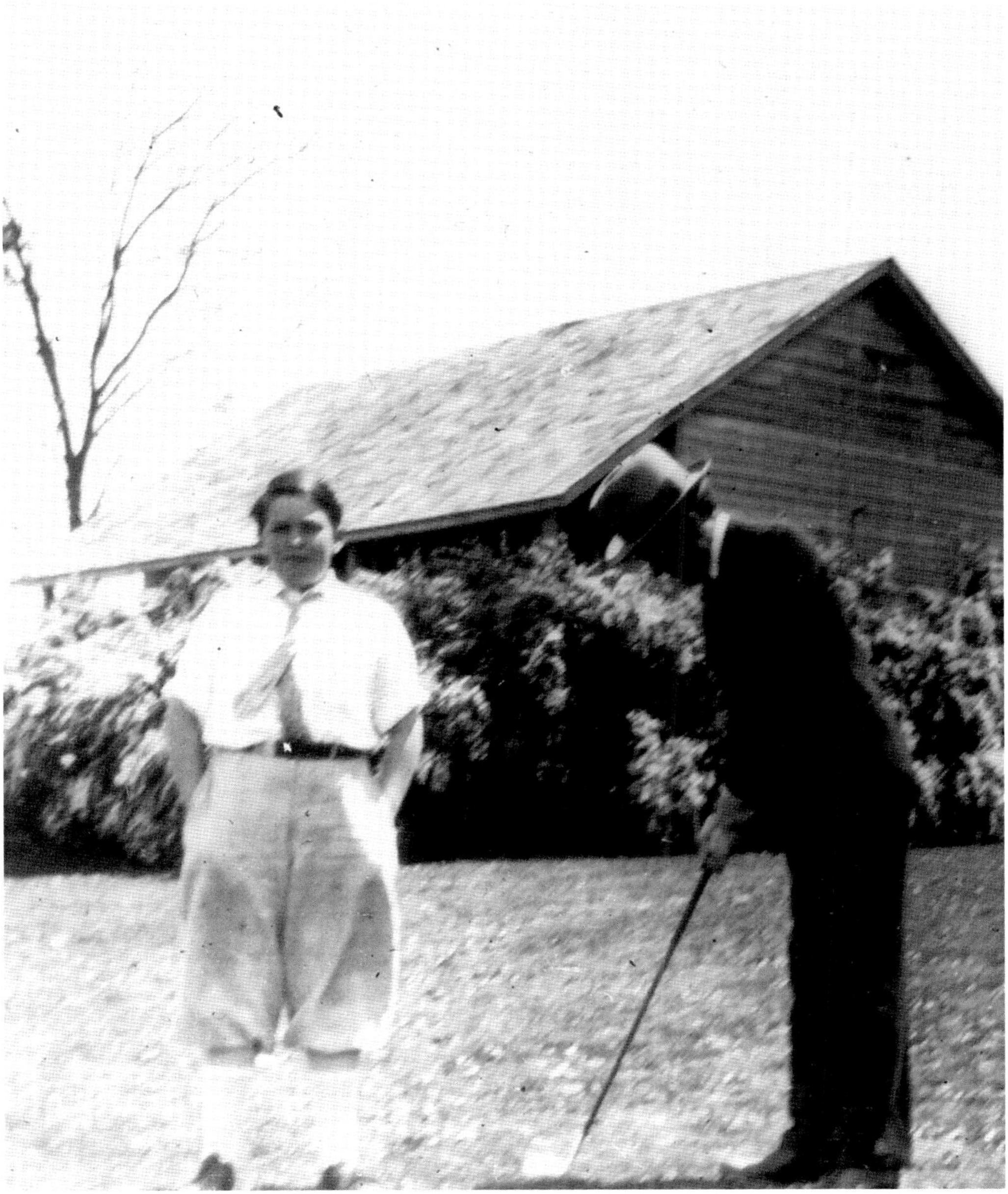

This is the oldest known photograph of Hickory Hills Country Club. The photograph shows John Woodruff (right) and a young man on the course that was built in 1926 on his farm located on the east side of Springfield. (Courtesy of Hickory Hills.)

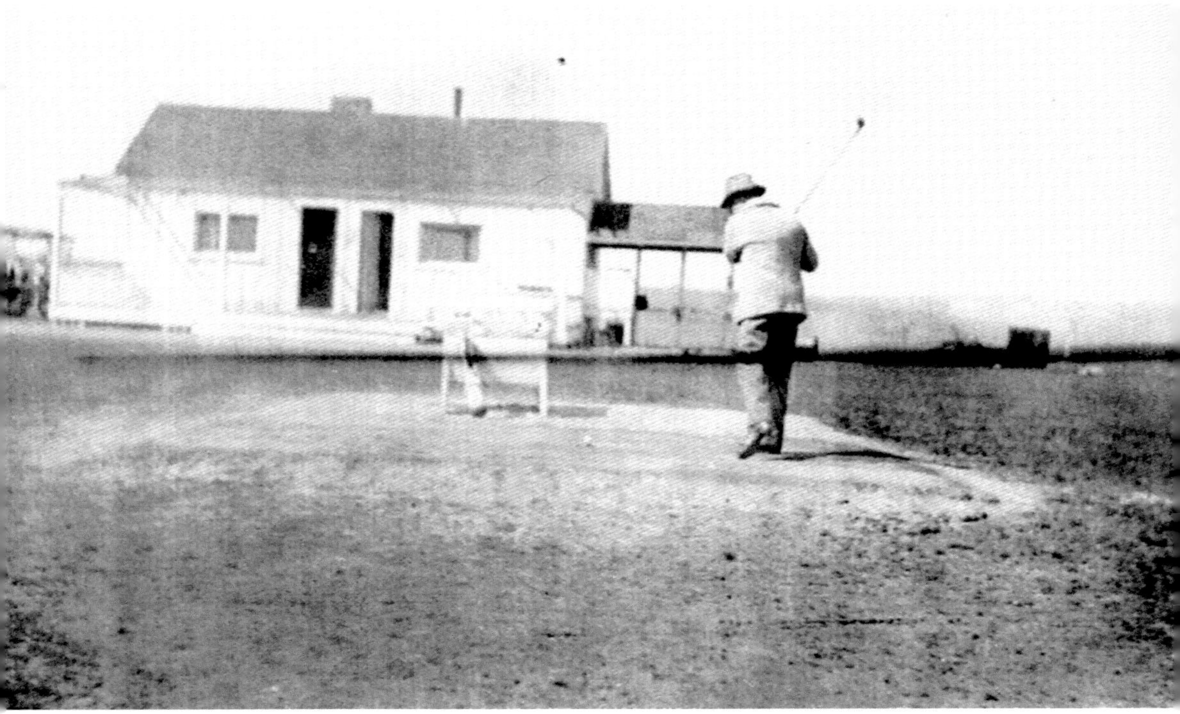

This is the oldest known photograph of Oak Hill, now Twin Hills, in Joplin. The golfer is Gabriel Neuberger on the first tee box of the then nine-hole course. This hole is now the seventh hole on the Twin Hills course. (Courtesy of Twin Hills.)

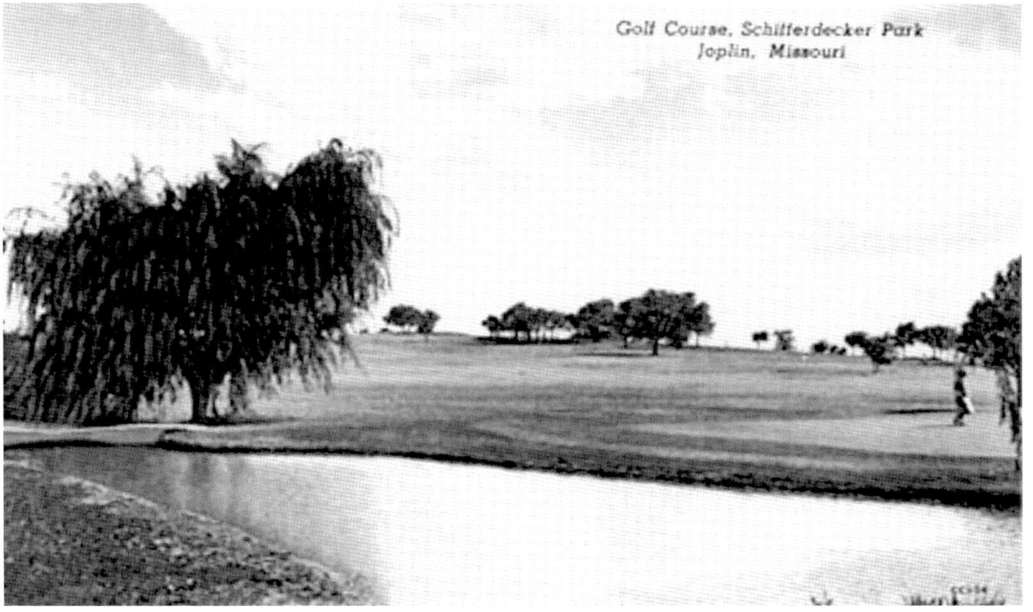

In 1921, 144 citizens and businesses donated the money for Schifferdecker Golf Course. The course started with nine holes, and in 1924, the course was expanded to 18 holes. Schifferdecker is the home to one of the oldest golf tournaments west of the Mississippi, the Ozark Amateur. A limestone clubhouse was added in 1930.

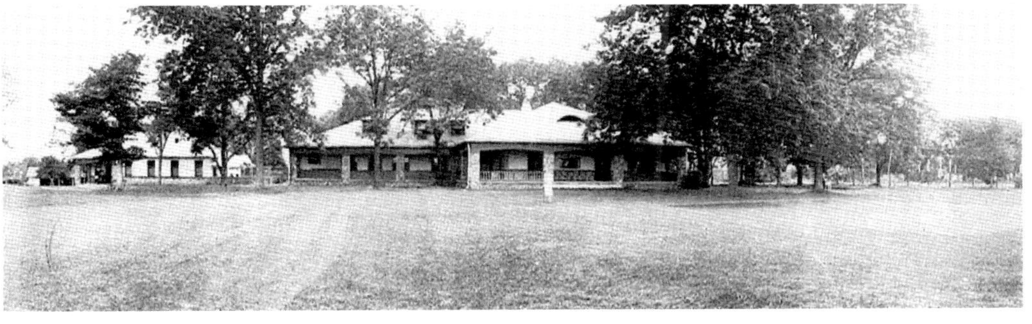

This shot of the original clubhouse of the Springfield Country Club was taken in 1929. Horton Smith would start his golfing career at this course in 1920. In 1925, Smith would become the caddie master and assistant to the professional.

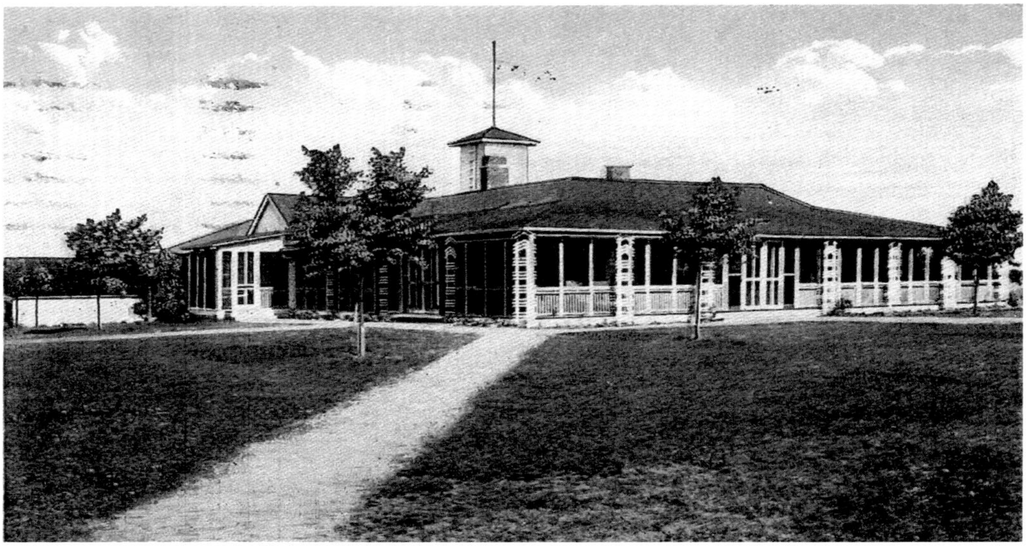

The original clubhouse from Oak Hill Country Club in Joplin, Missouri, is shown on this vintage postcard. The clubhouse was moved to the country club by Gus Mattes. (Courtesy of Twin Hills.)

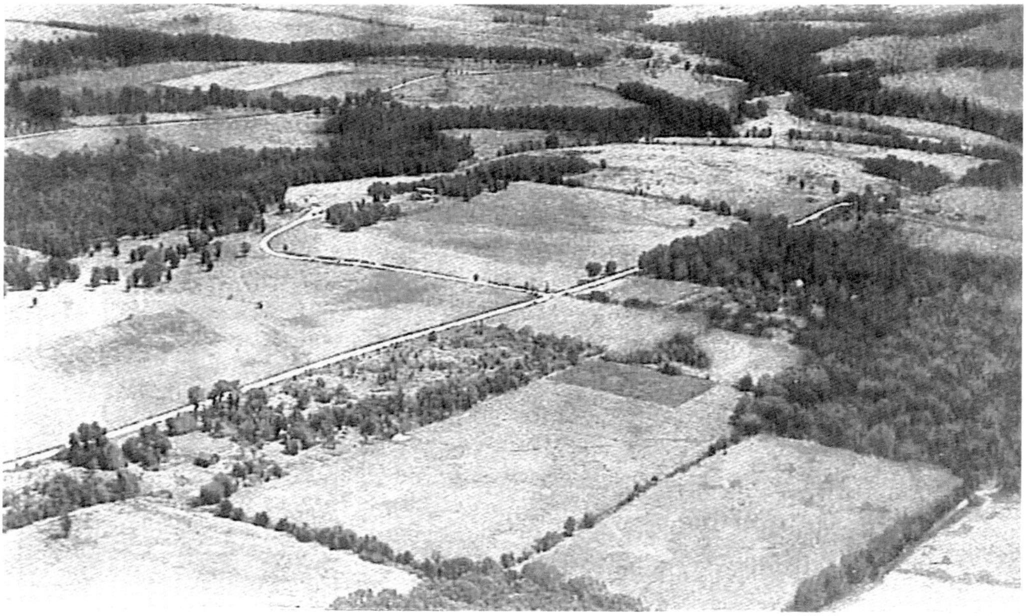

This vintage postcard depicts an aerial view of the old course and surrounding farms at Hickory Hills Country Club in Springfield. At the time, the course was located only on the north side of Cherry Street.

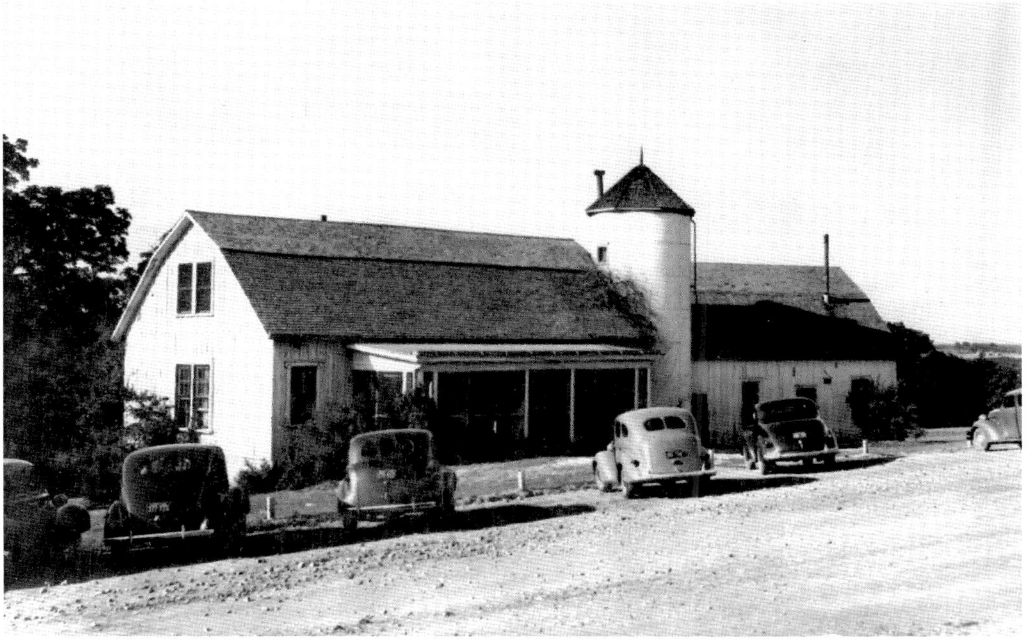

The original Hickory Hills clubhouse was built in 1926. At the time, it was the second private golf and country club in Springfield. (Courtesy of Hickory Hills.)

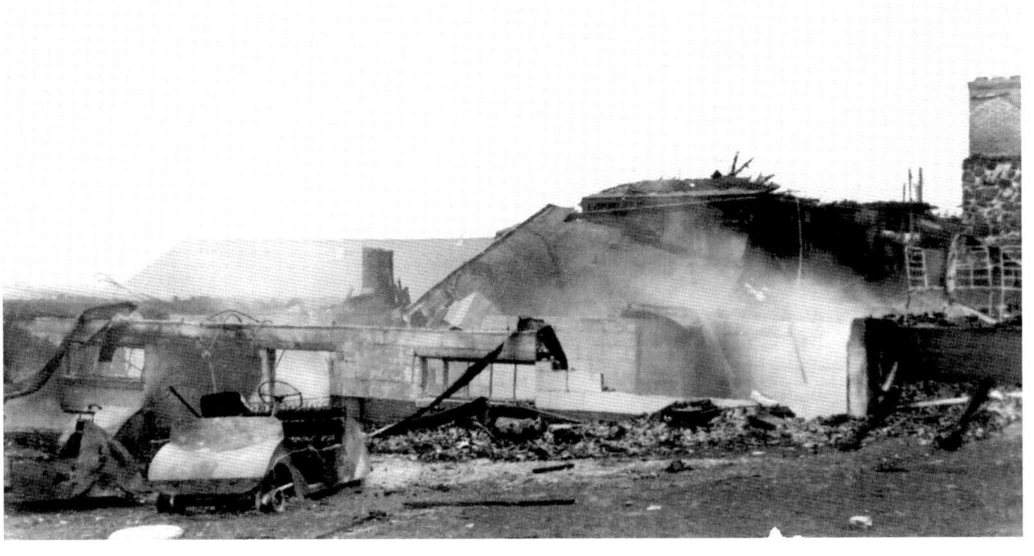

In 1939, a fire destroyed the original clubhouse at Hickory Hills. A new clubhouse was built shortly after. The second clubhouse would be lost to fire in 1954. Again, a new clubhouse was built and is still standing today. (Courtesy of Hickory Hills.)

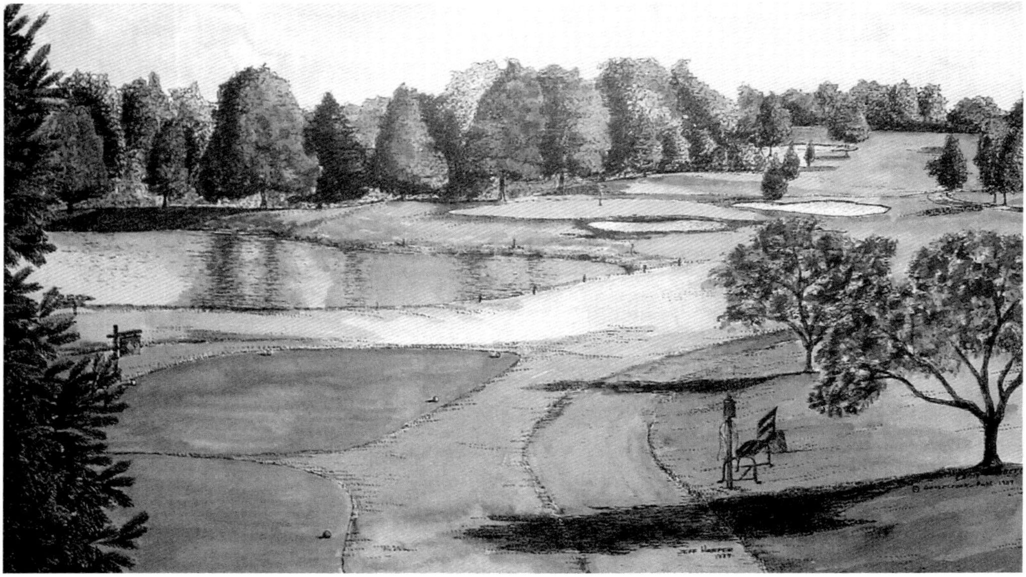

In 1989, Catherine Corbett and Jeff Harper would paint the second hole of Hickory Hills Country Club's 18-hole, 6,996-yard-long course. The print run was limited to only 250 pieces.

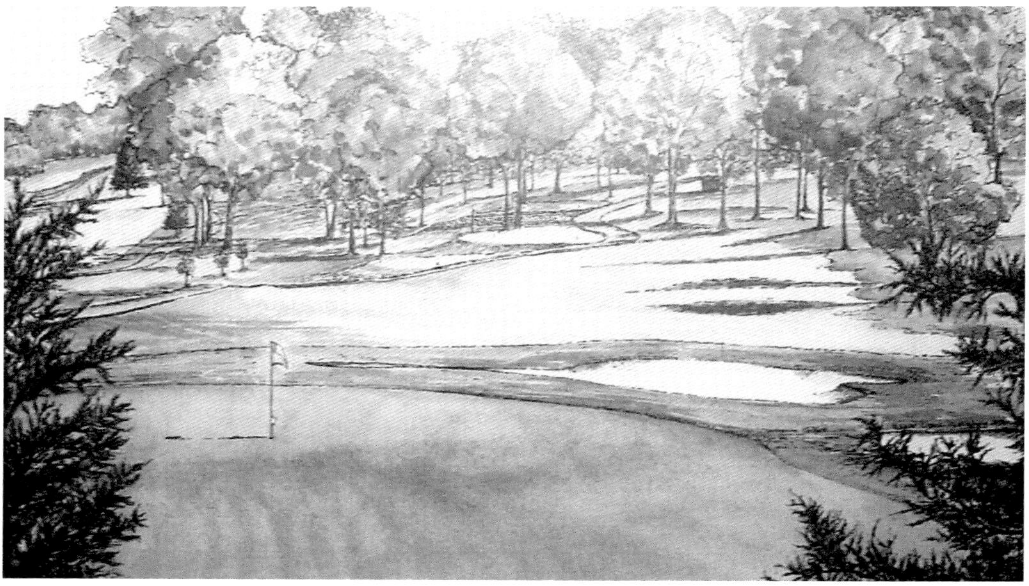

Catherine Corbett also created a watercolor painting of the 16th hole of Hickory Hills Country Club. The print run of this painting was limited to 250 pieces.

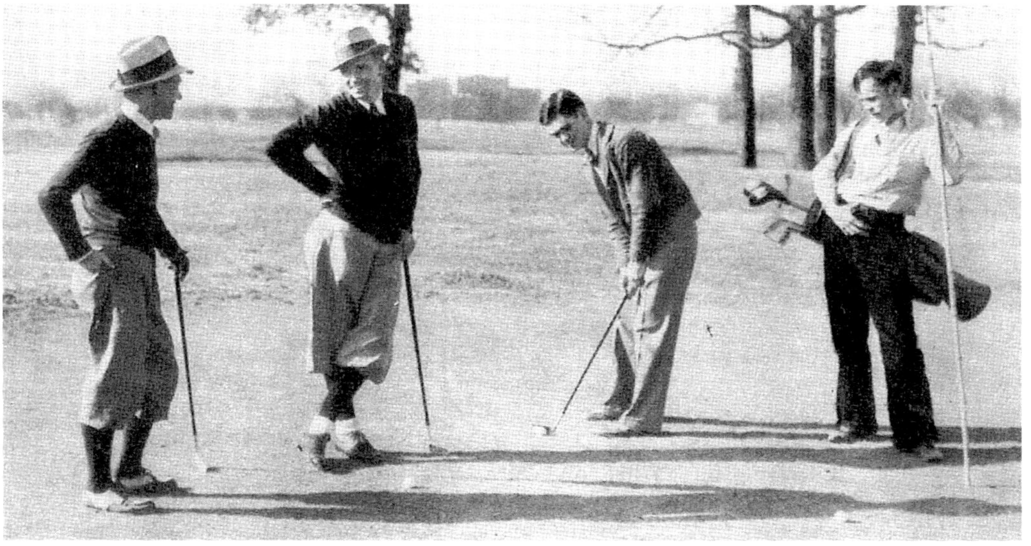

This photograph, taken at Glenstone golf course, was shown in the *St. Louis Post-Dispatch* on February 12, 1933. The players shown from left to right are Walter Thomas, the City Amateur champion; Tom Talbot, the City Open champion; John Ferguson, the All-Ozarks champion; and Jimmy Ewing, the caddy. (Courtesy of John Ferguson.)

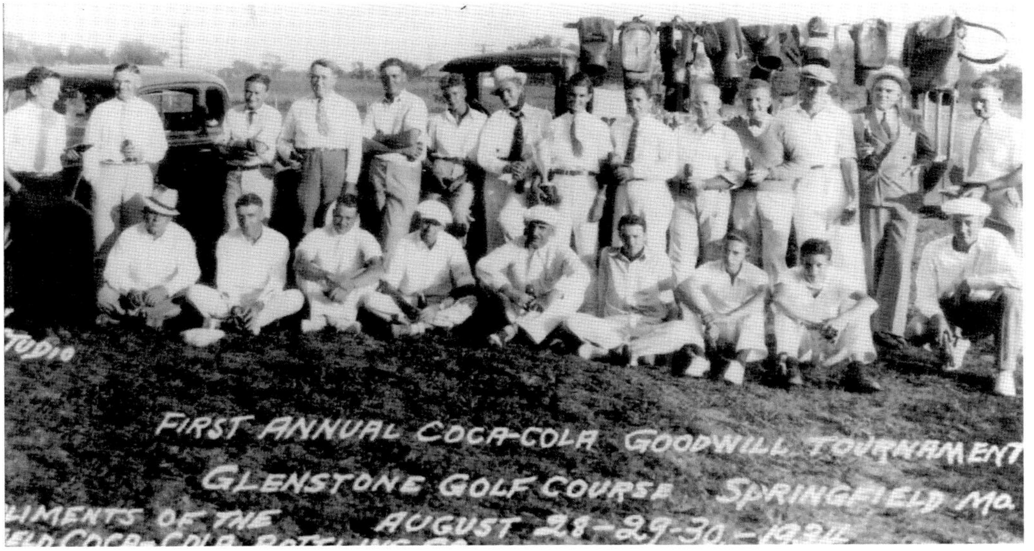

This vintage photograph was taken after the first annual Coca-Cola tournament held at Glenstone Golf Course in Springfield, Missouri. The tournament was held in August 1934. Everyone is shown holding a bottle of Coca-Cola, except John Ferguson, who is holding the championship trophy.

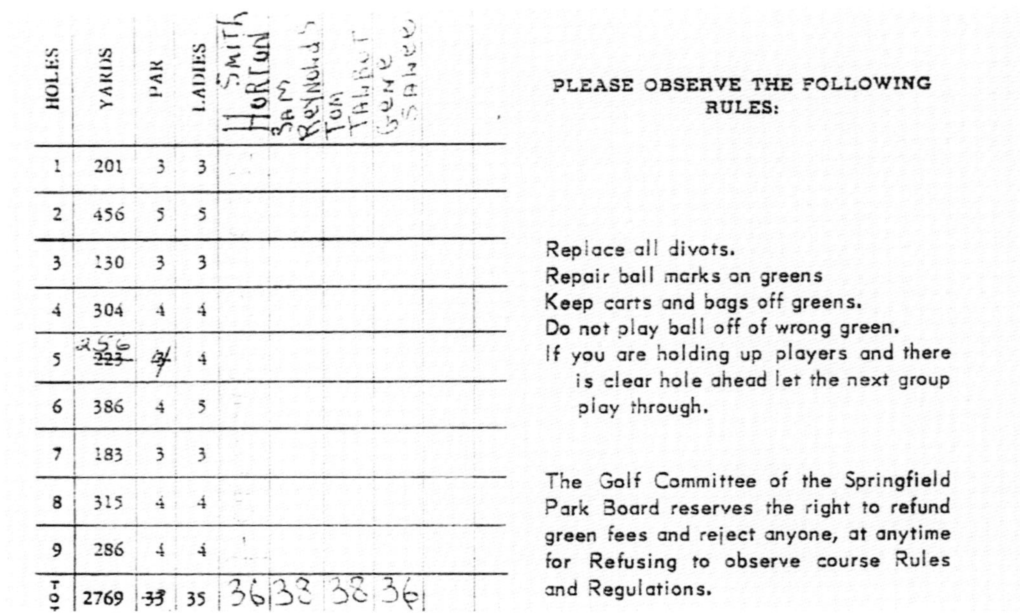

HOLES	YARDS	PAR	LADIES	H. Smith Horton	Sam Reynolds	Tom Talbot	Gene Sallee
1	201	3	3				
2	456	5	5				
3	130	3	3				
4	304	4	4				
5	~~223~~ 256	~~4~~ 3	4				
6	386	4	5				
7	183	3	3				
8	315	4	4				
9	286	4	4				
TOT	2769	~~33~~	35	36	33	38	36

PLEASE OBSERVE THE FOLLOWING RULES:

Replace all divots.
Repair ball marks on greens
Keep carts and bags off greens.
Do not play ball off of wrong green.
If you are holding up players and there is clear hole ahead let the next group play through.

The Golf Committee of the Springfield Park Board reserves the right to refund green fees and reject anyone, at anytime for Refusing to observe course Rules and Regulations.

This actual scorecard was used during the first round at Horton Smith golf course in Springfield. The inaugural foursome included Horton Smith, Sam Reynolds, Gene Sallee, and Tom Talbot. As one can see, Smith shot a 2 over par 36 during his first round on the course. (Courtesy of Dustin Raymond.)

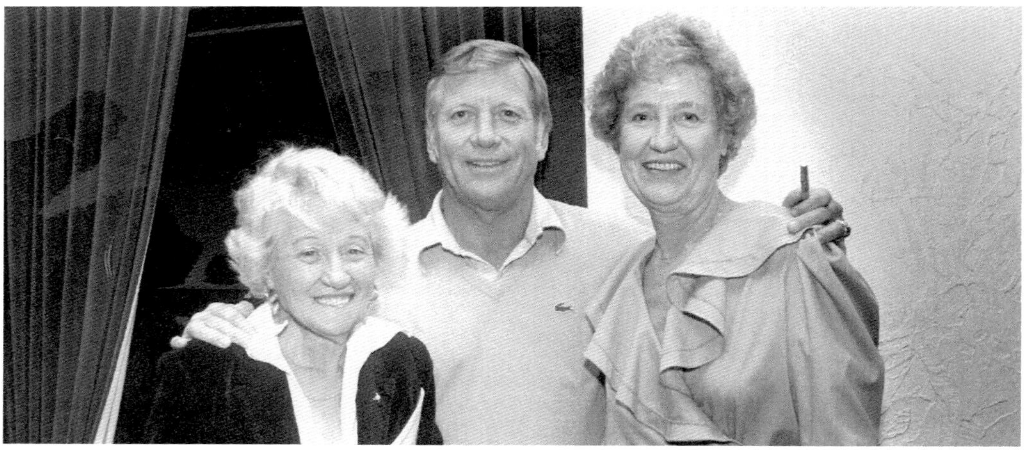

Mickey Mantle will forever be associated with the Ozarks, particularly Joplin. Mantle grew up in nearby Commerce, Oklahoma, and played minor league baseball for the Joplin Miners. Later in life, Mantle would have a home at Loma Linda Country Club. He would regularly play golf at Twin Hills Country Club, where he is photographed here with Fern Milligan and Cleo Watkins.

During the late 1980s and early 1990s, Mickey Mantle held charity golf tournaments at Loma Linda Country Club outside Joplin, Missouri. Players included Billy Martin, Yogi Berra, Warren Spahn, and Whitey Ford. The tournament would provide assistance to Oak Hill Hospital and Missouri Southern State College Department of Intercollegiate Athletics.

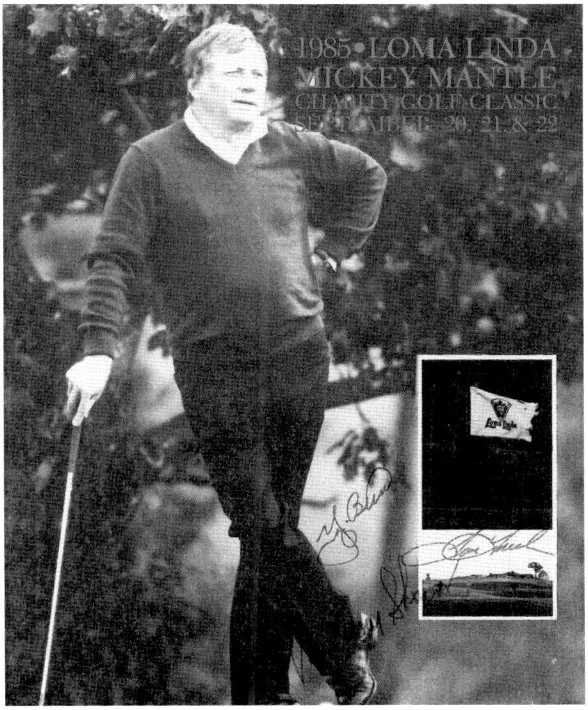

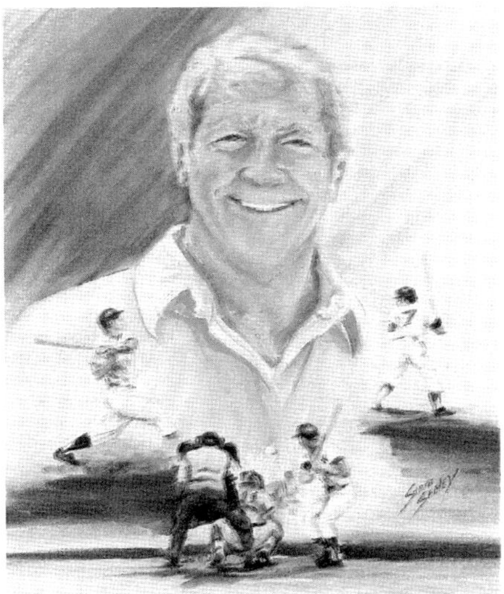

MICKEY MANTLE

Loma Linda

ESTATES & COUNTRY CLUB

Route #5, Box 1000 Joplin, Missouri 64801

(417) 781-2620

Mickey Mantle became a spokesman for Loma Linda and its housing development. Loma Linda would use his likeness to promote the housing, and Mantle was able to have his annual charity tournaments at the golf course.

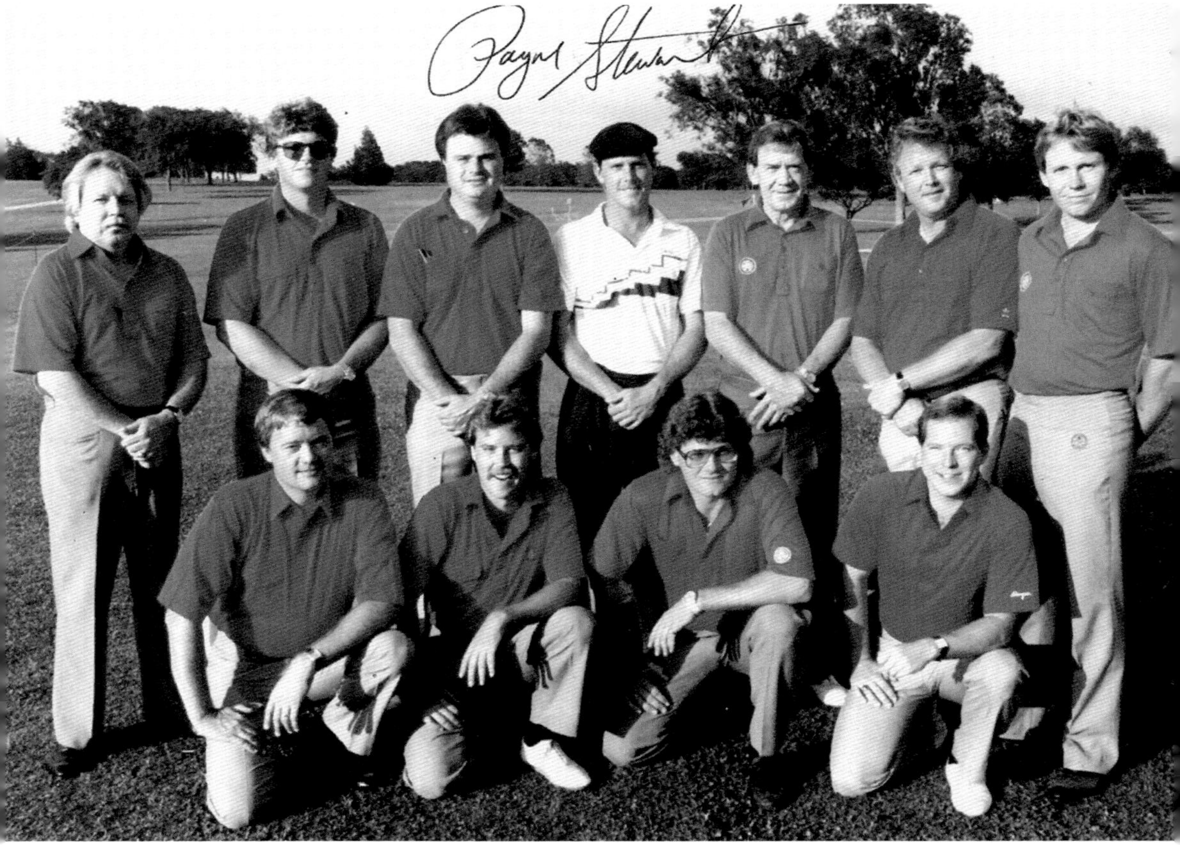

Payne Stewart would regularly come back to Springfield to give kids free golf clinics. This photograph was taken at a 1989 clinic at what is now the Bill and Payne Stewart Golf Course. The photograph includes Springfield golf professionals, from left to right, (first row) Max Arrowood, Mike Boring, Dale Fisher, and Tim Hacker; (second row) Ron Sweet, Bob Allen, Rick Grayson, Payne Stewart, Dorl Sweet, Perry Leslie, and Mike Reisenback.

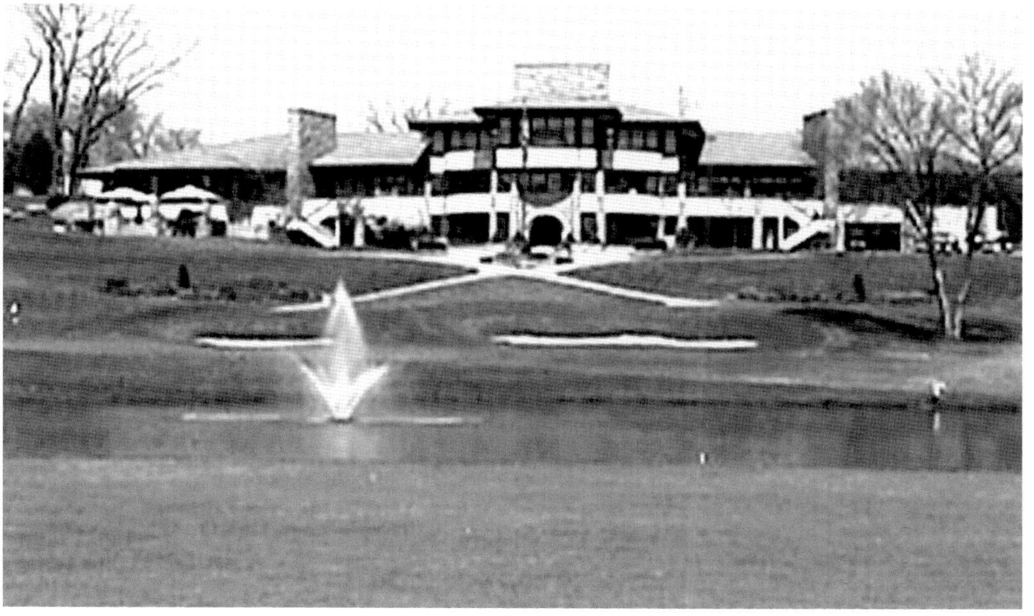

In 1989, John Q. Hammons built and developed Highland Springs Country Club. Hammons would have legendary golf course designer Robert Trent Jones design the 18-hole layout.

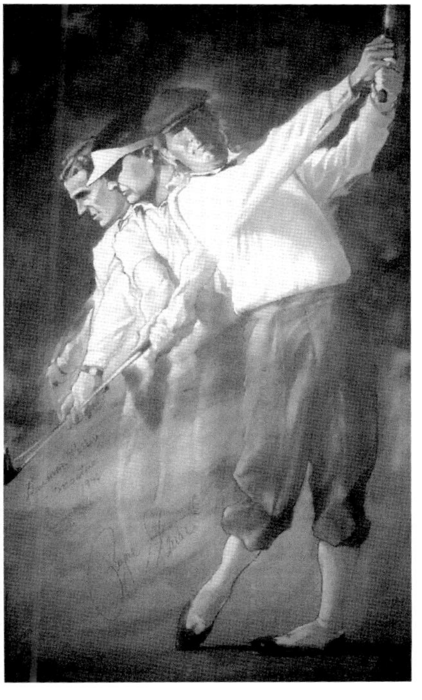

This painting was done by Gary Locke as the image used to promote the inaugural Ben Hogan Greater Ozarks Open held at Highland Springs Country Club in 1990. The painting includes Springfield's three most recognizable golfers Horton Smith, Herman Keiser, and Payne Stewart. According to Locke, the original painting showed the golfers in a different order and he had to paint over the original to correct it.

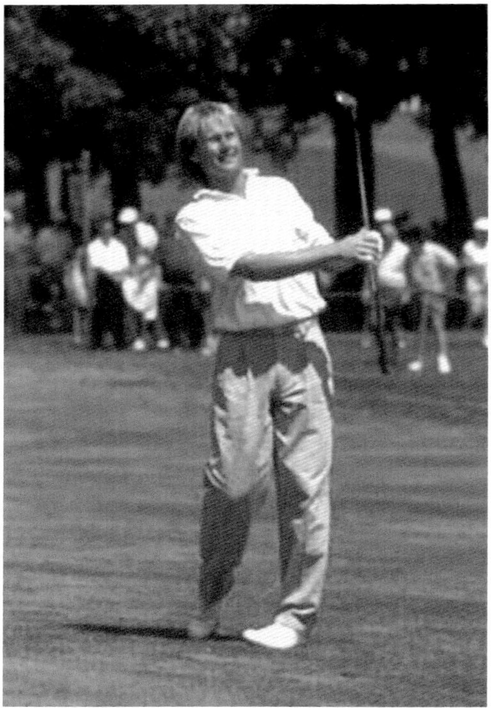

PGA Tour professional John Cook won the inaugural Ben Hogan tournament held at Springfield's Highland Springs in 1990. The tournament offers one of the largest purses and attendance on the Buy.com Tour.

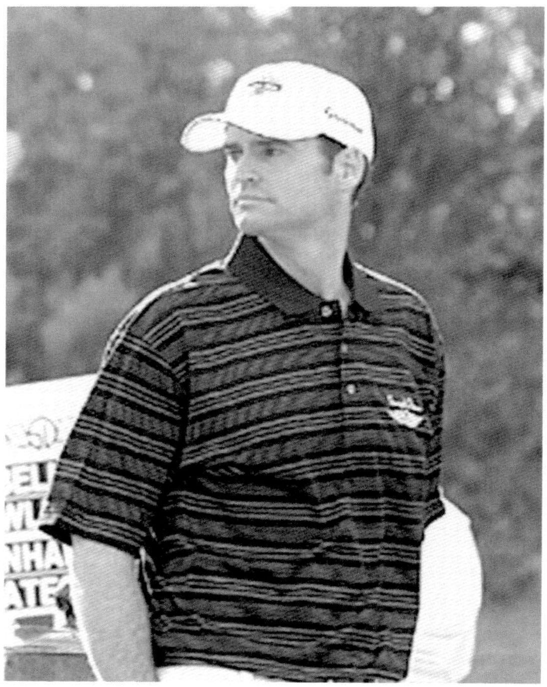

Roger Tambellini was the winner of the 2005 Buy.com Price Cutter Charity Classic by one stroke over David Peoples for a four-round total of 21 under par 267. The total purse in 2005 was $556,000 with Tambellini taking home $94,500.

8

Tournaments and Accolades

Horton Smith Cup Matches

The tournament that truly defines the Ozarks is the Horton Smith Cup Matches. In 1930, while Horton Smith was on the professional tour, Joplin and Springfield would both claim Smith was from their respective city. Smith suggested the two cities start teams to compete in a tournament. Smith would provide a trophy for the winning team, in addition to the claim of his hometown.

The first tournament was held in July 1930 at Joplin's Schifferdecker Golf Course and Oak Hill Country Club. Each team included 12 of the city's best golfers. The Springfield team included captain Tom Talbot, Norman Hinds, Horace Leslie, Claude Woodruff, Tommie Woodruff, Ralph Gardner, John Ferguson, Andy McDonald, Walter Cossey, C. L. Jarrett, Jack Boyd, and J. H. Keet. Joplin's team included James Porter, A. W. Knight, Jimmie O'Donnell, Brown Ransom, Carl Childress, Leonard Ott, Bob Andrew, Eddie Fowks, Arnold Levy, Fred Gulick, Wally Vancil, and Dane Catching. Despite Tom Talbot tying the Schifferdecker course record of 65, Joplin won the war on the links 11½ to 3½. The next year the Springfield team gained redemption with a 12½ to 2½ victory at the Hickory Hills Country Club in Springfield.

In 1932, the tournament was again held in Joplin. At the end of the match, the score was tied. They decided to come back the next weekend to settle the score. Thirty-six holes were played at Hickory Hills on Saturday and 36 more on Sunday at Schifferdecker and Oak Hill Country Club in Joplin. It was again a tie, which sent the cup back to Springfield. In 1933, Springfield would win again at Hickory Hills and Glenstone golf course. In 1934, Herman Keiser would join captain John Ferguson on the Springfield team to take care of the Joplin team on their own courses. In 1935 and 1936, Springfield would again prevail.

The tournament has continued over the years with the possession of the cup going to Joplin in 1998. In 1999, Springfield won the cup back on their turf. The 2000 cup was again won by Springfield by taking 11 of the 16 points. In the 2001 tournament, Springfield would win again, getting 13 of 16 points. The 2002, 2003, and 2004 cups were won by Springfield as well. Springfield would again win the 2005 Cup in Springfield with a final score of 15½ to 8½. Through 2005, Springfield leads the historic Horton Smith Cup competition 48–22–5.

Ozark Amateur Champions

1922 Charles Martin
1923 Carl Anderson
1924 Foster Naething
1925 Carl Childress
1926 Jimmy Porter
1927 Carl Childress
1928 Monk Wilson
1929 Leonard Ott
1930 Jim Bowers
1931 Alex Knight

1932 Dane Catching
1933 Bill Gilbert
1934 Herman Keiser
1935 Lloyd Wadkins
1936 Leroy Trotter
1937 Bob Hogeboom
1938 Bob Hogeboom
1939 Gene Webb
1940 Gene Webb
1941 Labron Harris
1942 Labron Harris
1943 Lebron Harris
1947 Podge Ferguson
1948 Charles Lewis
1949 Bob Hogeboom
1950 Jack Myer
1951 Chester Lloyd
1952 Speck Riggs
1953 Gene Sallee
1954 Dave Dennis
1955 Jim Scallety
1956 Jack Myer
1957 Dave Dennis
1958 R.V. Sikes
1959 Dave Dennis
1960 Jim Hatfield
1961 Jim Hatfield
1962 Bob Smith
1963 Dave Dennis
1964 Bob Smith
1965 Dave Dennis
1966 Jim Brown
1967 Ronnie Keeton
1968 Jack James
1969 Bruce Hollowell
1970 Odie Wilson
1971 Chris Strahan
1972 Odie Wilson
1973 Odie Wilson
1974 Odie Wilson
1975 Felix Fuentez
1976 Bo Dennis
1977 Odie Wilson
1978 Odie Wilson
1979 Mike Hammond
1980 Mike Hammond
1981 Bob Smith
1982 Stan Brewer
1983 James Saulsberry
1984 Ron Murray
1985 James Saulsberry
1986 Clyde Huff
1987 Marshall Smith Jr.
1988 Paul Ashe
1989 Marshall Smith Jr.
1990 Stacey Shiew
1991 Lee Larimore
1992 Jeff Westervelt
1993 Lee Larimore
1994 Robert Russell
1995 Robert Russell
1996 Kevin Muncrief
1997 Lee Larimore
1998 Lou Rapalino
1999 Lou Rapalino
2000 Blake Borello
2001 Lou Rapalino
2002 Mickey Carpenter
2003 David Pawlus
2004 Mike Maier
2005 Barrett Lais

Springfield Amateur Champions

1907 Felix Blackwell (Springfield CC)
1908 Frank Curran
1909 John Farrington
1910 John Farrington
1911 N/A
1912 N/A
1913 N/A
1914 Claude E. Woodruff
1915 Dr. Paul Talbot
1916 J.C. Graves
1917 Dr. Paul Talbot
1918 Dr. Paul Talbot
1919 Dr. Paul Talbot
1920 Dr. Paul Talbot
1921 Dr. Paul Talbot
1922 Dr. Paul Talbot
1923 Dr. Paul Talbot
1924 Horton Smith
1925 Claude E. Woodruff
1926 Norman "Red" Hinds
1927 Norman "Red" Hinds
1928 Norman "Red" Hinds
1929 Tom Talbot
1930 Tom Talbot
1931 Dr. John Ferguson
1932 Walter Thomas
1933 Tom Woodruff
1934 Herman Keiser
1935 Bob Hogeboom
1936 John Ferguson
1937 Gene Sallee
1938 N/A
1939 N/A
1940 N/A
1941 N/A
1942 N/A
1943 N/A
1944 N/A
1945 N/A
1946 N/A
1947 N/A
1948 N/A
1949 N/A
1950 Walter Cash
1951 Bill Stewart
1952 Bill Stewart
1953 Luther Snow
1954 Gene Sallee

1955 Bob Steury
1956 Bill Stewart
1957 Joseph Brown
1958 Ronald Ollis
1959 Lewis Hargis
1960 Bob Steury
1961 Bob Steury
1962 Bill Lucus
1963 Bob Hogue
1964 William Abney
1965 Bob Steury
1966 Jim Patton
1967 Jim Patton
1968 Bob Steury
1969 Larry Gooch
1970 George Thompson III
1971 Richie Gleghorn
1972 N/A
1973 N/A
1974 Bruce Hollowell
1975 John Hammond
1976 Bruce Hollowell
1977 Craig Withers
1978 Bobby Biser
1979 Joe Kremer
1980 Joe Kremer
1981 Bobby Biser
1982 Walter Powell
1983 Wayne Fredrick
1984 Vernon Bennett
1985 Chuck Greene
1986 Mike Krone
1987 Larry Wood
1988 Walter Powell
1989 Wayne Fredrick
1990 Walter Powell
1991 Alan Rosen
1992 Wayne Fredrick
1993 Brian Mitchell
1994 Mike Wood
1995 Bill Roberts
1996 Darren Pryor
1997 Mark Monroe
1998 Richie Gleghorn
1999 David Kirksey
2000 David Jenkins
2001 Richie Gleghorn
2002 Darren Pryor
2003 Richie Glenghorn
2004 Tim Holmes
2005 Justin Cox

Joplin Golf Hall of Fame

1985 Derril Tate
1985 Harold Kirk
1985 Horton Smith
1985 Jimmy Porter
1985 Jimmy Thomas
1985 Joan Thomas
1985 John Inman
1985 Ken Childress
1985 Ky Laffoon
1985 Mary Landreth
1985 Regina Townes
1985 Robert Smith
1986 Art Wadkins
1986 Clarence Houston
1986 Harold Thompson
1986 Harry Robeson
1986 Jack James
1987 Barry Franks
1987 Dan Tourtelot
1987 Jonne Laster
1987 Marvin Porter
1987 Terry Key
1988 Bill Parker
1988 Ethel Matter
1988 George Ott
1989 Eddie McKay
1989 Homer Halfield
1990 Clair Goodwin
1990 Gingy Lass
1991 Eddie Fowks
1991 Frankie Jacobs
1992 Bill Cox
1992 Larry Hickey
1992 Paul Ashe
1993 Woodson Oldham
1994 Bob Cox
1994 Lee Larimore
1995 Dave Pawlus
1996 Gary Phillips
1996 Joe McKenzie
1996 Rilla Miller
1997 Ed Spencer
1997 Jim Hatfield
1997 Robert Russell
1998 Charles Schifferdecker
1998 Marshall Smith
1998 Ron Johnson
1999 Dennis Goettel
1999 Mike Maier
2000 Leigh Ann Hackney
2000 Robert McKay
2001 Hale Irwin
2001 Mel Ipock
2002 Boyd Downey

Ozarks Golf Hall of Fame

2002 Bill Stewart
2002 Horton Smith
2002 Joyce Mahoney
2002 Sam Reynolds
2003 Rich Gleghorn
2003 Dorl Sweet
2003 Jim Morris
2003 Jim Patton

2003 Cathy Reynolds
2003 Ken Lanning
2003 Leon Faucett
2003 Jim Pearson
2004 Joan Thomas
2004 John Ferguson
2004 KG Wells
2004 Bruce Hollowell
2004 Leonard Dodson
2005 Charles Talley
2005 Gayle Runke
2005 Julie Wear
2005 Max Arrowwood
2005 Payne Stewart

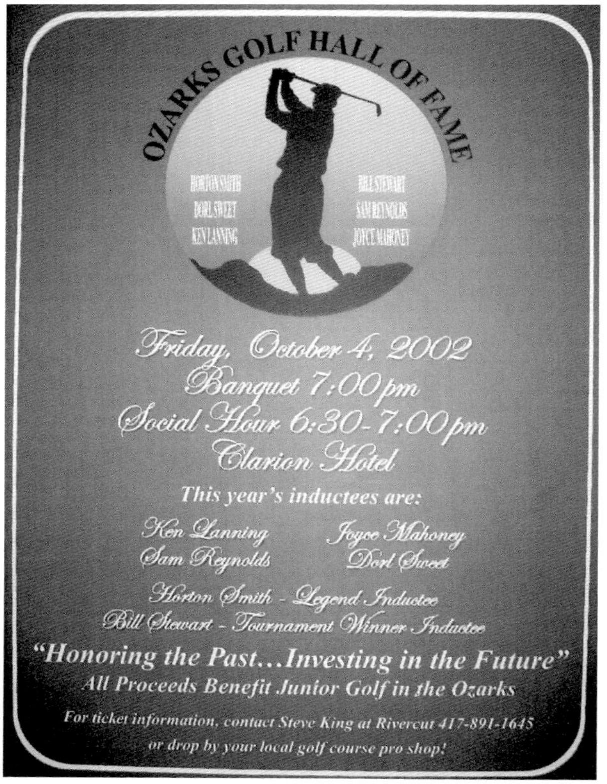

The inaugural Ozarks Golf Hall of Fame banquet was held October, 4 2002, in Springfield.

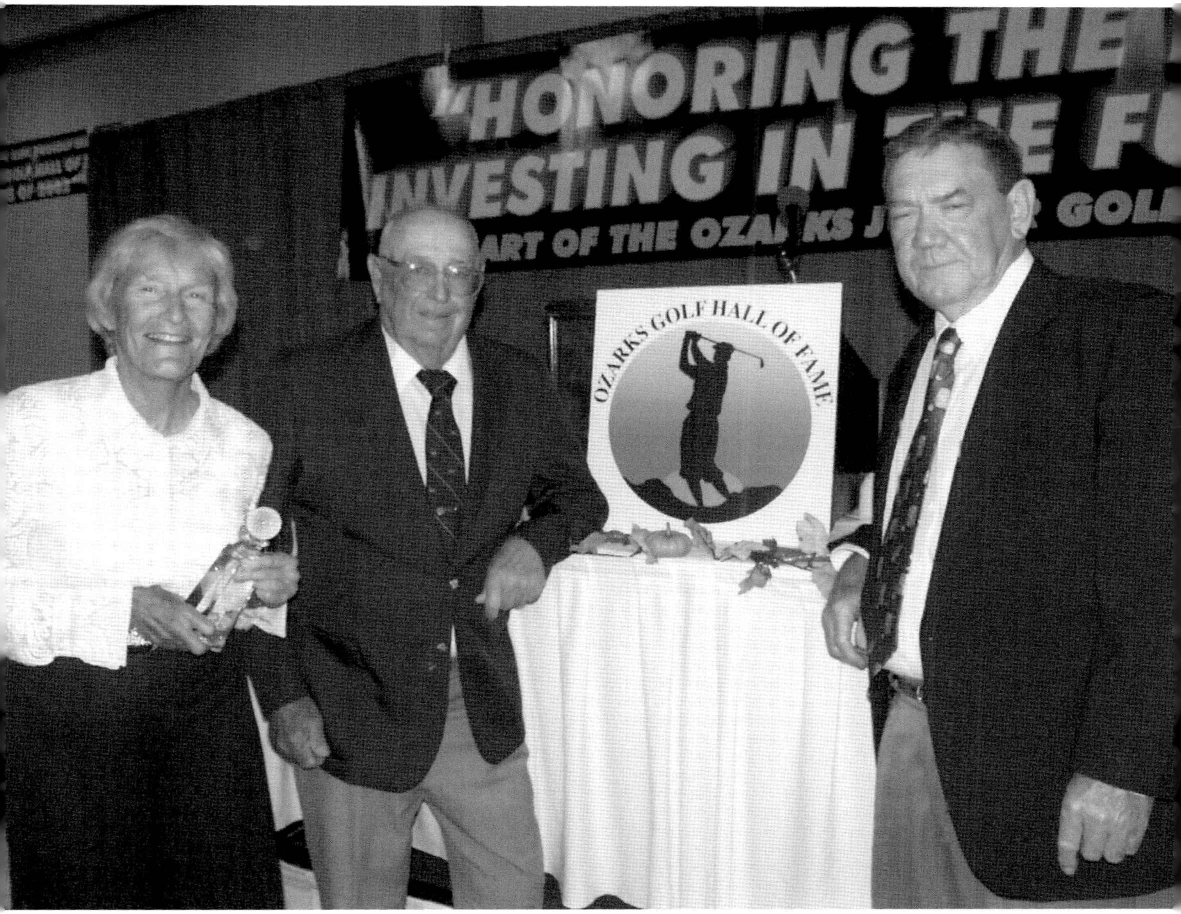

The Ozarks Golf Hall of Fame conducted its inaugural induction on October 4, 2002. The first members included Horton Smith, Dorl Sweet (right), Ken Lanning, Bill Stewart, Sam Reynolds (middle), and Joyce Mahoney (left). The proceeds from both the ceremony and golf tournament benefited Junior Golf in the Ozarks Foundation. (Courtesy of Tom Mast.)

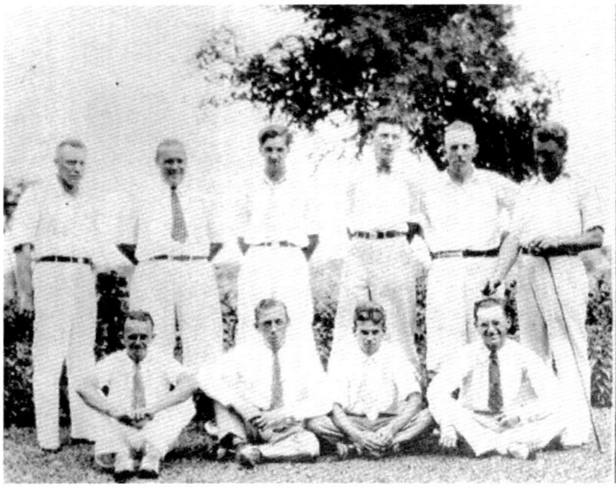

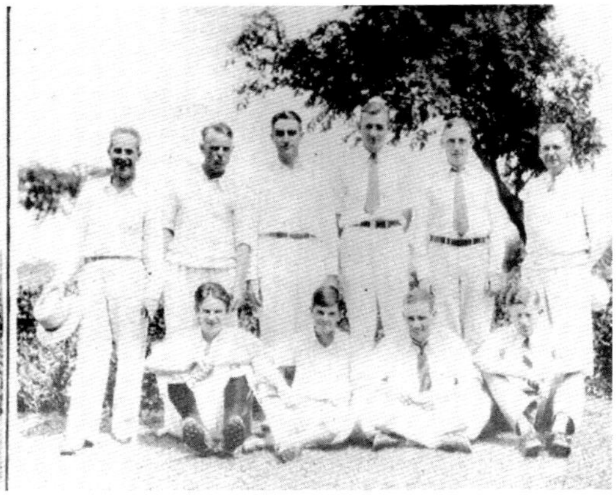

The inaugural Horton Smith Cup teams from 1930 are pictured here. The victorious Joplin team on the left was made up of (first row) Eddie Fowks, Carl Childress, Leonard Ott, and Jimmy Porter, (second row) Fred Gulick, Dane Catching, Wally Vancil, Arnold Levy, Alex Knight, and Bob Adams. The Springfield team on the right included (first row) Tommy Woodruff, Johnny Ferguson, Tom Talbot, and Horace Leslie, (second row) Claude Woodruff, Walter Cossey, Andrew McDonald, Ralph Gardner, Norman Hines, and Cliff Jarret.

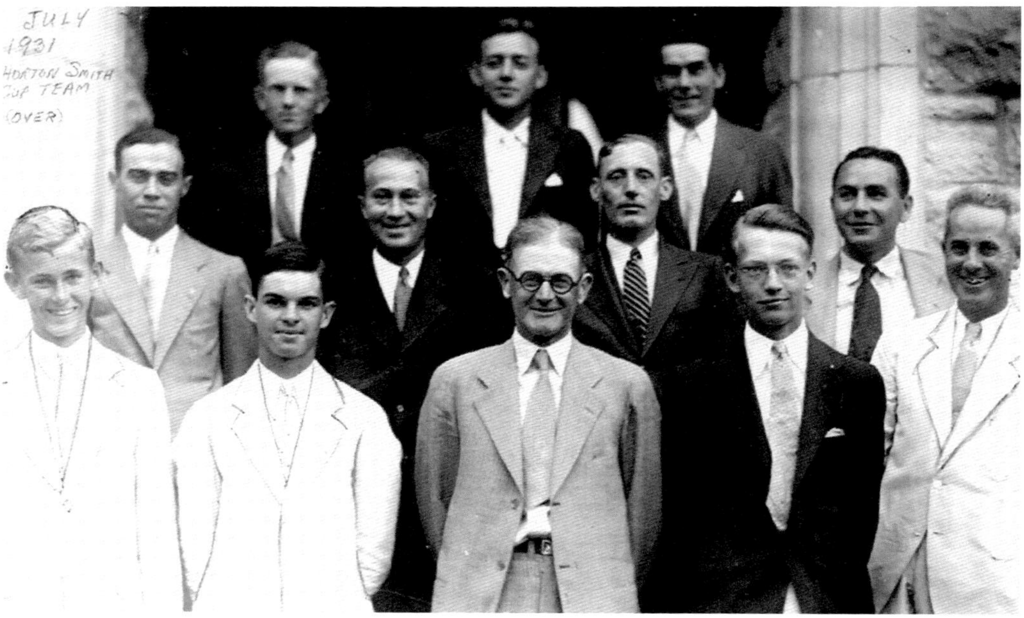

The 1931 Horton Smith team from Springfield included, from left to right, (first row) Jim Keet, Johnny Ferguson, Aubrey Hill, Joe Bill Hogeboom, and Claude Woodruff; (second row) Cecil Dawson, E. E. Moore, Norman Hinds, and Jack Boyd; (third row) Horace Leslie, Ralph Gardner, and Dan Wheeler.

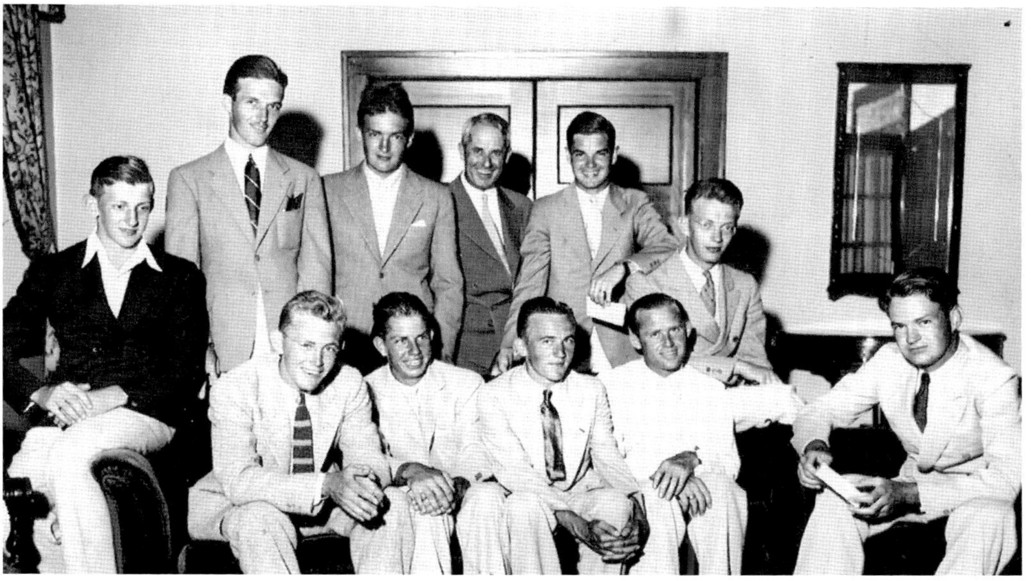

The 1935 Horton Smith team from Springfield included, from left to right, (first row) Bobby Hogeboom, Jim Keet, LeRoy Trotter, Gene Sallee, Clyde Hale, and Tommy Woodruff; (second row) Charles Winn, Dave Woodruff, Claude Woodruff, John Ferguson, and Joe Bill Hogeboom.

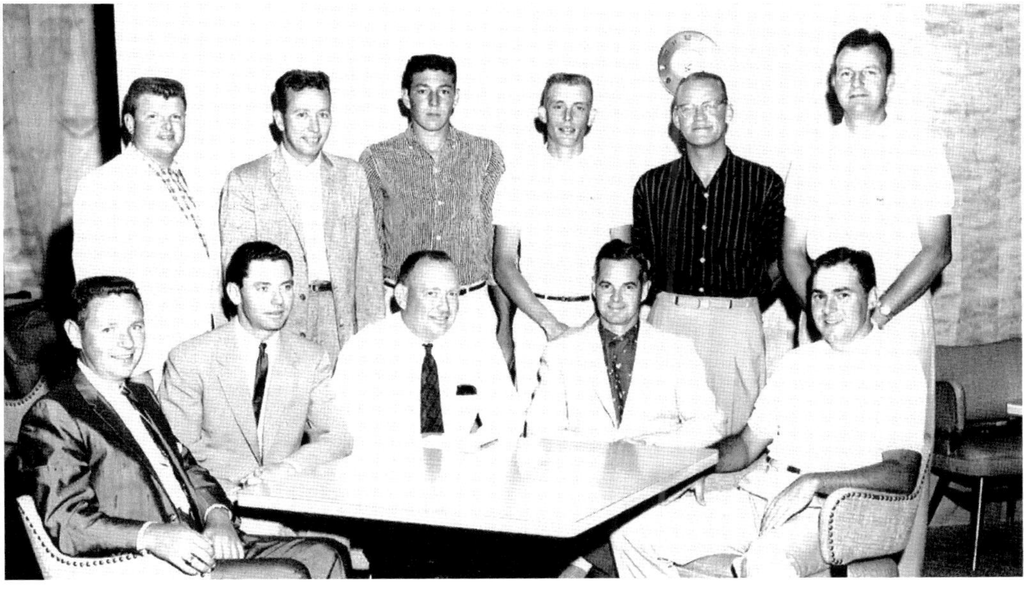

This vintage picture is of a Horton Smith Cup team in the very late 1950s. A few of the more notable players include Walter Cash, Milt Thompson, and John Ferguson.

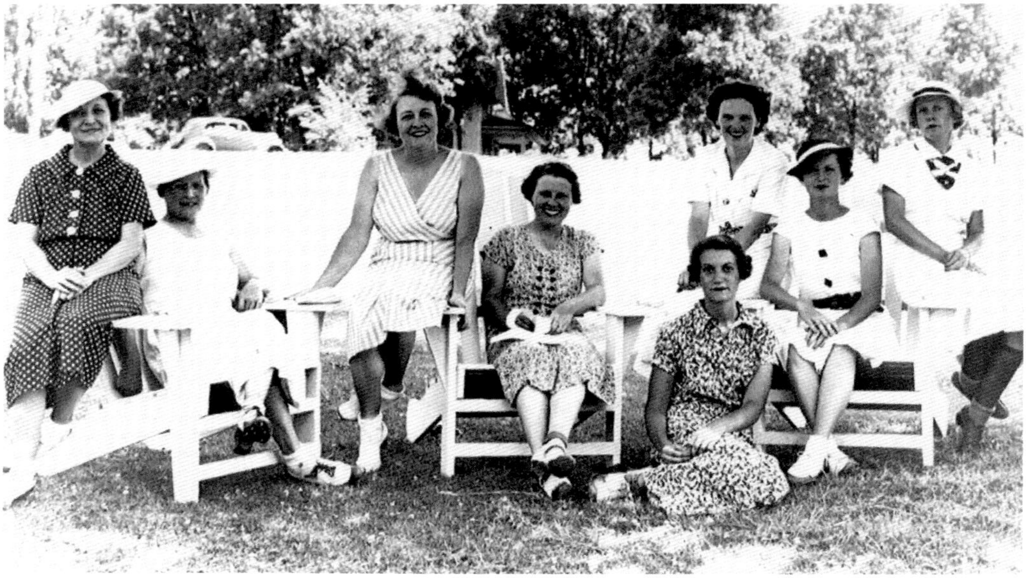

The 1936 Springfield women's Horton Smith team included (left to right) Grace Woodruff, Eva Mills, Cornell Hogeboom, Mildred Hogeboom, Rose Caroline Netter, Helen Dyer, Betty Woodruff, and Gladys Dickey.

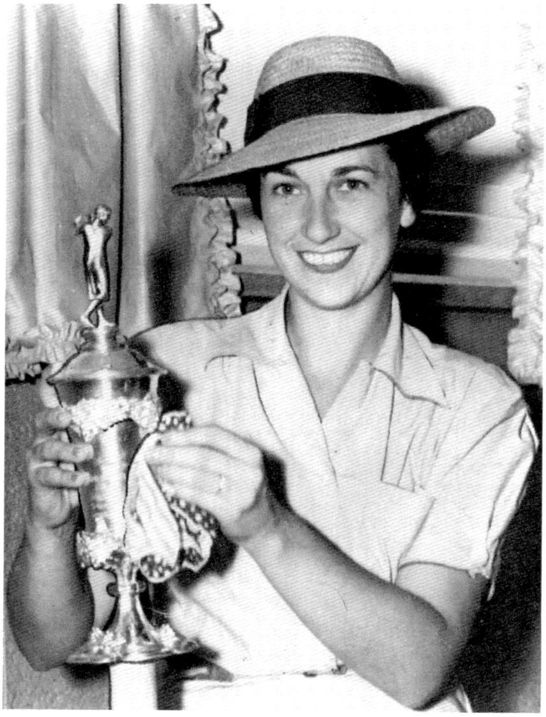

Mrs. Fred Farthing, captain of the 1940 Springfield Horton Smith women's golf team, is shown here. Springfield won in 1931, the year the women's tournament began, and in 1933, 1934, and 1935. Joplin won in 1932, 1936, and 1937 through 1939 due to default.

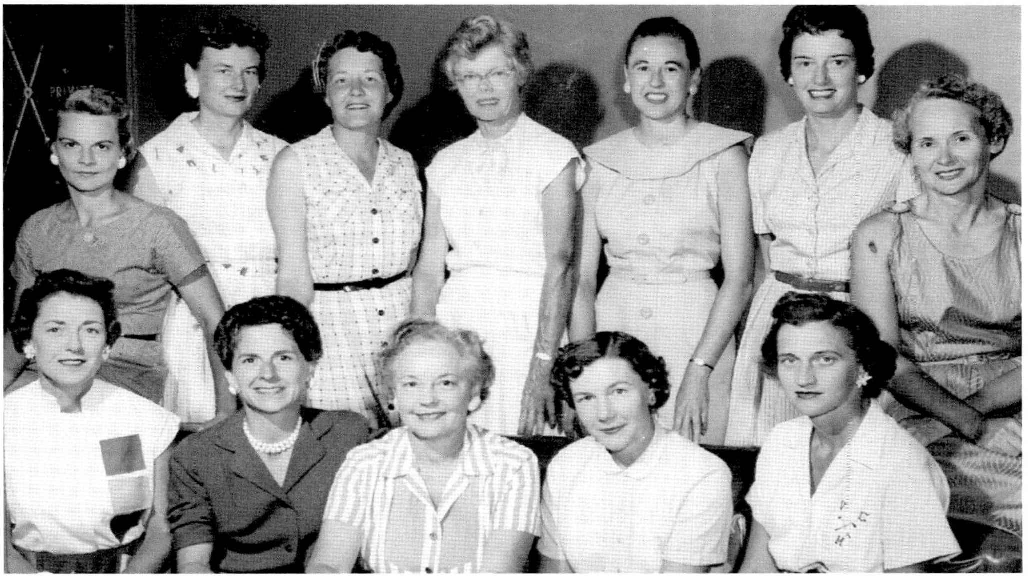

The 1956 Springfield women's Horton Smith team included, from left to right, (first row) Helen Ferguson, Sis Keet, Jessie Benson, Clara Hubbard, and Virginia Maher; (second row) Helen Engleman, Grace Dills, Mary Hoffman, Norma Johnson, Marian Bloemker, Judy, Forehand, and Cleo Johnson.

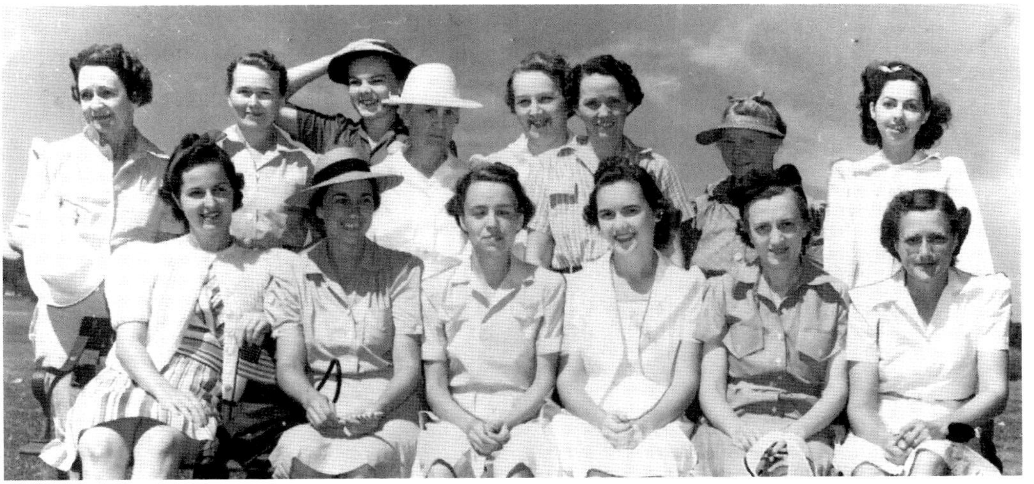

The 1940 Springfield women's Horton Smith team included, from left to right, (first row) Betty Woodruff, Mrs. Fred Farthing, Gladys Dickey, Jean Hogg, Mrs. Charles Moody, and Mrs. John Stark; (second row) Mrs. Claude Woodruff, Mrs. Ronald Elkins, Marjorie Mann, Mrs. Charles Newman, Mrs. Ben McDonald, Mrs. Ralph Elkins, Mrs. L. C. Snyder, and Jane Doggrell. Mrs. H. A. Lowe was absent.

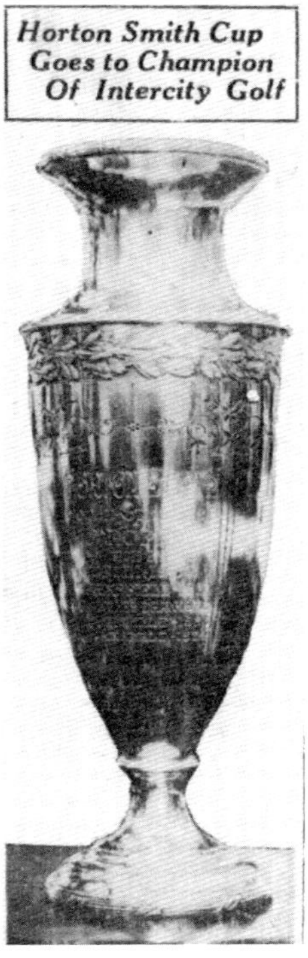

This vintage Horton Smith Cup was awarded to the Springfield team for their victory over Joplin. This is the original trophy donated by Horton Smith for the annual grudge match between Joplin and Springfield. (Courtesy of Dr. John Ferguson.)

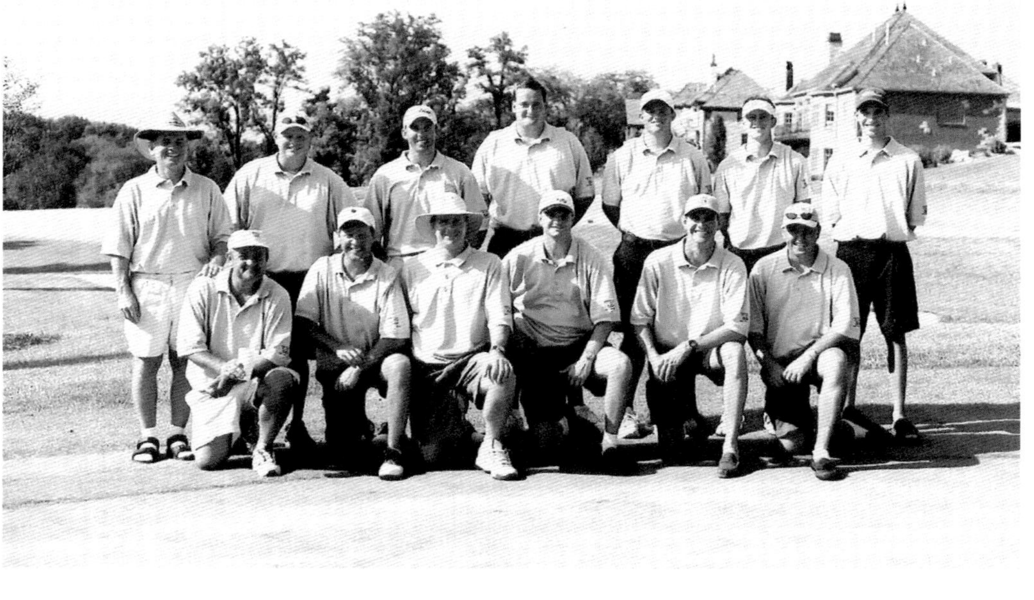

The 2001 Horton Smith Cup team from Springfield won by a score of 13 to 3. Players included Travis Mitchell, Larry Smith, Matt Morrison, Chuck Greene, Jeff Eiserman, and Todd Edwards. (Courtesy of Eugene Robinett.)

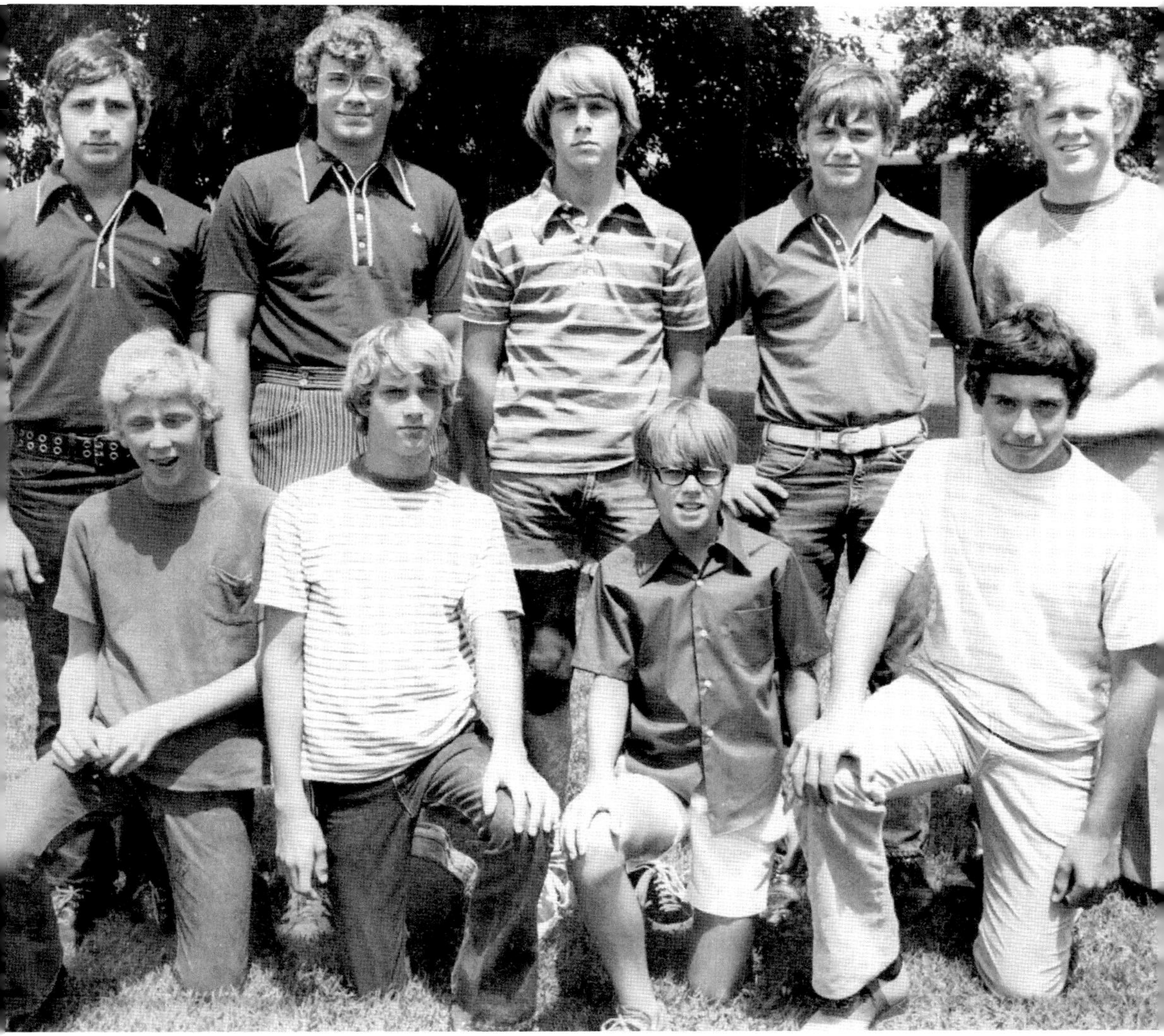

The 1971 Boys Horton Smith Junior Team consisted of several local stars of the future: (first row) Dave Bonham, John Gentry, Bill Gentry, and Monty Schneider; (second row) Gary Leuitch, Mike Schneider, Payne Stewart, Vernon Bennett, and Pat Mahoney.

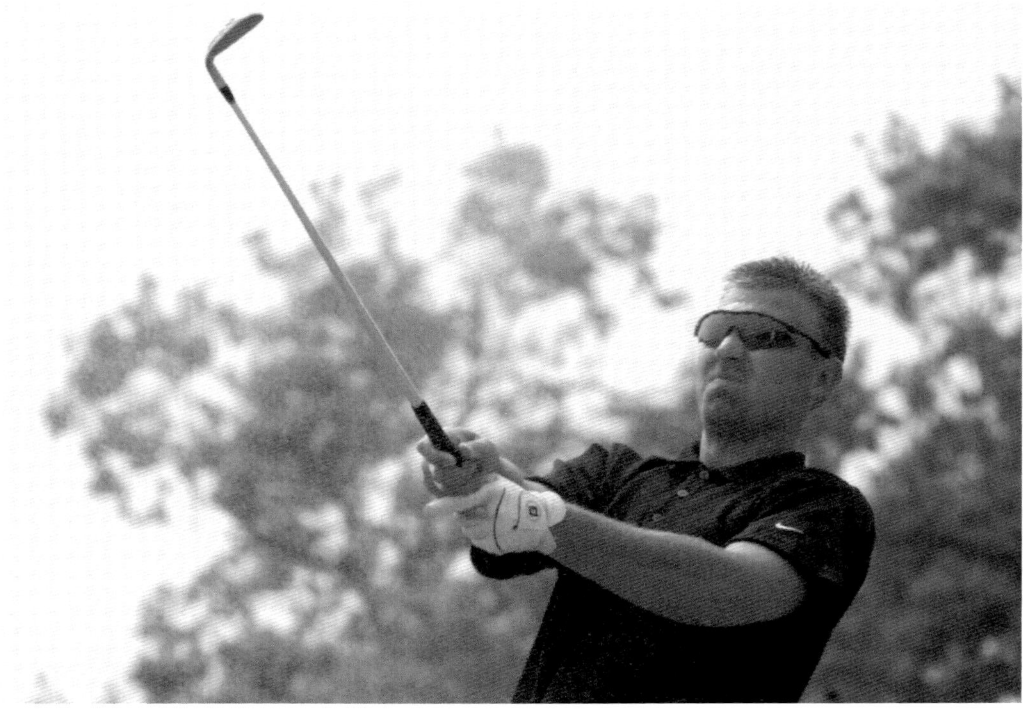

Robert Russell won the Ozark Amateur in 1994 and 1995. In 1994, he won the Michelob Golfer of the Year Award. (Courtesy of the *Joplin Globe*.)

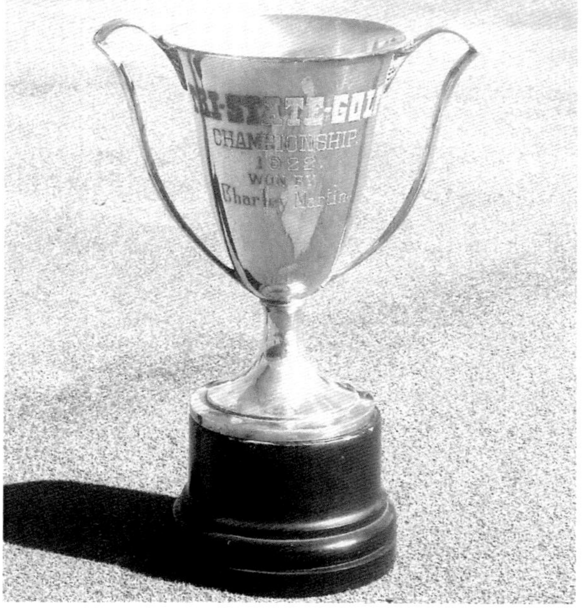

This trophy was awarded to Charles Martin for the inaugural Tri-State Amateur in 1922 held at Schifferdecker Golf Course in Joplin. The tournament would later be known as the Ozark Amateur in 1959.

The Springfield Amateur Championship began in 1907. This trophy was awarded to John Ferguson for his championship victory in 1931 over Dick Farrington. Ferguson won by an overwhelming margin of 10 up with nine holes to play.

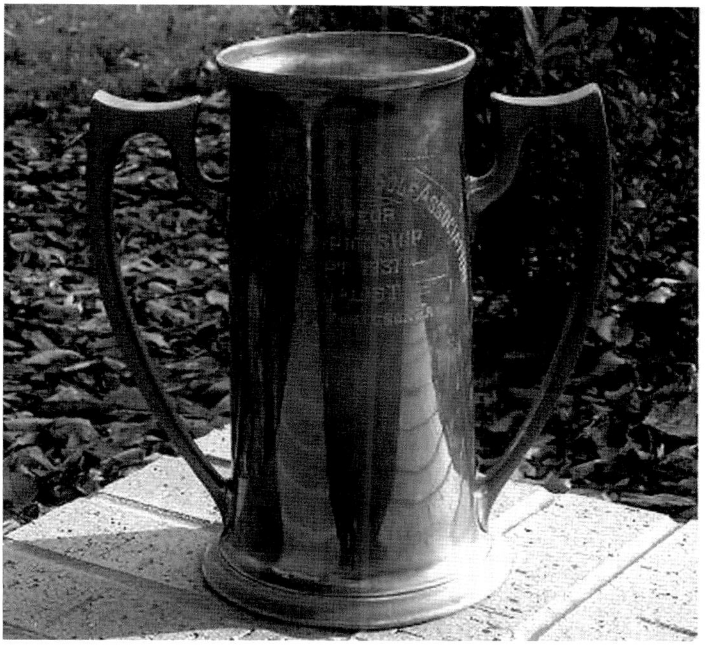

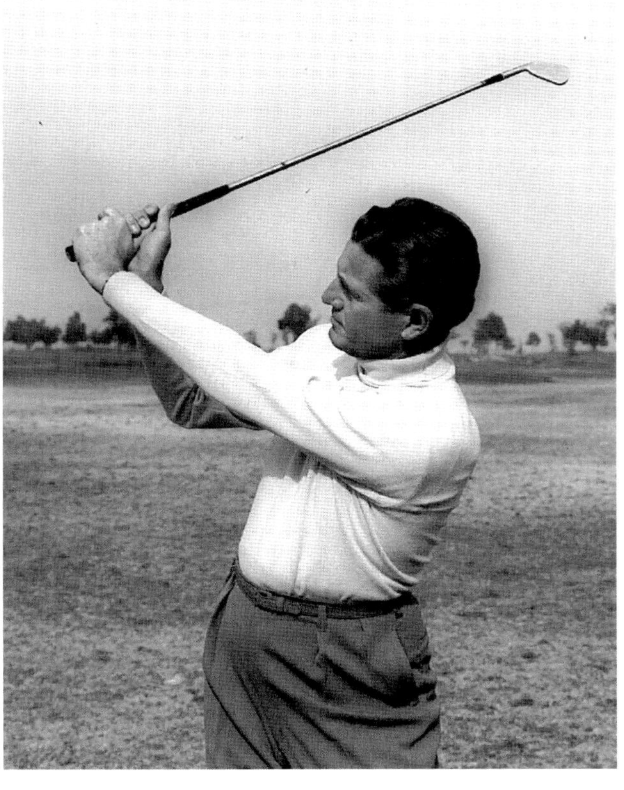

Horton Smith won the Springfield City Amateur Championship in 1924. The 1924 City Amateur Championship was the only one that Smith played in. (Courtesy of Photos From the Fairway.)

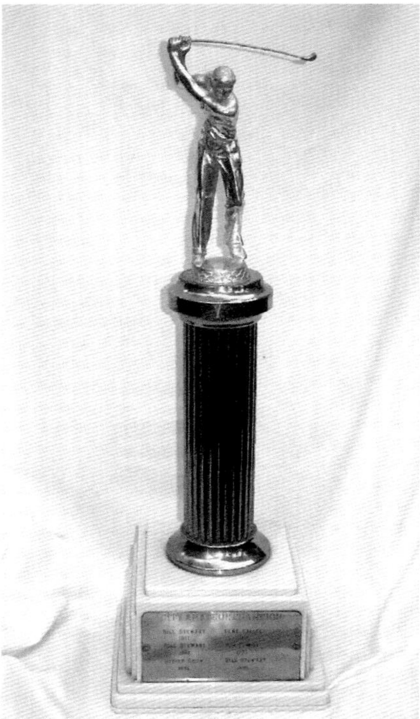

This Springfield City Amateur Championship trophy was awarded to Bill Stewart in 1956. It would be Stewart's third City Championship. He had already won the tournament in 1951 and 1952.

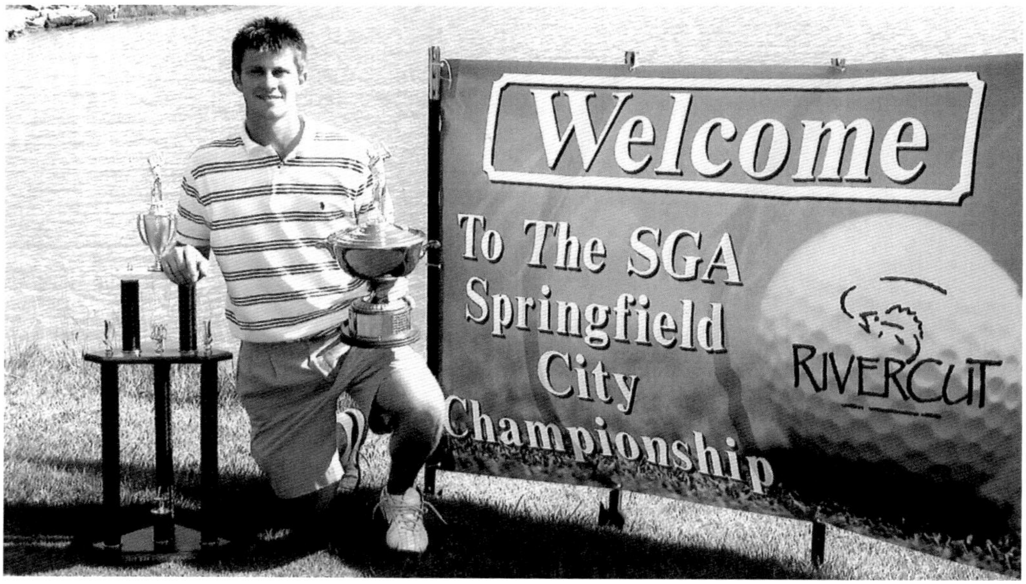

Justin Cox was the winner of the 2005 Springfield City Amateur Championship. The former Southwest Baptist University golfer defeated Wayne Fredrick in a playoff. His two round total was 141. (Courtesy of Eugene Robinett.)

1950 OZARK OPEN GOLF TOURNAMENT

HICKORY HILLS COUNTRY CLUB
SPRINGFIELD, MISSOURI

CO-SPONSORED BY SPRINGFIELD JUNIOR CHAMBER OF COMMERCE
AND HICKORY HILLS COUNTRY CLUB

PAIRINGS & STARTING TIMES - SUNDAY OCT. 1, 1950

FIRST TEE

A.M.	P.M.		PRIOR SCORE
8:00	12:30	(1) Fred Hawkins, El Paso, Texas	(72)
		(2) *Kenneth Lanning, Rolla	(73)
		(3) E. E. Buss Peele, Kansas City	(73)
8:07	12:37	(6) *Elmer Humphries, Stillwater, Okla	(71)
		(7) *John Garrison, Tulsa, Okla	(72)
		(8) Skee Riegel, Tulsa, Okla	(72)
8:14	12:44	(11) Arlin Stone, Springfield	(71)
		(12) Otto Greiner, Baltimore, Md.	(72)
		(13) *Dr. John Ferguson, Springfield	(72)
8:21	12:51	(18) E. J. Harrison, St. Andrews, Ill.	(70)
		(19) Tex Consolver, Wichita, Kan.	(71)
		(20) Chuck Klein, San Antonio, Tex.	(71)
8:28	12:58	(24) Bob Gajda, Birmingham, Mich	(70)
		(25) Ray Dodson, Springfield	(71)
		(26) Clarence Yockey, Kansas City	(71)
8:35	1:05	(30) Jim Turnesa, Briarcliff, N. Y.	(69)
		(31) Art Wadkins, Joplin	(70)
		(32) Tommy Bolt, Durham, N. C.	(70)
8:42	1:12	(38) Dave Douglas, Newark, Del.	(69)
		(39) Joe Kirkwood, Jr., Hollywood, Calif.	(69)
		(41) Bob Crow, Shreveport, La	(70)
8:49	1:19	(45) Buster Mills, Springfield	(68)
		(46) Wally Ulrich, Austin, Minn	(69)
		(47) Johnny Maloney, Shawnee, Kan.	(69)
8:56	1:26	(52) Ted Kroll, New Hartford, N. Y.	(68)
		(54) Walther Cash, Springfield	(69)
		(55) Marty Furgol, Albuquerque, N. M.	(69)
9:03	1:33	(59) Bob Toski, Northampton, Mass	(66)
		(60) Art Doering, Richmond, Va.	(67)
		(61) Labron Harris, Stillwater, Okla	(68)
9:10	1:40	(65) Ky Laffoon, Springfield	(65)
		(66) Pete Fleming, Hot Springs, Ark.	(67)
		(67) Ed Furgol, Royal Oak, Mich.	(67)

TENTH TEE

A.M.	P.M.		PRIOR SCORE
8:00	12:30	(4) *William Gillmoor, Kansas City	(76)
		(5) Eddie McKay, Iron Mountain, Mich.	(76)
8:07	12:37	(9) Leonard Dodson, Springfield	(76)
		(10) *Wilbur Bartells, Kansas City	(76)
8:14	12:44	(14) *Larry Etckorn, St. Louis	(76)
		(15) *Dr. N. Callahan, Kansas City	(76)
		(16) *W. J. Berkeley, St. Louis	(76)
8:21	12:51	(21) Paul McGuire, Wichita, Kan.	(75)
		(22) Al Stoehr, Arkansas City, Kan	(76)
		(23) *Clyde Hale, Lebanon	(76)
8:28	12:58	(27) *Tom Bramlett, Kansas City	(75)
		(28) *Curtis Collier, Fort Smith, Ark.	(75)
		(29) *Bill Stewart, Springfield	(75)
8:35	1:05	(34) Bill Jelliffe, Chattanooga, Tenn	(75)
		(36) *Bo Winniger, Stillwater, Okla	(75)
		(37) *Glen Oatman, Independence	(75)
8:42	1:12	(42) Horton Smith, Detroit, Mich	(74)
		(43) Ralph Ludlam, Wichita, Kan.	(74)
		(44) *Bill Smith, Tulsa, Okla	(75)
8:49	1:19	(48) *Jimmy Jackson, St. Louis	(74)
		(49) *Gene Sallee, Springfield	(74)
		(51) Pat Patton, Bimidji, Minn.	(74)
8:56	1:26	(56) Skip Carlson, La Grange, Ill.	(73)
		(57) Paul O'Leary, Bismarck, N. D.	(73)
		(58) Howard Capps, San Francisco, Calif.	(74)
9:03	1:33	(62) Bill Black, Independence	(73)
		(63) G. L. Leonard, Tulsa, Okla	(73)
		(64) Gerald Pepper, Overland Park, Kan.	(74)
9:10	1:40	(68) Jim Ferrier, San Francisco, Calif	(72)
		(69) Ernest Fortner, Joplin	(73)
		(70) Gib Sellers, Hot Springs, Ark.	(73)

* Amateur

Hickory Hills Country Club held the original Ozark Open from 1947 to 1951. This parings sheet was from the 1950 tournament. Professionals and amateurs in the tournament came from across the country. Players included Kenneth Lanning, John Ferguson, Joe Kirkwood, Bob Toski, Ky Laffoon, Leonard Dodson, Bill Stewart, Bo Winniger, Gene Sallee, and Horton Smith.

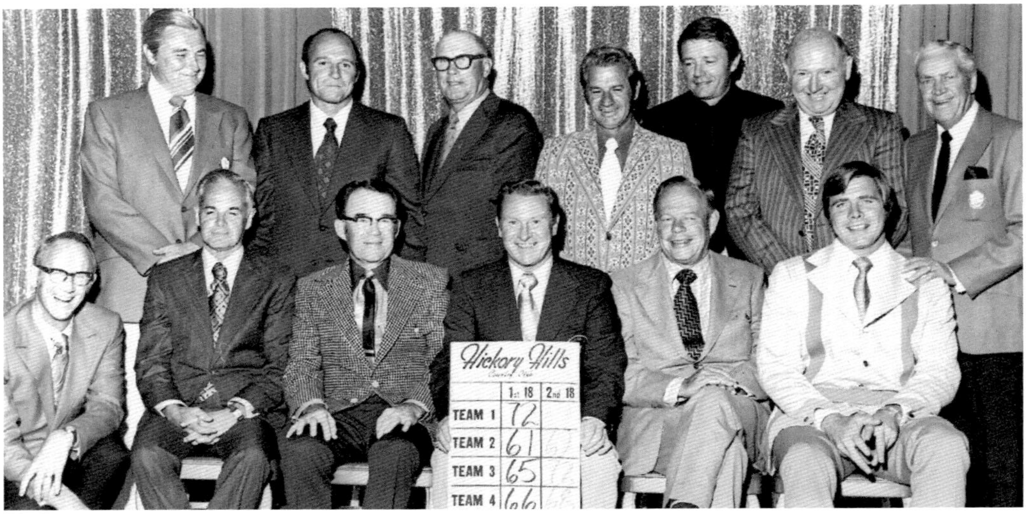

The Gold Cup was a team golf event held annually in Las Vegas. Hickory Hills would regularly send out a team of golfers for the event, and in 1969, Hickory Hills won the event with a team score of 522. Players included Jim Morris, Jack Frazier, Frank Campbell, Dave Williams, Johnny Ferguson, Eddie Clayton, Jack Hamlin, Bill Sanford, and Joe Greene. (Courtesy of Hickory Hills Country Club.)

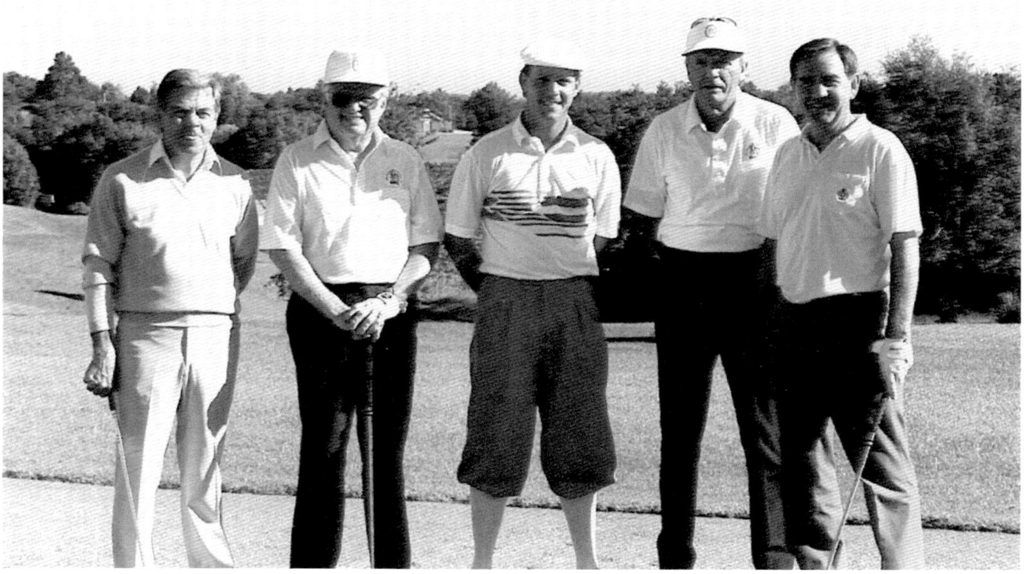

Pictured here at a Southwest Missouri State University golf tournament at Hickory Hills Country Club are (left to right) Harry Cooper, E. Rice, Payne Stewart, Jim Morris, and Ray Forsythe. (Courtesy of Hickory Hills.)

Hickory Hills would host the Women's Trans National Golf Association's golf tournament twice, in 1958 and 1991. Mrs. Claude Woodruff of Springfield, Missouri, was the first president of the association.

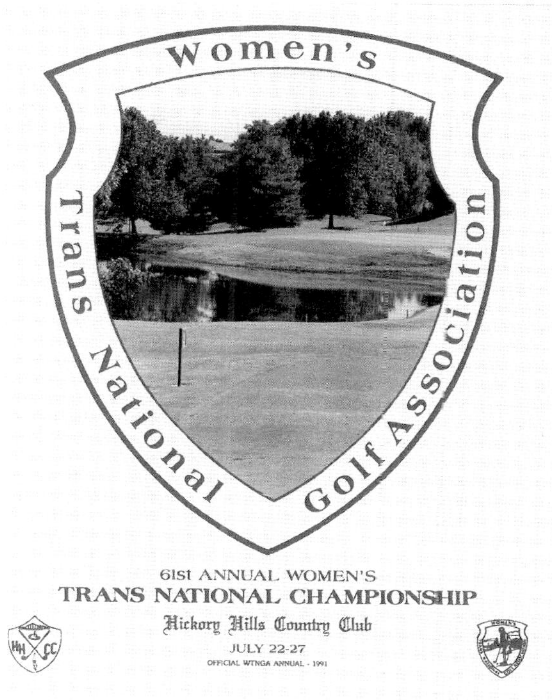

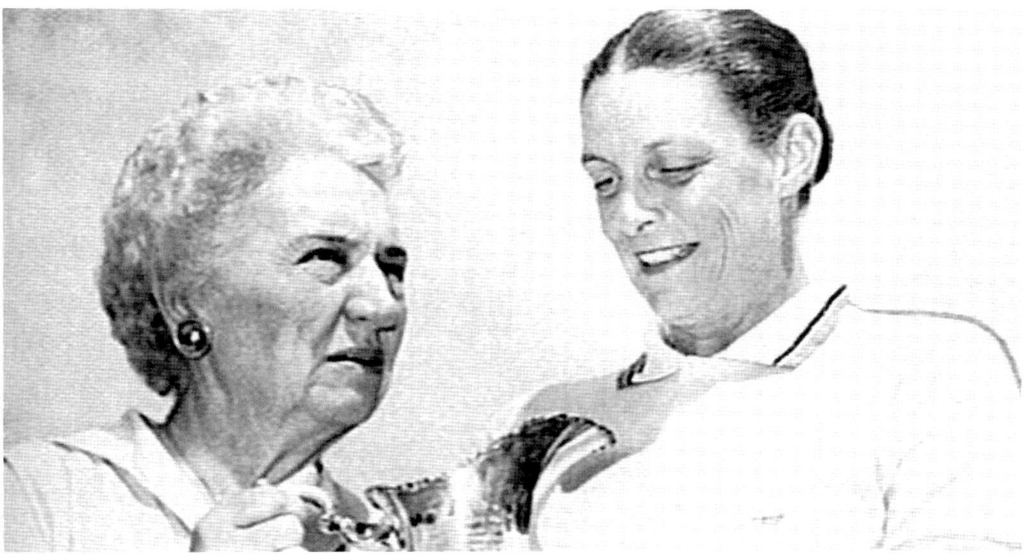

Marjorie Lindsay (right) of Decatur, Illinois, won the first Trans Championship at Hickory Hills in 1958. She is presented the trophy by Hickory Hills Club Chairman Mrs. A. B. Wyman. The 1991 tournament held at Hickory Hills was won by Vicki Goetze of Watkinsville, Georgia.

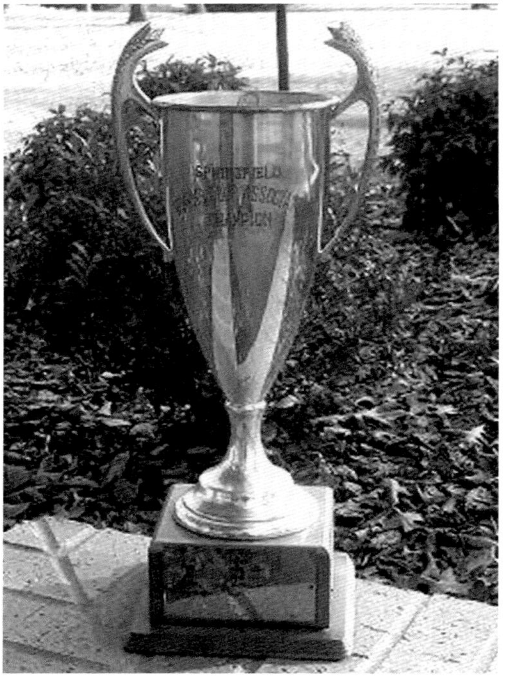

Pictured is one of the early Springfield Women's City Amateur Championship trophies awarded to Joyce Mahoney. Mahoney would win the championship a record 18 times. (Courtesy of Hickory Hills.)

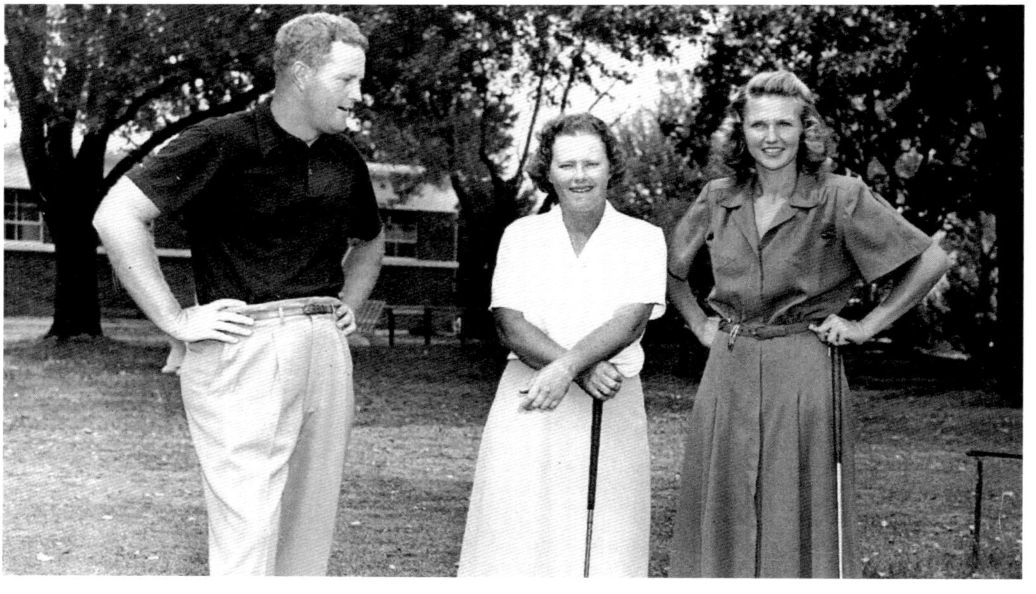

This picture, at Twin Hills Country Club during an exhibition, includes (left to right) the club's professional Art Wadkins, professional golfer Patty Berg, and Faye Sieler. Berg was the first president of the LPGA and the winner of more than 80 golf tournaments. (Courtesy of Twin Hills.)

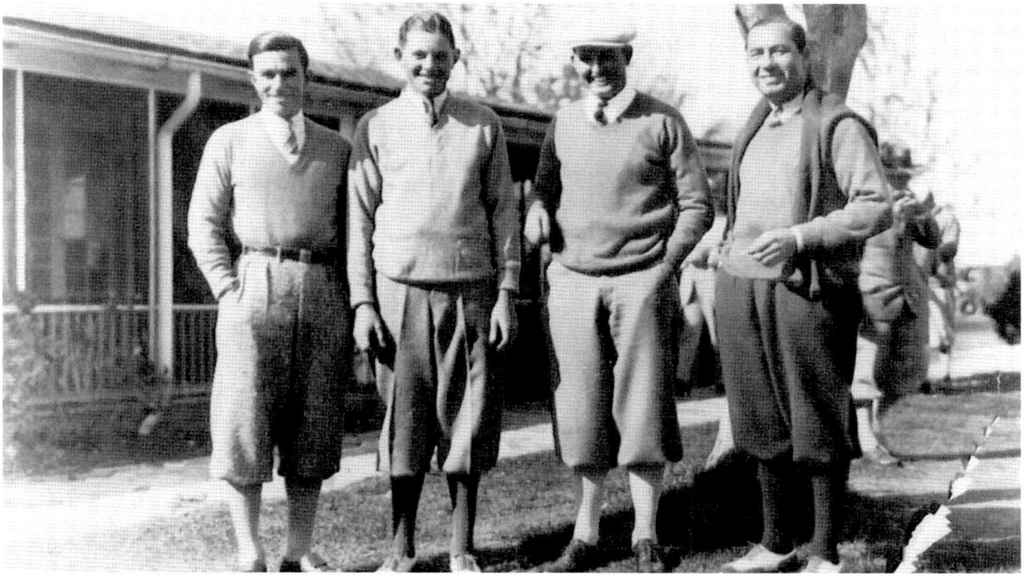

This photograph was taken during an exhibition event at Oak Hill golf club in Joplin, Missouri. The players photographed include (left to right) unidentified, Horton Smith, Ed Dudley, and Walter Hagen. Both Smith and Dudley were one-time club professionals at Oak Hill. (Courtesy of Twin Hills.)

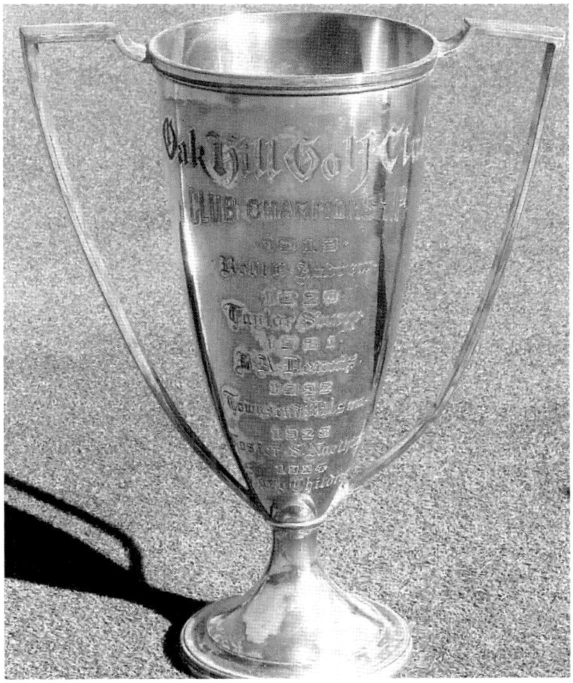

This is the earliest known Club Championship trophy from Twin Hills Country Club. This trophy was awarded to Robert Andrews in 1919, Taylor Snapp in 1920, B. A. Dennis in 1921, and Townsend Wilson in 1922. (Courtesy of Twin Hills.)

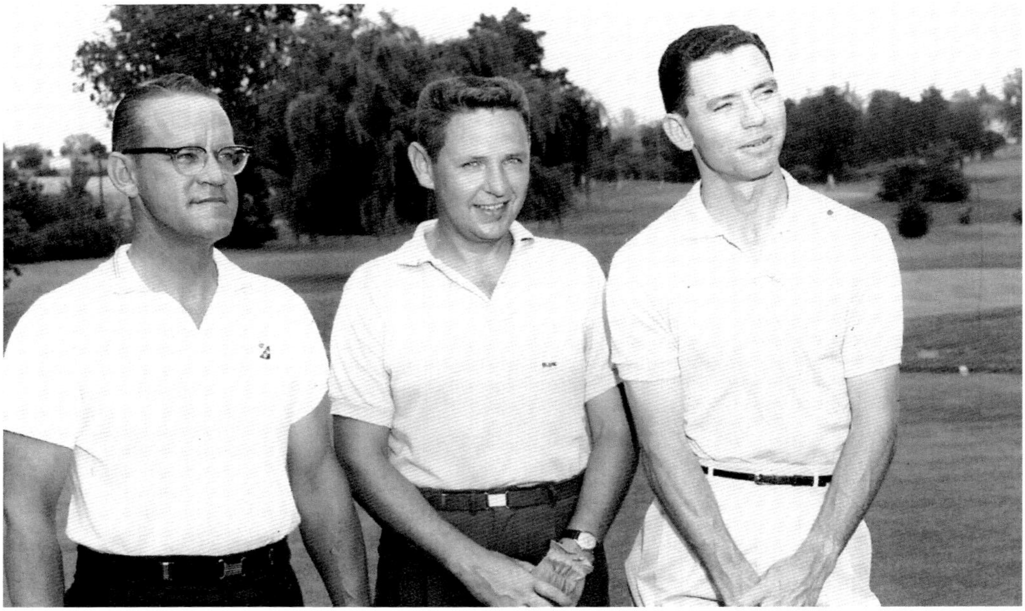

This vintage photograph is of former Hickory Hills Club Champions (left to right) Walter Cash, Don Gose, and Milt Thompson. Cash won the Club Championship four times and the Springfield City Championship in 1950. (Courtesy of Hickory Hills.)

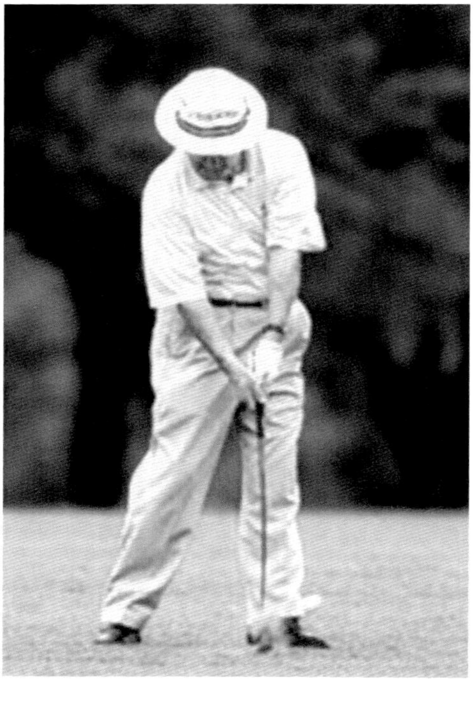

Marshall Smith is one of the most recognizable golf professionals in the Ozarks. Smith authored the book *Hit the Second Shot First*. Smith also is a regular contributor to *Golf Tips* magazine.

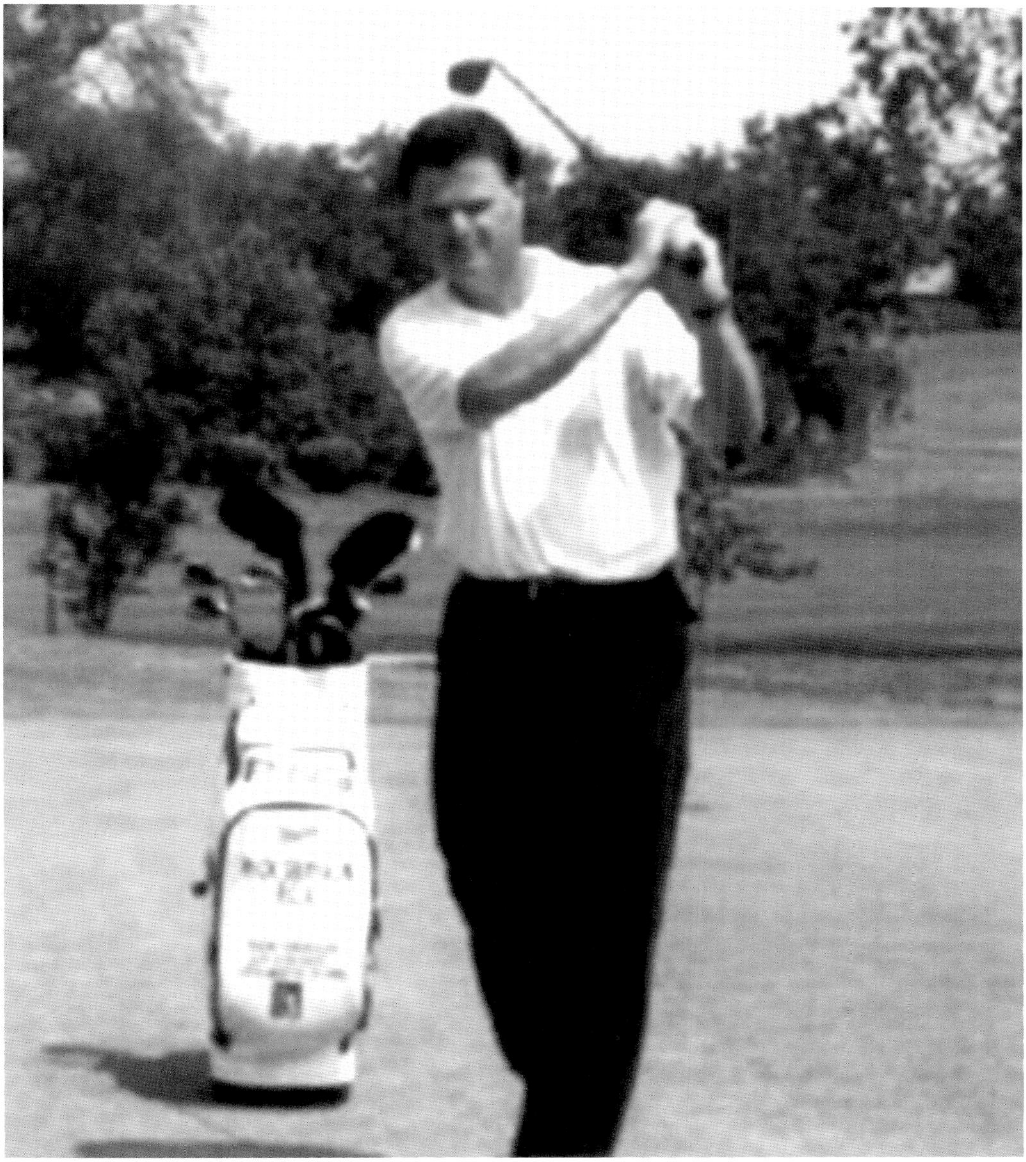

Rick Grayson was voted one of the top 100 golf instructors by Golf Magazine from 1996 to 2001. Grayson was also voted the Midwest Section of the PGA Teacher of the Year in 1991, 1998, 2000, 2002, and 2005. He coauthored *SuperGolf* with John Andrisani. Grayson currently teaches out of the Connie Morris Center at Rivercut Golf Course in Springfield.

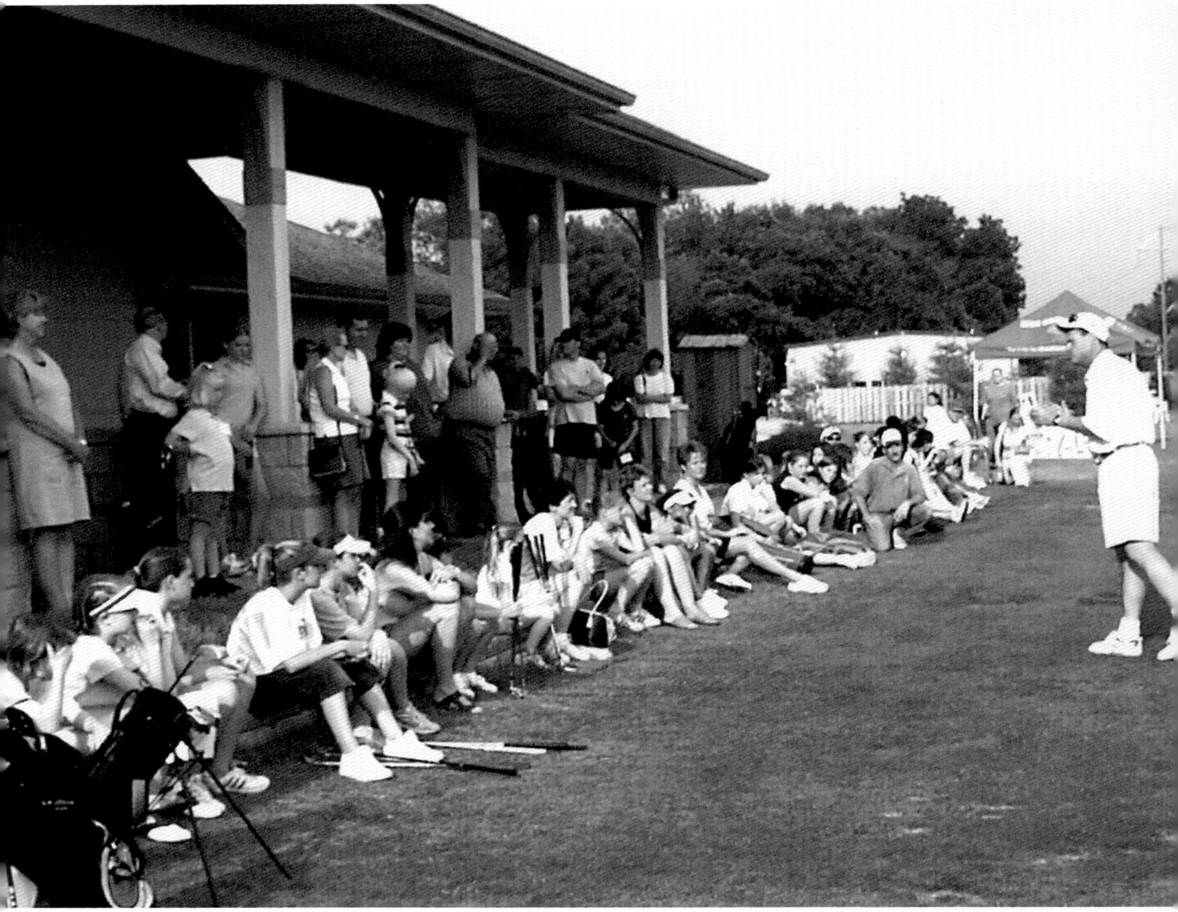

Rick Grayson is the head of the Heart of the Ozarks Junior Golf Foundation. The foundation has raised over $900,000 to develop youth golf in the Ozarks. Springfield offers two youth-oriented golf courses including the Betty Allison course at Rivercut golf course and Betty Allison golf course at Oscar Blom. (Courtesy of Rick Grayson.)

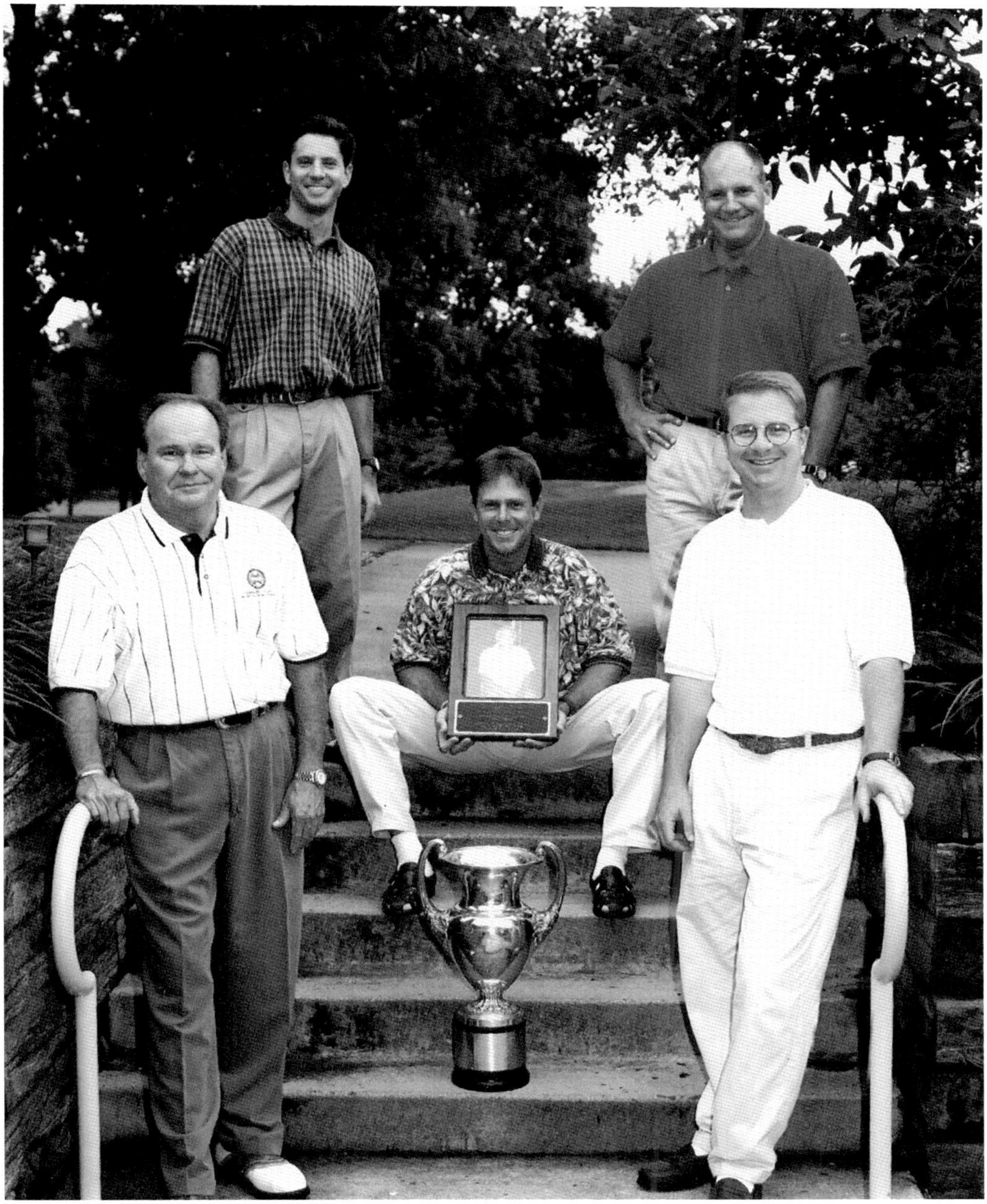

Pictured are all winners of the Missouri State Amateur Championship that played out of Hickory Hills Country Club. Top left is Alan Rosen (1991); top right is Wayne Fredrick (1996); bottom left is Bruce Hollowell (1975); in the middle is Payne Stewart (1979), with a photograph of Bill Stewart (1953 and 1957); and on the bottom right is Chuck Greene (1998). Hickory Hills boasts more Missouri State Amateurs champions than any other club. (Courtesy of Wayne Fredrick.)